PENGUIN CLASSICS

FRANCIS BACON: THE ESSAYS

FRANCIS BACON, philosopher, essayist, lawyer and statesman, was born in London in 1561. He studied at Cambridge and was enrolled at Gray's Inn in 1576. In 1584 he entered Parliament as the member for Melcombe Regis, subsequently representing other constituencies. Bacon made the acquaintance of the Earl of Essex, who endeavoured to advance him in his career. Nevertheless, having been appointed to investigate the causes of Essex's revolt in 1601, Bacon was largely responsible for the earl's conviction. Bacon was appointed Solicitor-General in 1607 and was successively Attorney-General (1613), Lord Keeper (1617) and Lord Chancellor (1618). He was created Baron Verulam in 1618 and Viscount St Albans in 1621. Later in that year he was charged with bribery and confessed that he had been guilty of 'corruption and neglect' but denied that he had ever perverted justice. He was deprived of the Great Seal, fined, imprisoned in the Tower and disabled from sitting in Parliament. Following his release, he retired to the family home at Gorhambury, Hertfordshire, and his remaining years were spent in literary and philosophical work. It was Bacon's ambition to create a new system of philosophy to replace that of Aristotle, and he has been justly acclaimed as an inspiration to later scientists, rationalists and materialists. Of his philosophical works, the principal and best known are *The Advancement of Learning, Novum Organum* and *De Augmentis*. He also wrote several professional works including *Maxims of the Law* and *Reading on the Statute of Uses*. Of his literary writings the most important are the *Essays* (1597; issued in final form in 1625), *De Sapientia Veterum, Apophthegms New and Old* and a *History of Henry VII*. Francis Bacon died in 1626.

JOHN PITCHER is Vice President of St John's College, Oxford, and Visiting Research Professor at the University of Ulster at Coleraine. He is General Editor of the Penguin Renaissance Dramatists series.

FRANCIS BACON

The Essays

EDITED

WITH AN

INTRODUCTION

BY

John Pitcher

PENGUIN BOOKS

PENGUIN BOOKS

Published by the Penguin Group
Penguin Books Ltd, 80 Strand, London WC2R 0RL, England
Penguin Putnam Inc., 375 Hudson Street, New York, New York 10014, USA
Penguin Books Australia Ltd, 250 Camberwell Road, Camberwell, Victoria 3124, Australia
Penguin Books Canada Ltd, 10 Alcorn Avenue, Toronto, Ontario, Canada M4V 3B2
Penguin Books India (P) Ltd, 11 Community Centre, Panchsheel Park, New Delhi – 110 017, India
Penguin Books (NZ) Ltd, Cnr Rosedale and Airborne Roads, Albany, Auckland, New Zealand
Penguin Books (South Africa) (Pty) Ltd, 24 Sturdee Avenue, Rosebank 2196, South Africa

Penguin Books Ltd, Registered Offices: 80 Strand, London WC2R 0RL, England

www.penguin.com

First published 1985
025

Introduction and Notes copyright © John Pitcher, 1985
All rights reserved

Printed in England by Clays Ltd, St Ives plc
Set in Linotron Aldus

ISBN-13: 978–0–14–043216–9

www.greenpenguin.co.uk

MIX
Paper from
responsible sources
FSC™ C018179

Penguin Books is committed to a sustainable
future for our business, our readers and our planet.
This book is made from Forest Stewardship
Council™ certified paper.

CONTENTS

CONTENTS

PRINCIPAL DATES IN BACON'S LIFE

Bacon's life, to adapt one of his own phrases, is a *dark saying*: concealed, reaching deeply within for its wisdom, and not a little dangerous. Even more, it is not yet expounded. It ought to be otherwise, if his long and considerable public career meant anything, for (as is not the case with so many Elizabethan writers) scores of his letters have survived, along with his personal papers, deeds, parliamentary reports, and accounts of his rise to and fall from great office. The documents fill seven volumes of the standard Victorian edition, besides the same number for his writings, literary, historical, scientific, philosophical and legal. Surely, of all the artists and writers who were lucky enough to begin their creative lives with one another in England in the 1590s, we should know most about Francis Bacon. Yet he still awaits his biographer, though many have told his life. Rather out of favour now, or simply more difficult to obtain, is the late-nineteenth-century life, *Francis Bacon* by E. A. Abbott. This is a well-written and well-documented study. Abbott can certainly be sniffy about the Jacobean court, and Bacon's venial and cardinal sins, but his prejudices are evident, and he is not an unfair critic. The biography by C. D. Bowen (1963) is quite a good modern one. Other lives, political and scientific, are listed in the primer by Vickers (see below, p. 49).

1561 Born, 22 January, at York House in the Strand, the son of Sir Nicholas Bacon, Lord Keeper of the Seal, and Anne Cooke (his second wife). Bacon was the youngest of eight children, six of whom were by Sir Nicholas's first marriage.

1573 April. Goes up to Trinity College, Cambridge, with his elder brother, Anthony.

1576 June. Admitted to Gray's Inn (again with Anthony). September. Goes to Paris with Sir Amias Paulet, ambassador to France.

1579 February. His father dies, and (in June) he returns to England. Left with only a small inheritance, he is forced to seek a career in the law.
Anthony Bacon sets out on a long tour of the continent.

1582 June. Admitted Utter Barrister at Gray's Inn.

1584 November. First appearance in Parliament, representing Melcombe Regis in Dorset. (He remains in the Commons, representing various constituencies, until 1618, when he is made a peer.)

c. 1585 Writes *Advice to Queen Elizabeth*, concerned chiefly with the recusants, and *The Greatest Birth of Time*.

1586 Becomes a Bencher of Gray's Inn.

1592 Writes four speeches*[1] for an entertainment, *A Conference of Pleasure*, celebrating Queen Elizabeth's accession day. Anthony Bacon returns from abroad and notes that his brother is 'bound and in deep arrearages' to Robert, Earl of Essex.

1593 In Parliament, speaks against a government proposal for subsidies, and as a consequence is forbidden to come into the Queen's presence.
With support from Essex, he begins his (unsuccessful) petition for the offices of Attorney-, and then Solicitor-General.

1594 Writes six speeches* for the Gray's Inn Christmas masque *Gesta Grayorum*. Begins to compile *Formularies and Elegancies*, a notebook of quotations and ideas; and writes legal and state pieces.

1595 Essex gives Bacon an estate (Twickenham) to console him on his failure to gain office.
Writes part of the device presented by Essex to celebrate the Queen's accession day (*Of Love and Self-Love*).

1596 Advises Fulke Greville on his studies and the Earl of Rutland on his travels.

1597 Publishes the *Essays*,* with *Colours of Good and Evil* and *Meditationes Sacrae*. Writes *Maxims of the Law*.

1. An asterisk by a title indicates that at least part of the work is to be found in the present edition.

Proposes marriage to Lady Hatton, who refuses and then marries his rival and enemy, Sir Edward Coke.

1598 Arrested for debt, but soon released.
Writes a pamphlet about a Jesuit conspiracy against the Queen.

1600 June. Takes part in proceedings against Essex after the Irish débâcle (in which the Earl, close to defeat by the Irish, abandoned his command and returned to England without the Queen's permission).
July. Offers his services to Essex, a fortnight after the Earl has been released but not restored to the Queen's favour.

1601 February. Essex is arraigned after his rebellion and executed as a traitor. Bacon assists the prosecution in his trial, and publishes a *Declaration* of the Earl's crimes.
May. Anthony Bacon dies. Mortgages Twickenham Park.

1603 After Elizabeth's death, tries (unsuccessfully) to obtain King James's favour.
July. Knighted at Windsor, along with three hundred others.
Deeply in debt, he is assisted by Sir Robert Cecil (later Lord Salisbury).
Writes *Valerius Terminus of the Interpretation of Nature, Temporis Partus Masculus* (The Masculine Birth of Time), and *De Interpretatione Naturae Proaemium* (Preface to 'Of the Interpretation of Nature'). Begins work on a series of writings about the union of England and Scotland.

1604 Publishes *Apology in certain imputations concerning the late Earl of Essex.*
August. Appointed King's Counsel.

1605 Publishes *The Advancement of Learning.*

1606 May. Marries Alice Barnham, the daughter of a rich London alderman. There are no children of this marriage.

1607 Writes *Cogita et Visa* (Thoughts and Conclusions).
June. Appointed Solicitor-General.

1608 Writes *Redargutio Philosophiarum* (The Refutation of Philosophies) and short historical pieces.

1609 Publishes *De Sapientia Veterum** (Of the Wisdom of the Ancients).

1610 His mother dies, several years after losing her wits.
Devises plans for a history of Great Britain, and in Parliament speaks for the King's right to impose taxes.

1612 Publishes second edition of the *Essays,** enlarged and revised.
Writes *Descriptio Globi Intellectualis* and *Thema Coeli* (Description of the Intellectual Globe and Theory of the Heaven).

1613 October. Appointed Attorney-General.
Provides an expensive masque for the wedding of the King's favourite, Robert, Earl of Somerset. Writes against duels.

1616 Helps to prosecute Somerset for the murder of Sir Thomas Overbury.
Writes a letter of advice to the new favourite, George Villiers (later Duke of Buckingham).
June. Made a Privy Councillor.

1617 March. Appointed Lord Keeper.
In and out of favour with the King and Buckingham for opposing them.

1618 January. Appointed Lord Chancellor.
July. Created Baron Verulam.

1620 Publishes *Novum Organum** (The New Organon) as the first part of the (uncompleted) *Instauratio Magna* (The Great Instauration).

1621 January. Created Viscount St Albans.
May. Sentenced by the House of Lords for taking bribes. Dismissed from the office of Chancellor. Fined and imprisoned briefly, he receives a limited pardon, and retains his title. Retires to his family home at Gorhambury.

1622 Publishes *History of Henry VII*, and (in monthly instalments) part of his proposed Natural History. Writes an *Advertisement touching an Holy War*.

1623 Publishes *De Augmentis Scientiarum*, a much enlarged Latin version of *The Advancement of Learning*.
Tries (in vain) to be made Provost of Eton.

1624 Writes *New Atlantis*, and publishes *Apophthegms* and a
     translation of some of the Psalms. Desperately short of
     money.

1625 Publishes the third edition of the *Essays*,* again enlarged
     and revised.

1626 Dies, 9 April, at Highgate, over £20,000 in debt.
     Less than three weeks later his widow marries one of his
     servants.

INTRODUCTION

One of the sure signs that there is something special about Bacon's *Essays* is that they look unbelievably easy to write. So easy, that if we try our hand at the Baconian manner, fragments of the imitation may seem to come out quite close to the originals:

The grain of man be like to wood; rubbed the wrong way doth but ruin the finish.

or

Brutes, we see, do strut apace before their betters, but are, by God's decree, then *named*: for Adam ruled the beasts by cases vocative, and every player can call a knave.

Yet if we put fakes like these (which I have written) alongside the genuine stuff, it becomes clear at once that there is something inimitable in Bacon's style. Words like figures in a tapestry, unfolded and spread out, was how one of Bacon's wise men defined speech,[1] and the unrolling of language into needle-sharp clauses, quotations and sunbright sentences is what keeps the *Essays* as alert and as readable as they were over three centuries ago. It also keeps them ahead of impersonations, as these extracts will show:

There is . . . great use of ambitious men in being screens to princes in matters of danger and envy, for no man will take that part, except he be like a seeled dove, that mounts and mounts because he cannot see about him.

(*Of Ambition*)

He that builds a fair house upon an ill seat, committeth himself to prison.

(*Of Building*)

---

1. From *Of Friendship*, p. 142 below. Page numbers for the *Essays* refer to the present edition.

. . . number itself in armies importeth not much where the people is of weak courage; for (as Virgil saith) *It never troubles a wolf how many the sheep be.*

(*Of the True Greatness of Kingdoms and Estates*)

The fact is that the writing in the *Essays* took Bacon almost thirty years to perfect, and that by the time he had finished with it (in 1625) it was one of the major achievements in prose to have come out of the Elizabethan academies and courts of law. Contemporary prose writers like Hooker and Nashe and Donne owed much to the universities and the inns of court, but with Bacon the debt was different and more profound, for he went directly to the dying heart of scholasticism, and there made something come alive after centuries of dreariness. Against everything one might expect, Bacon's style was born of Tudor school text-books, the university curriculum and the notebooks of keen young lawyers. Perhaps this is what makes it so vulnerable to mimicry,[2] for its own history is one of study, memorizing and imitation. If Cicero wrote a line thus, or thus, it was for the Elizabethan undergraduate to break down its grammatical structure, to point to its tropes, to memorize its arrangement, and to frame his own Latin accordingly. So with the law student and pronouncements from the Bench. It is in all these things that we must seek the origins of the *Essays*; that is, in the mental world which Bacon inherited from medieval book learning, disputation and jurisprudence. Only by reading into this world can we grasp just how much he had to do to arrive at that facility of writing which looks so effortless now.

1

The shape of a man's mind, so Bacon thought, either ventilated or sucked in knowledge. It could make him either full or empty, gassy or rarified. It could be inflated like a balloon, with vain opinions and nonsense, or draw in discoveries from nature, and from gullible chatterers: 'if a man be thought secret, it inviteth discovery, as the more close air sucketh in the more open'.[3] But if ever there was a

2. As Swift in particular discovered, and relished. There is a discussion of Swift's parodies of Bacon, and his dislike of him, in Brian Vickers, *Francis Bacon and Renaissance Prose*, Cambridge, 1968, pp. 240–45.

3. *Of Simulation and Dissimulation*, p. 77.

mind which could open and shut, and change shape, it was Bacon's own. When he was most closed (if we wish to read him in Karl Popper's terms), Bacon was an enemy, apprentice among many masters, of the Open Society: yet when fully dilated, no mind could have been freer than his. In one place he wanted the arts repressed;[4] in another, music and painting were to be especially honoured in his ideal state.

But how could he change the shape of other men's minds, that was the question for Bacon. To hand, he had a tradition of rhetoric over two thousand years old, and a rhetoric which, in its play against logic, might be able to persuade men to think aright. The open palm or the clenched fist, that was how the ancients had characterized the difference between rhetoric, manipulating men into truth, and logic, thumping them into it. The open, welcoming hand of persuasion, or the bunched knuckles of philosophical assertion.[5] Bacon was to try them both, and together, with varying success. In 1597, for example, along with the first versions of the *Essays*, he published a series of hackneyed propositions, subjects for school debate, which allowed him to gut and tear at the commonplaces, or deceits, or *colours*, of the mind. Sometimes the anatomy was a slow and bloody business. In one instance the colour put forward was that 'what consists of many divisible parts is greater than that which consists of few, because viewing things part by part makes them seem greater. Further, a lot of things put together give the impression of magnitude, but even more so if there is no order to their arrangement,

4. See *The Advancement of Learning* (1605), II.10.13. In 1623, in the corresponding passage in the Latin translation (*De Augmentis Scientiarum*, IV.2), Bacon still wants some of the arts suppressed, but he concedes that music and painting are virtuous pleasures for the ear and eye, and he distinguishes these from the voluptuary arts like cooking, and making perfumes and 'stimulants of lust' (*Works*, IV.395).

5. It appears, writes Bacon, 'that logic differeth from rhetoric, not only as the fist from the palm, the one close, the other at large; but much more in this, that logic handleth reason exact and in truth, and rhetoric handleth it as it is planted in popular opinions and manners. And therefore Aristotle doth wisely place rhetoric as between logic on the one side, and moral or civil knowledge on the other, as participating of both: for the proofs and demonstrations of logic are toward all men indifferent and the same; but the proofs and persuasions of rhetoric ought to differ according to the auditors' (*Advancement of Learning*, II.18.4). A good place to begin studying rhetoric (classical, Renaissance, and modern) is the brief introduction by Peter Dixon in the Critical Idiom series. There is a learned book on its relationship with logic in Bacon's day by W. S. Howell, *Logic and Rhetoric in England, 1500–1700*, Princeton, 1956 (see especially pp. 364–75). See also note 27, p. 34 below.

because the mind cannot take them all in at the same time'.[6] This is a
scholastic enough beginning, but then follow the reasons why an
average schoolboy with poor eyesight (and no one else, surely)
might find it credible:

This colour seemeth palpable, for·it is not plurality of parts without
majority of parts that maketh the total greater; yet nevertheless it often
carries the mind away; yea it deceiveth the sense; as it seemeth to the
eye a shorter distance of way if it be all dead and continued, than if it
have trees or buildings or any other marks whereby the eye may divide
it. So when a great monied man hath divided his chests and coins and
bags, he seemeth to himself richer than he was, and therefore a way to
amplify anything is to break it and to make an anatomy of it in several
parts and to examine it according to several circumstances.

This is an educative prose for dunces, written on the principle of an
abacus, with clauses on wires, but nevertheless there are some real
things in it. They become more evident in the *elenchus*, or refutation of the *colour*, even though the writing sheds none of its excess
weight of verbs and conjunctions. The *colour* deceives, so we are
told, if

the mind of him that is to be persuaded do of itself over-conceive or
prejudge of the greatness of anything; for then the breaking of it will
make it seem less, because it maketh it appear more according to the
truth: and therefore if a man be in sickness or pain, the time will seem
longer without a clock or hour-glass than with it; for the mind doth
value every moment, and then the hour doth rather sum up the
moments than divide the day. So in a dead plain the way seemeth the
longer, because the eye hath preconceived it shorter than the truth, and
the frustrating of that maketh it seem longer than the truth.

Clearly, with a style like this, *anything* will seem longer than the
truth, especially the time spent reading through its repetitions. At
every instant in this unreal Aristotelian domain, the clauses look as
though they are about to accumulate to a halt, and yet somehow the
writing manages to wind itself up and begin again. Appropriately
enough, there is a clock in Bacon's mind here, as if he were timing
our irritation with the prose, or seeing how long he could stay on his
feet, like a barrister in front of the judge, or a teacher in front of his
pupils. The idiom seems unalterable, even when (as in the next set

6. A translation of the proposition, which is in Latin. This, and the English text
which responds to it, are No. 5 in the *Colours of Good and Evil* (*Works*, VII.81–4).

of examples) there are subjects very close to Bacon's heart – heaps of money, smart gardens, and a lot of land. The colour deludes us, in this second case, so he persists, if

the matter broken or divided is not comprehended by the sense or mind at once, in respect of the distracting or scattering of it; and being entire and not divided, is comprehended: as a hundred pounds in heaps of five pounds will show more than in one gross heap, so as the heaps be all upon one table to be seen at once, otherwise not; or flowers growing scattered in divers beds will show more than if they did grow in one bed, so as all those beds be within a plot, that they be object to view at once, otherwise not; and therefore men whose living lieth together in one shire, are commonly counted greater landed than those whose livings are dispersed, though it be more, because of the notice and comprehension.

As might be expected, the *colour* is no less deceptive in a third (and fourth and fifth) respect, but it is noticeable that in these the examples become more literary, or at least are drawn from books and proverbs. To show that one thing is superior to many, Bacon quotes the remark of Jesus (in Luke 10.41–2), *Martha, Martha, you are busy about many things, but one suffices*, and he dusts off the old fable from Aesop about the fox and the cat: 'the fox bragged what a number of shifts and devices he had to get from the hounds, and the cat said she had but one, which was to climb a tree'. From this, with the assumed air of an old politic (he was thirty-six), Bacon derives the moral that 'a good sure friend is a better help at a pinch than all the stratagems and policies of a man's own wit'. Suddenly with that line we are very close to the late *Essays*, although the rest of the prose is still like some wobbly and over-large creature without vertebrae and with too many muscles. What we cannot fail to notice is that the writing has barely held out against the subject. We begin with a sophism about size and parts, followed by examples of why the proposal might seem believable, and then other instances that show us how easily it can mislead. Yet what matters here is not the finickiness of schoolroom debate, but the examples Bacon has used as illustration. There is that commonplace about foreshortening a distance with buildings and trees; then the great monied man dividing and laying out his bags and chests; then the sick man watching away the dreary hours of boredom and pain without a clock; then the heaps of money on the table; then the arrangement of flower-beds in some great garden; then the maps of wealth for landowners whose properties are compact and contiguous; and so on. We do not need to be Renaissance logicians to see the sharp end of the stick in this. In a refutation which claims that multiplicity of form and substance, introduced serially to the mind, is what confuses us, these heterogeneous and distinct figures are not at all neutral. They too are divisible parts in a unity, imaginative examples in a single rhetorical debate, and therefore they are also evidence presented within that debate. The rhetorical footwork is a bit cumbersome but we are supposed to see that the greater the difference between each illustration or imaginative specimen, where disunity and separation are more apparent than unity of argument, the more the refutation is suspect, even undermined. We know that Bacon is fully aware of this, because he gives up trying to falsify the proposition almost the moment he begins. When he acknowledges that the eye can be deceived by tricks of perspective, or scale, or a field of sight, he admits plurality of experience if not plurality of truth. If you stand in one position in a garden, then its flower-beds will support your argument; in another position, the eye cannot take in all the beds, and the argument doesn't hold. There aren't two truths here, or anything of that kind, but there are two (or more) vantage-points in the garden, and ways of viewing things in the head.

It is no wonder that Bacon's writing almost gives way at the knee joints in all of this. The clauses are broken up and carried around and around the syntax like some endless luggage belt at an airport until they bang into abbreviated phrases like *otherwise not*. Nonetheless the very clumsiness of the prose helps us to remember that it is an art form and not an instrument of philosophy, an art which pieces together (however badly) rather than one that takes apart. We may pose the distinction as a question. Is Bacon trying to demonstrate that this proposition about size is duplicitous, indolent and stupid, and should be expelled from the mind, or does his prose, even without a spine, trace out the figures, the perspectives and the (coloured) shapes of thinking itself? Interpreted one way, as a piece of dialectic, there is a choice between truth and falsehood, and a few suggestions on how to detect fraud or error in comparable cases: but read as an art form, a literary one, there is the experience of moving among the contradictions, the clutter, and (in philosophical terms) the *accidents* of the mind, the indeterminate but unavoidable properties of thought and language. In 1597, the writing is broken and dry, and looped unattractively around its subject, but even here, where his style is at its weakest, Bacon has an eye, one we can't resist, for restoring what is unnoticed, incidental and forgettable to some prominence in the mind. Our passage is from coins to flower-beds, from a sick-room to a map, from Christ's annoyance with Martha to a plain without trees. It is a rhetorical progress, although these imaginative bits are still only the flotsam of knowledge and they barely stay above the surface of the prose.

The suggestion that Bacon was concerned with accidents as much as with substantives, with words, rhetoric and the imaginative routes of thought just as much as scientific truth, may still be a heresy among Baconians, if no one else. Bacon himself would probably not have been too pleased at the notion. Year after year, in notebook after notebook, he attacked the Schoolmen, the medieval scholars who wrote their lectures with Aristotle instead of Nature before them, the graduates of an education which required only obedience to the classics, and their commentators, and an inventiveness with words. The very nature of words, so he wrote, being vague and ill-defined, was a source of illusion, for language embalmed in itself the mistakes and vulgar self-deceptions of the past,[7] and kept making imaginative wholes, or theories, or even poems in the present. Even so, it is still possible to argue, in spite of Bacon's insistent repudiation of the Schoolmen, and their fabrications, that his own writing was not always as unimaginative, or as mindless (I mean this exactly), as he proposed it should be. One instance of his attack on the mind, or at least its creative potency, shows just how much he could contradict himself. In *The Masculine Birth of Time*, which he wrote in Latin in 1603, he makes a father explain to a son how easy it is to conceive:

The human mind in studying nature becomes big under the impact of things and brings forth a teeming brood of errors. Aristotle stands for the tallest growth of one kind of error, Plato of another . . . Now you would like me to confute them individually . . . [but] that would be to sin on the grand scale against the golden future of the human race, to sacrifice its promise of dominion by turning aside to attack transitory shadows. The need is to set up in the midst one bright and radiant light of truth, shedding its beams in all directions and dispelling all errors in a moment. It is pointless to light pale candles and carry them about to

7. See below, pp. 278 and 283, aphorisms 5 and 21 in the 'Idols of the Mind' (from the *Novum Organum*, Book I).

every nook and cranny of error and falsehood. I would have you learn to hate that for which you ask. Believe me, it is to sin against the light.[8]

There are two tropes in this. One represents the study of nature as sexual intercourse, gestation, birth and growth to maturity; while the other divides a dark present from a golden future, and a room of obscure ignorance from one lit by understanding. Looked at separately, the tropes are neither unusual nor particularly effective, but when they combine with one another the result is much more disturbing. The formal conjunction is the father's refusal to be bothered by Plato and Aristotle ('you would like me to confute them individually') which links the brood of errors to the danger of sinning on the grand scale, and then to the transitory shadows. From there the images move in sequence through a single light expelling error, through nooks and crannies, and a candle in the dark, and on to sin again, this time against the light itself. The chain of images begins with the mind impregnated and growing big, passes through rooms of shadows and dark corners, and ends with the lights switched on. Even in translation, it is obvious that the two tropes, bonded together like this, are more inventive and interesting than they should be. They almost constitute a subtext, connecting the mind's fecundity and begetting to unlit rooms and sinful shadows. The rhetoric is probably not subversive enough for that, but it does demonstrate that the creative mind is more than a match for any attempts to curb creativity. Bacon's views on the imaginative or experiential life of writing are of no importance here. Whether or not, as he saw it, words, language, and the texts of Aristotle had been perverted by medieval writers, and by mankind in general, his own essays, advice and interpretation were still made out of, and are to be judged as, literate experience. Quite late in life Bacon seems to have realized this himself, and the term *literate* or *learned experience* (in the Latin, *literata experientia*) is his own.[9] It is applied to various kinds of experiment, rather than kinds of

---

8. Translated by Benjamin Farrington, in *The Philosophy of Francis Bacon*, Liverpool, 1964, p. 70.

9. Learned experience can 'hardly be esteemed an art or a part of philosophy, but rather a kind of sagacity' and when 'a man tries all kinds of experiments without order or method, this is but groping in the dark; but when he uses some direction and order in experimenting, it is as if he were led by the hand; and this is what I mean by Learned Experience' (*De Augmentis Scientiarum*, V.2; *Works*, IV.413). Not working to a method, but gathering and experimenting with an *instinct* of what might be

experience and verbal testimony (the Aesop fable, the exemplum of the clock-watching invalid), but it does place some trust in the subtlety of the mind, and its capacity to learn; and it does imply a deferral of mind, a putting off of conclusions, which is relevant to his own writing.

2

There were other types of language about which one could learn. Aphorisms, *sententiae*, maxims, proverbs – they formed a whole genus of writing which Bacon called broken knowledge.[10] They were the building blocks of his writing life, the primary verbal code out of which he made his style. They were so minimal, so atomic, that he was sure there was nothing smaller in language that made its own sense. Building up from these, from their irreducible base, there might be a new beginning. And this broken knowledge was simply everywhere, in the ruins of ancient books, and in the foundations of new ones. Bacon, just as much as anyone else in the Renaissance who read books, and marked them, and tried to use their reading, was constantly on the look-out for new aphorisms, in any language. He didn't mind making up a few, either. On one occasion he was watching some fishermen casting their nets in the Thames. He offered them a price for their catch before it came in, but they wanted more. When they drew up their net, and it contained only two or three small fish, Bacon told them 'it had been better for them to have taken his offer. They replied, they hoped to have had a better draught. But, said his lordship, hope is a good breakfast, but an ill supper.'[11] In his *Essays* and other literary writing the *sententiae* are certainly more polished, rounded, and they strike deeper, like musket-balls, but the metal is just the same, and from the same armoury as *hope is a good breakfast, but an ill supper*. Compare the velocity and thrust of these: *if a man look sharply and attentively, he shall see Fortune: for though she be*

right; relying on the experience of the senses, and acknowledging that man's five wits, however ruined, may make discoveries; and not rushing into conclusions at too early a stage in the experience of learning – all these things seem to be in Bacon's *literata experientia*.

10. See *The Advancement of Learning*, II.17.7.

11. *Aubrey's Brief Lives*, ed. Oliver Lawson Dick, Penguin edition, 1972, p. 174. The anecdote is recorded, in a slightly different form, in *Works*, VII.168 (No. 36).

*blind, yet she is not invisible; or Suspicions amongst thoughts are
like bats amongst birds: they ever fly by twilight; or extreme
self-lovers . . . will set an house on fire, and it were but to roast their
eggs.*[12] There can be no question but that these vindicate, however
indirectly, the hours sweated out by Tudor scholarship, teaching the
mind to pack and unpack its words. Yet if all Bacon had done was to
strike off a few more sentences and pithy sayings, he would not have
added much to the books already stuffed with extracts from ancient
authors, the equivalents in the Renaissance to our own crammer
notes and guides. What he did that was new, and he seems to have
been alone in this, at least in English sources, was to set up one
sententia against another and to conceive of the opposition as thesis
and antithesis, proposition and counter-proposition.[13] In 1623 he
published forty-seven sets of Latin sentences split down the middle
by a column of white page, a no-man's land where either, or neither,
side of the contraries could be true. Under *Cruelty*, for example,
were these:

For.	*Against.*
None of the virtues has so many crimes to answer for as clemency.	To delight in blood, one must be either a wild beast or a Fury.
Cruelty, if it proceeds from revenge, is justice, if from danger, prudence.	To a good man cruelty always seems fabulous, and some tragical fiction.
He that has mercy on his enemy has no mercy on himself.	
Bloodlettings are not oftener necessary in medicine than executions in states.	

Bacon does not give a very convincing account of why these
aphorisms, or *Antitheses of Things* as he calls them, are parcelled
and sewn up like this. He says that he got the idea from the
preparatory store of rhetoric, recommended by Cicero, in which the

12. From respectively pp. 181, 158 and 131 below.
13. For Bacon's place in the humanist tradition of teaching from such commonplaces, see Jardine, *Francis Bacon*, pp. 224–6 (full reference, p. 51 below). For the
connections between Tudor speaking and writing, see Walter J. Ong, *Rhetoric,
Romance and Technology*, Cornell, 1971, chapter 2.

orator was to have commonplaces ready at hand to debate a question on both sides. But where Cicero had devised his system for judicial oratory, Bacon wanted to take in everything. All topics were to be studied and prepared beforehand, in the form of a debate, with the case 'exaggerated both ways with the utmost force of wit, and urged unfairly, as it were, and quite beyond the truth'.[14]

Explained like this, Bacon's scheme sounds painfully threadbare, an old dodge for a hard-pressed and second-rate speaker, and it reminds us of those memoranda that he was forever writing down in his personal notes. Stop breathing too quickly when speaking at the Council table, he tells himself urgently in one note. Have a lake and island dug for a model garden, and impress Lord Salisbury with them, in another. Put together a history of marvels and contraptions, and find out just how much Salisbury is worth, in two more.[15] In 1623, in the *Antitheses of Things*, for everyone, whether lawyer, parliamentarian, moral adviser, scientific counsellor, Lord Chancellor or someone who was simply tempted to kick his dog, there were reels of advice on Cruelty to be memorized strip by strip ready for the occasion. This all seems so pedestrian, so hand-cranking a method, that one wonders if Bacon took the slightest notice of such laboured counsel. His own delivery on and off the Bench seems to have been pure silver. The poet Ben Jonson, not an easy man to please, declared that no one ever spoke 'more neatly, more pressly [precisely], more weightily, or suffered less emptiness, less idleness' in his speech than Bacon. His 'hearers could not cough, or look aside from him, without loss' and the 'fear of every man that heard him was lest he should make an end'.[16] But even if, after all, Bacon did acquire his volubility and compactness and ready speech from these lists, they were yet still more important to his art of writing. Indeed, many of the *Essays* begin with and are sustained by the sentences marshalled here. Under the audit of *Wife and Children*, say, there

14. *Works*, IV.472 (the *antitheses* for cruelty are listed on pp. 479–80).
15. *Letters and Life*, IV.93 (the breathing), 76–7 (the garden), 65 (the marvels), 52 (Salisbury's estate). All these are recorded in a notebook for 1608; but Bacon carried on making preparatory notes even in his last, tormented years. Even when he was convicted and done for, and had sought interviews with the King, Buckingham and Prince Charles, there he was again, scribbling down the exact phrase he should put to them. Some of the notes verge on being pathetic. To Prince Charles he intended to say, hoping for his own restitution, 'the work of the Father is creation, of the Son redemption' (*Letters and Life*, VII.352).
16. 'Explorata: or Discoveries', in *Ben Jonson: the Complete Poems*, ed. George Parfitt, Penguin, 1975, p. 401.

are five maxims *for*, and five *against*. Four of these appear in the essay *Of Marriage and Single Life*, two from either side of the account:

He that hath wife and children hath given hostages to fortune [*against*] . . . the best works . . . have proceeded from the unmarried or childless men [*against*] . . . Unmarried men are . . . not always best subjects, for they are light to run away [*for*] . . . wife and children are a kind of discipline of humanity; and single men . . . are more cruel and hard-hearted [*for*].

Once we appreciate that much of Bacon's writing is compounded from the acknowledged contradictions between such *sententiae*, then the *Essays* in particular can be understood as a rhetorical art form rather than a digest of popular philosophy or a set of fireside homilies. If the essay *Of Marriage and Single Life* is construed as counsel – that is, forensic debate designed to test the strength of a case one way *and* the other – then it can be distinguished from books giving *real* advice (like, don't marry, shoot your wife or invest in your children's education) and the other countless literary exercises going under the name of essays. This needs to be in our minds all the time if we are to avoid reading Bacon as though he were telling us something new, or verifiable, or as though he had penetrated the mysteries of human behaviour through his reading and close observation. In this same essay he writes that

Chaste women are often proud and froward, as presuming upon the merit of their chastity. It is one of the best bonds both of chastity and obedience in the wife if she think her husband wise, which she will never do if she find him jealous. Wives are young men's mistresses, companions for middle age, and old men's nurses.

The most comment that such passages normally attract is that they point up Bacon's tough reasonableness, or his misanthropy, or his reptilian nature, or his misogyny, or even (more surprisingly) his acuteness. Yet one hardly needs to read an essay by Lord Bacon to divide up a woman's life or the lives of women into mistress, lady companion and nurse. As for his remarks about chaste women, these should be useful or useless according to their accuracy, and the extent to which they can be tested. Just how one tests for chastity and correlates it with a woman's pushy behaviour is left to the imagination. Once we ask the really hard questions about marriage and single lives – are they pestered or lonely, savage or overcivilized, smothering or bleak – we will realize what this essay, and its companions, are *not* trying to do. Instead of having an emotional interior, into which we are invited, it makes a series of rapid intellectual passes across and conjunctions with the verbal knots and ties that have been taken out of books and which are called *sententiae*. Put it this way: in the *Essays*, Bacon tries to write a prose, or create a style, which can cross that ditch of blank whiteness between one maxim and its opposing number. The *Essays*, at their etymological root, are assays, attempts to hold together thesis and antithesis, love and hatred, marriage and single life. But for the most part Bacon doesn't seem prepared to give away much about marriage, love, or anything else. If we recall the exceptions, it is precisely because they are so rare, and because, in some cases, as Jonson again pointed out, Bacon couldn't resist a joke, especially at the expense of an enemy (as with the remark, pointing at the hunchbacked Robert, Earl of Salisbury – '*Deformed* persons are commonly *even* with nature: for as nature hath done ill by them, so do they by nature'[17]).

Yet still it is true that in the *Essays*, and other of Bacon's writings, the imaginative life is vested in a geometry of contradictory utterances rather than in the emotional densities or feelings the thought moves into. Consider another paragraph, in these terms, from *Of Friendship*:

A principal fruit of friendship is the ease and discharge of the fullness and swellings of the heart, which passions of all kinds do cause and induce. We know diseases of stoppings and suffocations are the most dangerous in the body, and it is not much otherwise in the mind: you may take sarza to open the liver, steel to open the spleen, flowers of sulphur for the lungs, castoreum for the brain; but no receipt openeth the heart but a true friend, to whom you may impart griefs, joys, fears, hopes, suspicions, counsels, and whatsoever lieth upon the heart to oppress it, in a kind of civil shrift or confession.

The line of connection here, the intellectuality poised in movement between one truth and another, crosses a divide between the body,

---

17. *Of Deformity*, p. 191 (my italics). In a letter of 17 December 1612, soon after the publication of the 1612 *Essays*, one of the court gossips, John Chamberlain, writes that 'Sir Francis Bacon hath set out new Essays, where in a chapter of Deformity the world takes notice that he paints out his little cousin [i.e. Lord Salisbury] to the life'. *The Letters of John Chamberlain*, ed. N. E. McClure, 2 vols., Philadelphia, I. 397.

or at least the heart, conceived of as an anatomical gadget, needing mechanical if not medical solvents to rectify its faults, and (in contradistinction) the heart as the meeting-place of spirit, psychology and emotion which can be opened by no medicines, but friendship. The assay in this instance passes between the heart as a vulnerable and physical bag of blood, and the heart as the source of unseen, unphysical but undeniable human energies. If this seems at all primitive to us, seems lost in alchemical half-truths and half-lies, we should remind ourselves just how early a mind Bacon's is. And more, we should make some allowance for a choice which does not seem to have been available to him. Without choosing to write poetry – or even being sure that poetry wasn't simply a falsifying of human understanding – he imitates the impossible and implausible connections the mind tries to make between yes and no, black and white, unity and diversity, open and closed.

Tracing back through the published sequence of *Essays*, from the final edition in 1625 to the one in 1612 and then to the first versions in 1597, we find everywhere a perceptible thinning out of the prose between this or that observation or maxim. In 1597 and 1612, *Of Suitors* begins 'Many ill matters are undertaken, and many good matters with ill minds', but in 1625 the alliterative doubling on *many*, *matters* and *minds*, and the single fulcrum of *undertaken* is changed into something very fancy indeed:

Many ill matters and projects are undertaken, and private suits do putrefy the public good. Many good matters are undertaken with bad minds; I mean not only corrupt minds, but crafty minds that intend not performance.[18]

The paragraph ends with *performance*, as it should, for this is a fugue made out of a simple melody. The words pass over and around and through and across one unchanging and perplexing contradiction: that bad minds can conceive of and accomplish good things. In 1597, in *Of Studies*, one set of injunctions (a famous one) begins as 'Read not to contradict, nor to believe, but to weigh and consider', but in 1625 the first two infinitives split open, and another clause branches its way into the sentence:

Read not to contradict and confute; nor to believe and take for granted; nor to find talk and discourse; but to weigh and consider.

18. The 1597, 1612 and 1625 versions of the essay (which was first entitled *Of Suits*) are printed below in parallel texts, pp. 242–7.

What starts as twelve words, in a brief symmetry of one imperative controlling two positives and two negatives, becomes twenty-four words: still a single imperative, but now four paired infinitives, made asymmetrical in total, three negatives against one positive. Evidently in 1625 it is the scheme of the words, the rhetorical design upon the reader, which interests Bacon. As he himself observed in that *colour* about divisibility and size, breaking up something can make it seem less, and this is certainly true of stylistic analysis, but in this case it does explain how the *Essays* changed shape, on occasions out of all recognition, moving away from notebook readings towards reading itself. Moving, in other words, from reading which has finished and is displayed in a literary mortuary (where men have thought this aphorism, or that, or that; and they have left it dead or rootless) to readings which *cannot* be finished because the writing can't cross the interstices so finally that these conflicting aphorisms, maxims and other verbal authorities are reconciled. In 1625, the *Essays* are like an expanding universe, moving outwards, filling space so as to be able to join up within what is irreconcilable matter: the conjunctions striven for are impossible, but the words continue to flow in. So much so, in some instances, that the prose can become heavily literary, or even flatulent. There is no 1597 text of the essay *Of the True Greatness of Kingdoms and Estates*, but even by itself the 1625 version (twice the length of 1612) makes this point about the plenitude, if not surfeiting of words. It opens with:

The speech of Themistocles the Athenian, which was haughty and arrogant in taking so much to himself, had been a grave and wise observation and censure, applied at large to others. Desired at a feast to touch a lute, he said, *He could not fiddle, but yet he could make a small town a great city*. These words (holpen a little with a metaphor) may express two differing abilities in those that deal in business of estate. For if a true survey be taken of counsellors and statesmen, there may be found (though rarely) those which can make a small state great, and yet cannot fiddle: as, on the other side, there will be found a great many that can fiddle very cunningly, but yet are so far from being able to make a small state great, as their gift lieth the other way – to bring a great and flourishing estate to ruin and decay.

In this everything depends on the aphorism, quarried from Plutarch, *He could not fiddle, but yet he could make a small town a great city*. The sentence is exact and quite self-evident, yet the prose massages it as if it were some conundrum or mystery of language. Playing the fiddle, or fiddling the state, or having fingers to make nations but not draw the bow, are phrases which bristle to get out and sting the reader, but Bacon slows everything down because he wants to show how lubricious his style has become. The rhymes are one sign of decadence (*state/great*, *great/estate*, *way/decay*), as is the pedantry about needing help from a metaphor, and the pairings, more for the ear than the sense, *counsellors* and *statesmen*, *haughty* and *arrogant*, *observation* and *censure*. Fortunately, in the late *Essays* Bacon does not falter very often, but where he does it is because he has failed to distinguish between sentences and sententiousness, between a style approaching judgements, and the mannerisms of the judge. The last is a phoney, an assumed *gravitas* which tries to usher the reader past a problem (here, that some statesmen can make a kingdom, and others unmake it). By contrast, in, say, the essay *Of Ceremonies and Respects*, there is a style made out of *literata experientia*, the experience of learning, of making up and remaking one's mind with subtle and elegant qualification:

> Not to use ceremonies at all is to teach others not to use them again, and so diminisheth respect to himself (especially they be not to be omitted to strangers and formal natures); but the dwelling upon them and exalting them above the moon is not only tedious but doth diminish the faith and credit of him that speaks. And certainly there is a kind of conveying of effectual and imprinting passages amongst compliments, which is of singular use, if a man can hit upon it.

3

Bacon's education in words and things, and how to put them together, began early. In the long gallery of his family home at Gorhambury, in Hertfordshire, were tall windows in which were set stained-glass figures of beasts, trees, plants and flowers from the four known continents. On the walls and wooden panelling between each window there would have been, as in most Elizabethan great houses, a set of portraits, and perhaps mythological paintings, and just possibly a continental landscape. At Gorhambury, though, there was something else, for above each panel, painted on to a wooden frieze, were Latin inscriptions, the maxims and *sententiae* which Bacon's father had culled from Seneca and Cicero. Sometimes single, sometimes paired, on *fortune*, *law*, *ambition*, *injustice*, *benefits*, and *poverty* and *riches*, the inscriptions were as predictable and as laconic as ever. In one place, *De Amore* was squeezed into *Amor, insana amicitia: illius affectus: istius ratio, causa: at ea sola amicitia durat, cui virtus basis est.*[19] We have seen already that the truth of these mottoes was not of the first significance. As the Bacon family walked the length of their gallery, all sides of the chamber posed for them the difficulty of the inwardness and veracity of things, pictures and words. What substance was there, other than paint, to the figures and surfaces on the walls – were they more deceitful and vain than the Latin phrases, retrieved from the past and made to crown each part of the woodwork? Language and pictures, each medium was impenetrable, but there were also those windows, shot through with light, in which the whole world's natural history might be displayed. Portraits in oils, words in gold lettering on dark wood, glass images of nature lit from behind by daylight: the panelled room at Gorhambury, by no means exceptional, was a Tudor allegory of the mind's perplexity, and of its longing to get into things, and language, and make them reveal their inner truths. There was an urgency to this, even a nervousness, grabbing at understanding, with which the room collaborated. Not a space on the walls to be wasted, not a moment of leisure squandered in mere promenading. Every inch, and every moment to be educative: inscriptions to be verified against representations of nature, and man, from one alcove to the next. Whether or not this was exactly how the young Francis's mind was formed is not all that important, but that gallery and its long panels and windows *are* emblematic of the way his thought was to develop, reading and testing the words of antiquity against the light within and from outside solid bodies. This is as true of his rhetoric, shapes of words to name and create words, as of his science.

Light, as much as time and space, bends so much in the universe envisaged for us by Einstein that it scarcely seems worth asking what Bacon made of it, whether light for him was alert or inert, a dead or a live substance. In our century unimaginable equations

---

19. 'Love is friendship gone mad: passion is the motive of one, reason the other; but only that friendship lasts, whose foundation is virtue'. The Latin text and translation by Elizabeth McCutcheon, *Sir Nicholas Bacon's Great House Sententiae*, English Literary Renaissance Supplements, No. 3, Amherst, Massachusetts, 1977, pp. 74–5. McCutcheon gives full details about Gorhambury and its *sententiae* (pp. 5–36). There are more notes about Gorhambury in Aubrey, pp. 177–9 (edition cited in note 11).

have made infinitude and its retreating and curving perimeters so
incomprehensible that Bacon's notion of light as a divine revelation,
or as an instrument of discovery, has now become suspect. Yet even
now in our uncertainties the sundering of darkness by light still
figures for us the triumph of truth over falsehood, of wisdom over
ignorance, of good over bad. For Bacon, four centuries ago, the light
in men's heads had begun as pure knowledge (God had put it there),
but it was also a physical substance, porous and capable of being
stained by fear and sloth. Our understanding, he explained in the
Novum Organum,

is no dry light; it is drenched and steeped in our will and feelings . . .
We turn away from things hard to discover because we cannot bear the
pains of research, we turn away from what is cooling to the imagination
because it narrows our hopes, away from the deeper secrets of Nature
because we have superstitious fears, away from the light that comes
from doing experiments because we are too arrogant and proud to allow
the mind to be occupied by low concerns . . . In a thousand ways . . .
our minds are dyed and stained by our feelings.[20]

Writing like this, Bacon is most distant and closest to us at one
and the same moment. His pleas for experimental research have
certainly been answered in the centuries that separate us, but if
we think for an instant too long of the physiological explanations
here, the whole proposition dissolves into a mush of pre-Galenic
absurdity. It appears by this that the imagination can be cooled
down by the friction of research (where the work of experiments
apparently restricts and counteracts energy of mind), while light
passes in and out of the head through a wash of feelings, and is
saturated in the process. It won't do to suggest that Bacon is only
writing figuratively here, because he isn't. In the fourth book of *The
Advancement of Learning*, he complains that light has not been
studied scientifically, and that it has been extruded too quickly from
physics. He rejects confused theories that arise from attributing
false origins to what are its unstudied physical properties, and he
proposes that men of science inquire into what it is that 'is common
to all lucid bodies; in other words, into the Form of Light. For see
what an immense difference of body there is . . . between the sun

20. Book I, aphorism XLIX (from the 'Idols of the Mind' passage). Quoted here
from the translation by H. A. Mason in *The Cambridge Quarterly*, VII (1976–7),
359–71 (364–5). This should be compared with Spedding's translation of the same
Latin original, printed below, p. 280.

and rotten wood, or even the putrefied scales of fish'.[21] Scientists should also ask 'why some things take fire and throw out light when heated, and others not'. On a hot night at sea, what causes the water on the oars to glitter and shine, why do glow-worms and fireflies give off light, and why do the eyes of certain animals glow in the dark? The questions are interesting, but they begin with a premise, endemic in the Renaissance and before, that light is emitted by all substances, whether human or animal, liquid or solid, alive or decaying. What is to be identified is the factor of light in every material structure, not (as we might now ask) what are the reflective properties of a substance as it receives visible emissions, or electromagnetic radiation from the sun or firelight or an electric bulb. When he writes of the light of understanding Bacon is describing a property within the human body, located within the head, constituted by the physical activity of human organs (worked upon by the sensible soul, itself the agent of the rational soul, inspired into man by God).

Is this a scientific naming of light, then, or at least a show of how science might name something like light? Before we make up our minds, it is worth noting that Bacon's idea of *dry light* is based not on any observation or measurement (other than glancing at the scales on a dead fish), but on yet another piece of ancient writing, this time an apophthegm from Heraclitus, the pre-Socratic philosopher who lived five hundred years before Christ:

Heraclitus the Obscure said; *The dry light was the best soul.* Meaning, when the faculties intellectual are in vigour, not wet, nor, as it were, blooded by the affections.[22]

To us this may be valuable or misleading (especially as a first principle for a science), but it was a remark that Bacon couldn't leave alone. In *The Advancement of Learning* he wrote that 'Heraclitus the profound said, *Lumen siccum optima anima*',[23] and in the essay

21. *De Augmentis Scientiarum*, IV.3 (*Works*, IV.403–4).
22. *Works*, VII.163 (No. 268).
23. I.1.3. The saying itself is based on a misunderstanding. In his edition of the *Advancement* (1974, p. 251), Arthur Johnston explains that Heraclitus 'is reported to have said that "the dry soul is the wisest and best". By a corruption in the Greek the sentence became "the dry light (*lumen siccum*) is the wisest soul". Heraclitus believed that the soul was a mixture of fire (the noble part) and water (the ignoble). The soul which has most fire he calls "dry".' The saying and its later corruption are discussed in *The Art and Thought of Heraclitus* by Charles H. Kahn, Cambridge, 1979, pp. 245–54.

Of Friendship he could find no higher praise for a friend's advice than, once more, the enigma, *'Dry light is ever the best'*, because the light a man receives in 'counsel from another is drier and purer' than that from his own judgement. According to Bacon this saying is from a source profound, obscure and enigmatic, the very opposite of *dry light*, and this if nothing else should make us suspicious. The pure light of understanding appears to come out of a dark well of thought. We must not dismiss this as confused thinking. The remark from Heraclitus conceals something which Bacon wants to draw up out of it, to make his science strong and holy.[24] What we must recognize is that this involves a rhetorical activity as much as a scientific one, the naming of things unimaginable (or unrevealed) as much as the description of real things. Bacon worried at this distinction for years, but although he kept them apart in theory, rhetoric and science were always in collusion in his writing.

There are names for non-existent objects as well as for real things, he argues in the *Novum Organum*, and some objects are nameless because they have not yet been identified. But some unreal figments of the imagination 'are treated as if they were real and named as such. Some names refer to real things but they do it in a confused way. Some definitions of qualities are based on aspects not permanently characteristic of real objects. Examples of the former sort are Fortune, the Prime Mover, Planetary Orbits, the Element of Fire, and such-like fancies based on meaningless or false theories'. These last, the rhetorical names for unreal things, can be dismissed easily, he claims, if only we are rigorous enough in challenging them. But it is more difficult to undo mistakes in naming real things. For example, *humidum*, the Latin word for *moist* or *wet*, stands for too many different things:

> It is applied, firstly, to whatever flows easily round another body; secondly, to what has no fixed shape or consistency; thirdly, to what yields to pressure from any direction; fourthly, to what is easily divisible and is easily scattered; fifthly, to what readily joins up and forms into a continuous substance; sixthly, to what readily flows and is easily set in motion; seventhly, to what easily sticks to and wets the

24. It is true that in 1607, in *Thoughts and Conclusions*, he wrote that 'truth must be sought from the light of nature, not recovered from the darkness of antiquity' (translation cited in note 8; p. 87), but the pre-Socratic philosophers were important exceptions to even this rule. And in any case what is important is not what Bacon says he is doing (relying on things rather than words), but what he actually does.

surface of another body; eighthly, to what is easily liquefied and melts easily.[25]

When each of these properties has a separate name assigned to it, men will be able to eliminate absurdities of definition (whereby a flame can be *humid*, as well as glass and fine dust). So much for the scientific naming, but we should not miss the rhetorical one which accompanies it. What links all of these things together is not just the surcharged word *humidum*, but the unwritten words *liquidity of form*. Bacon knocks *humidum* on the head, but he can't stop all these things making another coherence, in which each substance is measured in terms of its internal freedom, its capacity to stick, flow, resist pressure, reshape, react, melt, join up and liquefy. Certainly this is not good science, but it shows how irrepressible Bacon's words are in making unreal (or at least unrevealed) categories, even when he is trying most vigorously to scotch them. Despite himself, he arranges these (allegedly) disparate elements in a rhetorical figure which compares their inner resistance.

This is a clue for understanding the apophthegm about *dry light*, and its place in the mind. In the passage from the *Novum Organum* quoted above (p. 30), Bacon tells us that human understanding is light suffused and defiled by will and feelings. Because we dislike hard work we avoid 'the pains of research', because we have big ambitions we keep away from the narrower horizons of science, and because we are timid and superstitious we shun 'the deeper secrets of Nature'. In all, we hide from 'the light that comes from doing experiments'. This barely registers as a scientific account of intellectual activity compromised by emotion, but its rhetorical shape is much more visible. It figures impatience, pride, fear, a longing for knowledge, pain and hard work, and a light from which we turn – in short all the elements of the story of sin and disgrace in Genesis. The unwritten words this time are *Man's Fall in the Garden of Eden*, and the passage is a trope, or rhetorical transformation, which brings forward the Biblical story of disobedience and lost purity, and roots it in Bacon's new way of thinking, the new organon. But the past is part of the Baconian future as well as the present, because the old pure light which Adam knew in Eden is also the goal of the new science.

This is not an easy notion, and to understand it we need to know

25. Mason's translation (cited in note 20), p. 369. See also below, p. 284.

something of Bacon's theory of rhetoric. In this, the mind can be thought of as a balance, on one side the *affections*, on the other *reason*, with the pivot, the *imagination*. Mental health is achieved when the scales are in equilibrium, but there is a fundamental difference between the weights, because the

affection beholdeth merely the present; reason beholdeth the future and sum of time. And therefore the present filling the imagination more, reason is commonly vanquished; but after that force of eloquence and persuasion [i.e. *rhetoric*] hath made things future and remote appear as present, then upon the revolt of the imagination reason prevaileth.[26]

Rhetoric makes the future, the not yet real or even imaginable 'appear as present': it corrects the deficiency of reason, which can envisage only the future (and sum of time) and corrects the affections, which are immobile in the present. When Bacon writes of *dry light* and fallen man's search for knowledge, and fear of it, his rhetoric is a trope for the unimaginable. What he is imagining is purity of thought, dry light in Adam's mind, lost in Eden but which science will bring back to man. (Just how distant this purity has become is the subject of the essay *Of Truth*, also grounded in Genesis. See the discussion below, pp. 43–4.) The future is only a name here, something which cannot even be depicted, but it is no less real than the things which scientists are to describe and measure. Indeed, Bacon's literary understatements, meaning beneath the surface, prefigure what science cannot yet deal with. What he only half perceives and intuitively responds to is traced in rhetorical outlines before the science of measurement, observation and tabulation can even begin. In this sense rhetorical tropes are very close to scientific hypothesis, the faculty of theory which Bacon is often accused of having undervalued.[27] As he put it himself in

26. *The Advancement of Learning*, II.18.4.

27. Karl R. Wallace, in two very good studies, *Francis Bacon on Communication and Rhetoric*, Chapel Hill, 1943, and *Francis Bacon on the Nature of Man*, Urbana, Chicago, 1967, has done much to explain what Bacon understood by the imagination and reason, and how rhetoric worked upon them. According to Wallace (1943, Chapter 12) Bacon's major contribution to rhetoric was to free it from its old inferiority to logic. Rhetoric was to direct the imagination, rather than just deploy language in everyday circumstances. Nevertheless there were to be strict limits to its inventiveness: it was not supposed to create anything it pleased. What is claimed in this Introduction is that Bacon's own rhetoric slips the leash and discovers what no scholastic logic or simple-minded induction could arrive at. Margaret Willey has

1603, 'the knowledge which we now possess will not teach a man even what to wish for'.[28] The device of rhetoric, a proleptic naming, was to supply exactly that deficiency.

In the *Essays*, too, in subjects not normally thought of as at all scientific, there is evidence of words anticipating things. In the essay *Of Riches*, the things themselves are of limited practical value:

> Of great riches there is no real use, except it be in the distribution; the rest is but conceit. So saith Solomon, *Where much is, there are many to consume it; and what hath the owner but the sight of it with his eyes?*

You can pick up gold bars, or look at them, or count coins into bags, or weigh them, or put them into strong boxes or on tables, or move them upstairs or from one side of the room to the other, but there is little else to riches as tangible objects. So few other practical uses have they, that most of the essay is given over to the various ways, good and bad, of obtaining, augmenting and accepting riches. It concerns itself with the transactions of wealth, the activity of men passing money between themselves, and the most efficient ways of doing it.

> The improvement of the ground is the most natural obtaining of riches, for it is our great mother's blessing, the earth's; but it is slow. And yet where men of great wealth do stoop to husbandry, it multi-plieth riches exceedingly. I knew a nobleman in England, that had the greatest audits of any man in my time: a great grazier, a great sheep-master, a great timber-man, a great collier, a great corn-master, a great lead-man, and so of iron, and a number of the like points of husbandry: so as the earth seemed a sea to him, in respect of the perpetual importation.

The real things are soon put aside here. The earth and man working with it, a natural alliance, give way to an earth transmogrified into the sea, bringing in (importing) rather than giving out from the roots. The sleight of hand that achieves this is in the phrase 'men of great wealth do stoop to husbandry', because this stooping has nothing to do with bending one's back and planting, but taking time to look in ledger books, diversify investment and outpace the return of the land. This nobleman's activity is not in rearing, mining, growing, smelting and selling, nor in wood, metal or wool. It is in

some very interesting things to say on this subject in her paper 'Bacon: Induction and/or Rhetoric' in *Studies in the Literary Imagination*, IV (April 1971), 65–79.

28. From the Preface to 'Of the Interpretation of Nature' (*Letters and Life*, III.87).

the intangible audits and planning and management of the estate. What Bacon glimpses here, as elsewhere in the essay, is that wealth is a calibration of human relationships rather than bags of money piled up in a treasury or corn stored in a barn. Even the language of service and labour, real enough in Jacobean England, gives way to jargon, and wheeling and dealing:

. . . the gains of bargains are of a . . . doubtful nature, when men shall wait upon others' necessity, broke by servants and instruments to draw them on, put off others cunningly that would be better chapmen, and the like practices, which are crafty and naught. As for the chopping of bargains, when a man buys not to hold, but to sell over again, that commonly grindeth double, both upon the seller and upon the buyer.

Grinding, chopping, waiting on, holding, putting off, drawing on – the verbs remind us of their physicality, but are at once submerged into the language of commerce and sharp dealing in the market-place. It is a vocabulary quickly slipping from the real to the invisible. The smooth operator doesn't buy to possess, doesn't deal directly with his customers or rivals, doesn't touch the realness of money or merchandise. What is anticipated here is a time – our own – when all the substance of riches, metals and grain, will have disappeared into bank statements and rates of exchange.

Bacon is not always as prescient as this about money matters. In *Of Usury* he is still stuck with medieval ideas of wealth as a fixed commodity, a predetermined total to be divided among a set of players (king, government, merchants and financiers). All the same, in *Of Riches* he clearly recognizes that, say, market values can be manipulated by moving and delaying capital: 'when a man's stock is come to that, that he can expect the prime of markets, and overcome those bargains which for their greatness are few men's money . . . he cannot but increase mainly'. In total, the essay makes its way rhetorically towards the relational or social science of economics even when (as at the beginning and end) it is still weighed down with respectable junk about avarice, classical advice about begging inheritances, and pious notes on charities. It is not by chance that Bacon begins the essay with riches as *impedimenta*, or baggage, for his own thought and speculation is as encumbered by their clumsiness as the army itself. What he cannot quite make out, and neither could most of his contemporaries, is how sharing risks, or doubling bargains by not touching the purchase, merely buying or selling it, links the individual to the army, the one to the many, as the secret of generating wealth. He lived before registered banks, limited liability, and the Keynesian Multiplier, so this is not all that surprising. But the enterprise of his English nobleman, the accelerated profits on these primitive stock markets, and the multiplication that comes from dividing up and distributing money, all suggest that Bacon is writing ahead of what he knows, and that he is finding words for the unimaginable science of economic activity.

4

We might have guessed that Queen Elizabeth, the most parsimonious and unforgiving of Renaissance princes, would never really take to Francis Bacon, young or middle-aged, sycophant or loyal critic, lawyer or prophet of science. He had the nerve to want to spend her money (on schemes for a zoo, a laboratory and a natural history museum[29]), and he opened his mouth too much, and too early, as a backbencher in the Parliament of 1593. She never forgot his smart protests against increasing taxes for that year, and despite all his efforts, and those of his patron, the Earl of Essex, he never quite made it into Eliza's charmed court circle. Looking back, some of her judgements about him seem cruel and even impertinent: for one thing, she said he was shallow in the law, which he certainly was not. But she also said, and he relished it, that he was her watch-candle, because he burnt continually.[30] This was an acute, if a rather over-pretty conceit. Throughout his life Bacon wrote and worked steadily, and was awake at all times, waiting to illuminate his monarch's darkness and measuring the passing of time. But there was also in him a tendency to be extinguished after a while, to be snuffed out or simply to go out if he didn't make headway in his

29. See below, p. 263, in the speech 'Advising the Study of Philosophy', which was delivered at Christmas 1594 to a Lord of Misrule elected by the students of Gray's Inn. The plans Bacon wrote down for a play prince would certainly have been what he thought the real Queen of England should do.

30. Recorded in a letter he wrote to her successor, King James, on 31 May 1612 (when, after Salisbury's death, he was looking to be the King's minister in Parliament): '. . . my offering is care and observance: and as my good old mistress was wont to call me her watch-candle, because it pleased her to say I did continually burn (and yet she suffered me to waste almost to nothing), so I must much more owe the like duty to your Majesty, by whom my fortunes have been settled and raised' (*Letters and Life*, IV.280).

career. It is true that he had more than his fair share of disappointments, but he was a man of genius, and he knew it, and some of his dithering points to a feebleness of will. At least twice he resolved to give up public life, and return home to study philosophy, and yet somehow he hung on at court, waiting for the main chance, avoiding the big decision about an active or a contemplative life. In 1607 he got what he wanted (he was made Solicitor-General), and he burned brightly enough after that until Parliament finally did the choosing for him, by excluding him from public office.

To accuse Bacon of inconstancy to his own greatness may be unfair: but to suggest it of his work in the *Essays* would be a gross injustice. In them, as in nothing else that he wrote, there is the compulsion to make whole, to finish the design of something, to perfect it. W. B. Yeats was right enough when he said that a man had to decide between perfection of the life or of the work, but Bacon nearly failed to get either of them right. He messed up the end of a great career, and he didn't complete one major philosophical, historical or scientific plan. For all his brilliance, and industry, so much of what he had started had to be finished by others. Only in the *Essays* was there a constancy of his genius. He called them his 'recreations' of his 'other studies',[31] as if to slight their importance, but he meant what he said: they were attempts to remake or *re*create, from sentences and syntax, the lines which held together body and mind. For someone like Bacon, with no mathematics and very little practical experience, his genius could only really fulfil itself in words, by reading or translating the outer motions of the body into the inner motives of the mind. Confronted by a deformed man or woman, he is not interested in what is wrong with their joints, or backbone, but in the language which tries to join up exterior and interior:

Certainly there is a consent between the body and the mind, and *where nature erreth in the one, she ventureth in the other: Ubi peccat in uno, periclitatur in altero*. But because there is in man an election touching the frame of his mind, and a necessity in the frame of his body, the stars of natural inclination are sometimes obscured by the sun of discipline and virtue.[32]

31. In a letter to Lancelot Andrews in the summer of 1622 (*Letters and Life*, VII.374).

32. *Of Deformity*, p. 191.

Whatever consent or agreement there is between the Baconian body and mind, it is not one described explicitly in this passage. Instead, what brings them together are the symmetries in vocabulary and phrasing: *erreth* against *ventureth*, *election* against *necessity*, *man* against *nature*, the quotation in Latin against its translation; and so on. The *frame* here is not so much in the mind or body, but in the writer's determination to be regular, to construct a perfect surface. It is not a beautiful shape, but then all that matters is that it avoid being deformed. Bacon holds on to the symmetry until almost the final line, but then what was merely a bit dainty becomes ornamental and leaden: 'the stars of natural inclination are sometimes obscured by the sun of discipline and virtue'. There is neither life nor wit in this analogy, only a fetish for congruity. Bacon is simply paying too much attention to the shape of the line. To say that its meaning is metaphoric makes no difference. No matter whether the stars are the engines of fate, or the sun the source of inner light, this conjunction is still only a dead limb fastened into place to make the passage look right.[33] The subject of the essay is the malformed body, and how the mind responds to it, but in this case Bacon's writing itself makes no concession to irregularity and disproportion. The words remain figurative, able to make a way into more words, but not into the substance, or the body of meaning.

From a number of sources, including the essay *Of Regiment of Health*, we know that Bacon was intensely interested in his own body, and its regularity. He suffered fainting fits at every eclipse of the moon, he reckoned his health to be most vulnerable at around four o'clock in the afternoon, and he experimented with all kinds of potions, ointments and diets.[34] He was not unusual in this, nor in his persistent efforts to keep his bowels open. The thing he dreaded

33. Thomas Hobbes, who is said to have acted as Bacon's secretary on occasions, could evidently be just as insensitive to the difference between dead sentences and live ones. He reused the comparison in *Leviathan*, I.2.5, where the 'light of the sun obscureth the light of the stars'. There are other shapes in the *Essays* which are still to be considered by literary students. For example, the first essay, *Of Truth*, opens with a spoken question and giddiness in men's minds, while the last essay closes with more giddiness and the word *writing*. And it tells us something about the design of the *Essays* that in the last sentence the study of language, *philology*, is linked to a *circle of tales* – a turning wheel of study, contemplation and narratives, the form of the *Essays* perhaps.

34. The fainting is recorded by his chaplain, Dr William Rawley (see Arber, p. xvii: full reference, p. 47 below). His attention to the times and cures of his body, and his fears for it, are recorded in a notebook of 1608 (see *Letters and Life*, IV.78–80).

was a stoppage, a closing up of the body, which would shut in the humours and ferment them as in a vat. So he administered purge after purge, and was surprised at how weak he felt. All of this was what any Elizabethan physician could have prescribed for him. What is strange, given how little he knew about his own insides and those of most of the physical structures around him, is that he chose to describe the *Essays* (in a Latin translation) as *interiora rerum*,[35] the insides of things. Normally when he spoke about being inside or looking into things, it was with despair. The senses unaided were so ineffectual and so insensitive that men were as good as blind and deaf. When we cease to see, he observed, we cease to think. Our eyes are unable to see into the invisible workings within tangible bodies, and so we miss the more subtle changes of form that are taking place.[36] The alimentary canal, the urinary ducts, the veins, the capillaries, these are what Bacon wants to see, and beyond, to the corpuscles, bone marrow and nucleic acids. Yet if he is shut out from these, for want of a microscope, what kind of insides can he be thinking of for the *Essays*, what interiors are there to masques, custom, envy, death or love?

The question is tricky because they can't have any inner space or meaning that isn't made by Bacon's mind, and the very vocabulary he invites us to use – spaces, interiors, insides – is the language of bodies, perimeters drawn around two- or three-dimensional areas. In the *Essays*, books enter the body through the digestive system, envy radiates out through the eyeball, litigation is spewed out through the courts, ambition gnaws into the stomach, merchants are veins of blood to the liver, and speech seeps through the head into the mind.[37] Everywhere, words and names penetrate the body or are projected out of it. The insides, the *interiora rerum*, are spaces of language forced in among the bones, flesh and viscous humours. The physicality of opening up or sealing or even eating the body disgusts Bacon, but this is the way to true meanings:

35. The full title of the translation, first printed in 1638 in the collected edition *Operum Civilium et Moralium*, is *Sermones Fideles, sive Interiora Rerum* (Faithful Discourses or the Insides of Things).

36. See aphorism 12 from the *Novum Organum*, p. 280–81 below.

37. *Of Studies*, p. 209 (tasting, swallowing and chewing books), *Of Envy*, p. 83 (envy irradiating from the eye), *Of Judicature*, p. 222 (the litigation), *Of Ambition*, p. 173 (ambition as a malign, inward humour), *Of Usury*, p. 184 and *Of Empire*, p. 119 (merchants as *vena porta*, the gate vein in the body politic), *Of Truth*, p. 62 (lies sinking and settling into the mind).

Philip of Macedon dreamed he sealed up his wife's belly, whereby he did expound it, that his wife should be barren: but Aristander the soothsayer told him his wife was with child, because men do not use to seal vessels that are empty.[38]

Her womb was full, but no fuller with child than with a meaning to be interpreted and delivered. This was even more obvious to Bacon in the myth of how Jupiter gave birth to Pallas, goddess of wisdom:

... they say, after Jupiter was married to Metis [goddess of counsel], she conceived by him and was with child, but Jupiter suffered her not to stay till she brought forth, but ate her up; whereby he became himself with child, and was delivered of Pallas armed out of his head. Which monstrous fable containeth a secret of empire: how kings are to make use of their council of state.

Bacon domesticates the story into a parable of wise government, but the real 'secret' is that counsel was taken into the body through the mouth and that it swelled into meaning in Jupiter's insides. Deep within the body there are some meanings so obscure and so frightening that they cannot be tamed at all. In *Of Friendship*, probably the greatest of the *Essays*, Bacon comes very close to saying that words lacerate the body, wound it, eat it within when it refuses to disclose meaning:

The parable of Pythagoras is dark, but true: *Cor ne edito*, 'Eat not the heart.' Certainly, if a man would give it a hard phrase, those that want friends to open themselves unto are cannibals of their own hearts.

To read into one of these essays, which Bacon calls the interiors of things, should be to reach into a body, into an inner presence of meaning. Not that this has anything to do with Bacon's own body, or his inner self. Quite the opposite, for his corporeal being is almost entirely absent from the writing, as if he wanted to ignore the sensations in his fingertips and the tastes in his mouth. We have only to compare him with Montaigne to realize just how much he keeps hidden. In a few pages of his essay *On Experience*,[39] Montaigne informs us that the insides of his ears are sometimes itchy, that he prefers unsalted bread, that he likes his meats rare and his fish tender, and that he has a habit of polishing his teeth with a

---

38. *Of Prophecies*, pp. 169–70. The next quotation is from *Of Counsel*, p. 120.
39. *Essays*, III.13, Penguin translation by J. M. Cohen (pp. 383, 386, 388–9). The currently received view about the relationship between Bacon and Montaigne is that, apart from the titles, their essays have little in common.

napkin, both in the morning and before and after meals. Needless to say we are also told that the teeth are in excellent condition, given his age. There is nothing at all like this in Bacon, and what is revealed in the *Essays* appears by chance, and not by design. In *Of Building*, Bacon tops out a plan for a house with an upper floor to be reached by an open spiral staircase. His only caution is that none of the lower rooms be made into a dining place for servants. 'For otherwise you shall have the servants' dinner after your own: for the steam of it will come up as in a tunnel'. Good enough advice perhaps, but for Bacon there is more to it than that. His nose is deeply offended. In court dances, when the company begins to sweat and smell a little, he considers that 'sweet odours suddenly coming forth without any drops falling' would be things of great refreshment. When he writes of a good name as *unguenti fragrantis*, a fragrant ointment, he recalls that 'the odours of ointments are more durable than those of flowers'. When he lays out a path in a garden, even an imaginary one, he smells the scents of burnet, thyme and water-mint, perfuming the air as they are walked upon and crushed into fragrance.[40] John Aubrey said that Bacon's sense of smell was so acute (or over-nice) that none of his servants dared 'appear before him without Spanish leather boots; for he would smell the neat's leather, which offended him'.[41] His sight is almost as sharp and fastidious. He notices that diamonds cut with facets give 'the quickest reflection', and he is choosy about colour and how it is arranged. In court entertainments, the 'colours that show best by candle-light are white, carnation, and a kind of sea-water-green': in needleworks and embroideries, 'it is more pleasing to have a lively work upon a sad and solemn ground, than to have a dark and melancholy work upon a lightsome ground'. He is just as discriminating about the shapes of things. A face is not to be judged by a painter's rules, because there is 'no excellent beauty that hath not some strangeness in the proportion'.[42] But if sight and smell can be traced in the *Essays*, this is not so with the other senses. There are

40. From *Of Masques and Triumphs*, p. 176 (the sweating courtiers), *Of Praise*, p. 215 (the fragrant ointment), *Of Gardens*, p. 199 (the crushed thyme and mint).

41. *Aubrey's Brief Lives*, p. 172 (edition cited in note 11). Aubrey also claimed that 'at every meal, according to the season of the year', Bacon 'had his table strewed with sweet herbs and flowers, which he said did refresh his spirits and memory.'

42. From *Of Honour and Reputation*, p. 219 (the diamonds), *Of Masques and Triumphs*, p. 176 (colours in court entertainments), *Of Adversity*, p. 75 (needleworks), *Of Beauty*, p. 189 (strangeness in proportion).

one or two comments about music and singing, but the sensations of tasting and feeling are only literary. When bread is eaten it is in the sweat of one's face, in a line from Genesis, *'in sudore vultus tui comedes panem tuum'*,[43] and even the most explicit physical agony is derived from a book, with only the briefest coda from Bacon himself:

> You shall read in some of the friars' books of mortification that a man should think with himself what the pain is if he have but his finger's end pressed or tortured, and thereby imagine what the pains of death are when the whole body is corrupted and dissolved; when many times death passeth with less pain than the torture of a limb; for the most vital parts are not the quickest of sense.[44]

The vitals proper – lungs, heart, brain and liver – are not the quickest of sense: but in the *Essays* neither are the limbs, skin and genitalia. No, the eyes and nose are the parts most vital to Bacon, the organs most alive, most quick with sense. For Bacon is a hunter, whose primary need is to follow a scent, and watch, and wait, and conceal himself. It comes as no surprise that his own doctor said that he had *viper's eyes*.[45]

The body is present in the *Essays*, then, but it is not Bacon's body – which is an odd displacement of authorial presence, and which contributes to a sense of numbness, of thought without feeling, of a brain unconnected to the nerves and senses. L. C. Knights was on to this when he accused Bacon of cutting the instincts away from the intellect, a lobotomy which ended for good and all the integrity of mind and matter. But there were also theological and philosophical implications to this absenting of his own body. He tried to evade them, but they are unmistakable in the essay *Of Truth*:

> *What is truth?* said jesting Pilate, and would not stay for an answer.

The sentence has been quoted so often that it has worn thin on examination papers and in academic chat but it is not at all the faded abstraction we have made of it. It alludes to nothing less than the essaying or trial of Christ, the trial by man under Roman law of man's Saviour, the Son of God, the embodiment, the *body* of Truth.

43. 'In the sweat of your face you shall eat your bread' (3.19), *Of Usury*, p. 183.
44. *Of Death*, p. 64.
45. Recorded by Aubrey (see note 11), p. 174. The doctor was William Harvey, who discovered the circulation of the blood (a theory which Bacon probably dismissed, and which he certainly omitted to mention in any of his works).

It begins a sequence of essays, which in their root sense are concerned with testing, or assaying, making trial of metals, valuing their purity, trying the metal of men. In *Of Truth* this is the first sentence of man against Christ, and it is matched by a last sentence, where Christ on the Day of Judgement returns to earth to test men, to try their faith:

Surely the wickedness of falsehood and breach of faith cannot possibly be so highly expressed, as in that it shall be the last peal to call the judgements of God upon the generations of men; it being foretold that when Christ cometh, *He shall not find faith upon the earth.*

The essay begins in legality, a Roman trial of a Jew, where Christ is prosecuted by man, and it ends in a supralegality where the Creator, in His Son, brings man to judgement. Truth is theological and philosophical and even 'of civil business' in the essay, yet it is always hedged in or justified by law. Furthermore, the sentence passing judgement by refusing to listen must for Bacon in 1625 have had other resonances. As Attorney-General, and chief prosecutor and adviser to the Crown, Bacon himself – in trials as fixed as the one before Pilate – had sent down royal favourite after royal favourite. He had deserted the Earl of Essex, and helped to send him to the block, and he had fitted up the Earl of Somerset – and in the end, four years before the essay was published, he himself had been tried and convicted because King James couldn't, or wouldn't, stick by him when he was charged with taking bribes. Banging inside his head, day after day, in the courts of princes must have been that contemptuous question, what *is* truth? He knew the answer, though – truth was Christ's body, the flesh sacrificed for the sins of old Adam. It was the other body, not Bacon's, and in *Of Truth* it showed up in the vocabulary: veins, blood in them, devil's wine, naked daylight, God's making of man in the Garden, the serpent going on its belly, love-making, man giving God the lie, challenging and deceiving his Maker. This is the language of man losing paradise in Eden, and the occasion for the divine body to be substituted, sacrificially, for the human one. In the essay *Of Truth* itself, for all its intelligence, Bacon fails inwardly because, in the same way, he puts another body in place of his own. He edges out of the writing and leaves a surrogate flesh and blood, a presence which isn't his. It is the same in a good many of the other *Essays*. The Christian theology of redemption – another man bears my guilt – allows him to swerve from his own being, to evade the here and now of his flesh and senses. And in the centuries of rationalism to follow, not even that other body will survive. By the end of the nineteenth century, the *Essays* will be praised for their abstractions and philosophical loftiness, and the language of the body, its mess and movement, will be ignored or unnoticed.[46]

Perhaps this is what C. S. Lewis was getting at when he described the *Essays* as sterile. No one doubts that they are alive, in spite of their beginnings in pedantry, rote-learning and superfine rhetoric, because Bacon made them tensile. They are strong but able to stretch out beyond themselves, and beyond this or that received wisdom or seemingly unshakeable truth. But they don't have any generative powers, they don't offer anything from within to their successors, to writers (or readers) who might want to learn from them, or learn how to write. It is possible to catch at their manner, or even to imitate them, but what they say would never make or break our lives. There are no secret joys in them, to recall Bacon's own remark about parents and their children. It may be that where there is so much intelligence, and nothing felt, the mind, contracted to its own bright eyes, simply feeds on its flame and consumes itself.

46. In his notes on the essay *Of Truth*, for example, E. A. Abbott in 1878 writes, revealingly, 'Christ appears to Bacon typical of the Truth, and Pilate the type' of the sceptical, cynical questioner (II.108). Types they may be, but for Bacon they were first the flesh and blood of God surrendering to His human inquisitor.

A NOTE ON THE TEXT AND ANNOTATION

The Text

1. The first edition of the *Essays* was published in 1597, with the title *Essayes. Religious Meditations. Places of perswasion and disswasion.* This contained ten essays, the *Meditationes Sacrae* and the *Colours of Good and Evil.* [1597]

2. Some time between 1607 and 1612 a manuscript collection of the *Essays* was prepared with the title *The Writings of S' ffrancis Bacon Kn': the Kinges Sollicitor Generall in Moralitie Policie, and Historie.* In this manuscript (Harleian MS 5106 in the British Library) there were twenty-four new essays, as well as the original ten. [*MS*]

3. The second edition appeared in 1612 as *The Essaies of S' Francis Bacon Knight, the Kings Solliciter Generall.* This contained thirty-eight essays: nine from the original ten, twenty-three of the additional ones in the Harleian MS, and six new ones. Many of the 1597 and MS texts were altered and enlarged for this edition. [*1612*]

4. The third edition, and the final one in Bacon's life-time, was published in 1625, entitled *The Essayes or Counsels, Civill and Morall, of Francis Lo. Verulam, Viscount S'. Alban.* This edition added twenty new essays, making a total of fifty-eight, and revised and expanded most of the existing ones. [*1625*]

The present Penguin text is taken from a copy of the 1625 edition in the Bodleian Library, Oxford. (This copy was presented as a gift to George, Duke of Buckingham, to whom Bacon dedicated the *Essays* – see below, p. 57.) For this text, the spellings of 1625 have been modernized, and so too the punctuation wherever the sense and pace permit. Bacon's punctuation, for all its value in determining some of the rhythms and weighting in the prose, is likely to be a hindrance to the majority of modern readers. There are examples of the original spellings and punctuation in the parallel texts of three essays, *Of Suitors*, *Fortune* and *Vainglory*, printed below, pp. 242–55.

It is important to remember that many of the *Essays* were altered greatly before achieving their final form in 1625. There is a complete record of the revisions in the parallel-text edition, *A Harmony of the Essays*, by Edward Arber, London, 1871 (and 1895). Arber also gives details of seventeenth-century and later reprints, and he has a note on the Latin translation of the *Essays* published in 1638 as *Sermones Fideles, sive Interiora Rerum*. Most of this translation was completed before Bacon's death in 1626, and its readings are useful for glossing and interpreting the English text. More detailed descriptions of the early editions are provided by R. W. Gibson in *Francis Bacon: A Bibliography of his Works and of Baconiana to the year 1750*, Oxford, 1950 (supplement 1959).

The Annotation

The annotation in this edition is at the foot of the page. It contains:

a. A note showing in which of the early texts each essay appears. So, under *Of Friendship*, there is 'Texts: MS, 1612, 1625', indicating that the essay made its first appearance in the Harleian MS and is to be found in all but one (*1597*) of the four versions of the *Essays* listed above.

b. Brief historical notes; glosses of archaic words, or ones peculiar to Bacon; and explanations and renderings of difficult sentences and phrases. Words listed in the *Concise Oxford Dictionary*, sixth edition, are not normally glossed.

c. Translations of the Latin, Italian and Spanish quotations and sayings, except where Bacon has already translated them (and it is obvious at once that he has done so).

d. Sources for Bacon's quotations from the Bible and ancient and modern writers. Knowing where Bacon has got things from, and what he has done to them, can sometimes be important. There are obvious examples at the beginning and end of the essay *Of Truth* (see notes 1 and 15). Another, more subtle instance is in *Of Nature in Men*, where Bacon quotes from Ovid, *Remedies for Love*, and later makes a brief comparison: 'nature will lay buried a great time, and yet revive upon the occasion or temptation. Like as it was with Aesop's damsel, turned from a cat to a woman, who sat very demurely at the board's end till a mouse ran before her' (p. 178). The interesting thing is that Bacon has changed the setting and circumstances of the fable: in Aesop, the cat-woman pounces on the mouse when she is in the nuptial bed, not seated at the table (see *Fables of Aesop*, Penguin translation, No. 96, p. 100). It is possible that Bacon had another version of the story in mind, but more likely that he swerved from the sexual element in the original. He certainly extracts Ovid's lines from their context of sexual restraint (resisting mistresses who drive their lovers mad with desire). Bacon's response to his sources, conscious or not, may lead us on to another question: in an essay about self-control in men, is it at all surprising that there is nothing explicit about sexual desire? Perhaps these sources, once we know them, open up new ways of reading the whole essay. This may also be true of his use of Tacitus, Machiavelli and Lucretius in other essays.

A distinction has been made in the notes between accurate quotations and those which Bacon has adapted or obviously misquoted. So, in *Of Seditions and Troubles*, note 4 gives the source as simply '*Aeneid*, IV. 178–80', meaning that this is a correct (or very nearly correct) quotation. In note 6, however, the source, in Tacitus, is cited as 'from *Histories*, I.7', indicating that this is some way from being an exact quotation.

In preparing the annotation, I have consulted, learnt from, and adapted the commentaries in earlier editions and selections of the *Essays*. Those of Abbott (2 vols., 3rd edition, London, 1878), Reynolds (Oxford, 1890), Max Patrick (New York, 1948) and Johnston (London, 1965) were particularly useful.

FURTHER READING

Editions

The standard edition is *The Works of Francis Bacon*, ed. James Spedding, R. L. Ellis and D. D. Heath, 14 vols., 1857–74. The first seven volumes are the philosophical, literary and professional pieces (abbreviated throughout the present edition as *Works*), and the second seven are the letters, private papers and notebooks, with a commentary (abbreviated as *Letters and Life*).

Editions of the *Essays* are referred to on pp. 46–8. There are useful editions of *The Advancement of Learning* by Arthur Johnston (Books I–II, Oxford, 1974) and William Armstrong (Book I, London, 1975). Both of these are well-annotated, and Armstrong writes a good introduction for the beginner in Renaissance science, logic and learning. Johnston's edition also has the *New Atlantis*, the utopian fable Bacon wrote in 1624. Each edition contains a list of books which place Bacon's work in an intellectual and scientific context. A valuable set of translations, noted above in the Introduction, is included in *The Philosophy of Francis Bacon*, by Benjamin Farrington, Liverpool, 1964.

Primers

Bacon's reputation is currently as glossy among some academics as it was among some scientists in the seventeenth century. Brian Vickers, for example, is so keen to rehabilitate Bacon as a great prose writer (which he is) that he can sometimes be uncritical of his duplicities and shortcomings. This should be borne in mind when using his otherwise helpful pamphlet *Francis Bacon* in the Writers and their Work series (1978). Professor Vickers is one of the most knowledgeable of Bacon's critics, and yet he does not record any of the important essays which have attacked Bacon's writings and morals. Anthony Quinton also knows enough about Bacon, but he doesn't sound especially interested in the subject in his short introduction in the Past Masters series (Oxford, 1980). This is good on Bacon's philosophical strengths and weaknesses, but has little to say about his imaginative life.

The Essays

The list must begin with the things not mentioned about the *Essays* in the Introduction: their variety, their styles (Ciceronic, Senecan, mixed), their concerns with Bacon's plans for the advancement of knowledge and society, and so forth. In her essay 'Francis Bacon', in *The English Mind*, Cambridge, 1964, pp. 7–29, Anne Righter (Barton) points out, among other things, just how much difference there is between, say, *Of Gardens* and *Of Seditions and Troubles*, and she argues that the *Essays* are intended to elicit varying responses from their readers. This is a stimulating piece of criticism, and one which gives Bacon his due, even if it is a little overgenerous on his feelings for poetry. Perhaps the single most important study of what it is like to read the *Essays* is by Stanley Fish, 'Georgics of the Mind: the Experience of Bacon's *Essays*' in *Self-Consuming Artifacts*, Berkeley and Los Angeles, 1974, pp. 78–155. This is an extended exercise in reading, and arguing, and so it is rather long, but students of the *Essays* cannot fail to learn much from it.

Historical studies of Bacon's styles are not as learnedly dusty as one might fear. The number of times Bacon quotes from Tacitus, Seneca and Cicero in the *Essays* alone calls for some explanation. Morris W. Croll in *Style, Rhetoric and Rhythm*, ed. J. Max Patrick and others, Princeton, 1966, and George Williamson in *The Senecan Amble*, London, 1951, give their versions of why and how Bacon (and others) wanted to write like the ancients, but improve on them. Brian Vickers in *Francis Bacon and Renaissance Prose*, Cambridge, 1968, Chapter 4, refines and corrects some of these earlier judgements, and subjects Bacon's syntax to minute and often interesting scrutiny. Smaller contributions, about sources and the form of the *Essays* etc., are made by R. C. Cochrane, 'Francis Bacon and the Architect of Fortune', *Studies in the Renaissance*, 5 (1958), 176–95; A. P. McMahon, 'Francis Bacon's Essay *Of Beauty*', *Publications of the Modern Language Association*, 60 (1945), 716–59; G. Tillotson, 'Words for Princes: Bacon's *Essays*', *Essays in Criticism and*

Research, Cambridge, 1942, pp. 31–40; and M. Walters, 'The Literary Background of Francis Bacon's Essay "Of Death"', *Modern Language Review*, 35 (1940), 1–7. See also D. S. Brewer, 'Lucretius and Bacon on Death', *Notes and Queries*, 200 (1955), 509–10.

The political implications of the styles need more attention. After all, Tacitus was writing under the Roman emperors, while Cicero was put to death when the Roman republic was just about on its knees. For an Englishman in the Renaissance to admire and quote and imitate this or that ancient writer was not just a question of style, but how one should think of oneself in court and Parliament, and how far royal authority should extend. The influence of Montaigne on Bacon is now thought to have been less than that of, say, Machiavelli (see J. Zeitlin, 'The Development of Bacon's Essays', *Journal of English and Germanic Philology*, 27 (1928), 496–512, and V. Luciani, 'Bacon and Machiavelli', *Italica*, 24 (1947), 26–40). The way the *Essays* fit into Bacon's social and educational plans is discussed by R. S. Crane in 'The Relation of Bacon's *Essays* to his Program for the Advancement of Learning', *Schelling Anniversary Papers*, New York, 1923, pp. 87–105. Lisa Jardine in *Francis Bacon: Discovery and the Art of Discourse*, Cambridge, 1974, has a chapter on 'The method of Bacon's essays'. This is a scholarly book on Bacon's dialectic and methods of communication, and a good piece of intellectual history, but it is difficult to agree entirely with Dr Jardine that the *Essays* were 'carefully constructed to put across practical precepts which Bacon believed to be of value to men of all intellectual backgrounds' (p. 228). Did those Jacobeans who planted out gardens, or designed new houses, or ruled in government circles, or were thinking of having children, really look to Bacon for advice on how to do things? And did he think they would? Surely they were intended for readers more than doers, for people who like to read about precepts, or scan lists of which fruit to plant, or read about how to disarm a political opponent by fixing one's eye on him.

The case against Bacon's writing is made by several literary heavyweights. C. S. Lewis and Douglas Bush both come down sharply on the *Essays* in the *Oxford History of English Literature*, Volumes III and V, which amounts to a kind of official black-balling. But much more devastating is the evergreen 'Bacon and the Seventeenth-Century Dissociation of Sensibility' which

L. C. Knights first published in 1943 (reprinted in *Explorations*, London, 1946). Developing a notion from T. S. Eliot, Knights identified Bacon as the chief culprit in the break-up of the imaginative life of seventeenth-century Englishmen. Brian Vickers (1968) takes him on over this, but with no great success (as John Carey points out in the few, highly charged pages he is able to give to Bacon in the *Sphere History of Literature in the English Language*, Volume 2 (1970), 393–7).

General

Coleridge, in the twelfth chapter of the *Biographia Literaria*, observes, as a golden rule, that there are two types of philosophical writer: those of whose understanding we are ignorant, and those whose ignorance we understand all too well. Few people who have written on Bacon, even his detractors, have doubted that he was in the first category. Coleridge himself said that the *Novum Organum* was one of the three great books since the coming of Christianity (the others were Spinoza's *Ethics* and Kant's *Critique of Pure Reason*), and he insisted on calling Bacon the British Plato. As so often, a few thoughts from Coleridge, however unusual, can be worth a book from some others, and the remarks on Bacon gathered in *Coleridge on the Seventeenth Century*, ed. Roberta F. Brinkley, Durham, N.C., 1955, pp. 41–58, will repay close attention.

What people *have* said against Bacon is that he was as base as he was talented. Pope's description of him as the *wisest, brightest, meanest of mankind* has become a commonplace. In the nineteenth century several writers, each great in their own way, took issue over Bacon's character and genius. Lord Macaulay vilified him in an essay in the *Edinburgh Review* in 1837 (reprinted in *Critical and Historical Essays*, ed. F. C. Montague, 3 vols., London, 1903, II.115–239), while S. R. Gardiner, in the entry in the *Dictionary of National Biography*, portrayed him as the only Englishman who could have averted the Civil War. Spedding's contribution, and the one that has outlasted all others, was of course his edition of the works and life. He is an apologist for Bacon (he was spurred into action by Macaulay's attack), but with such erudition, industry and fair-mindedness that he has made his view of Bacon an indispensable one. Some of this debate spluttered on into Lytton Strachey's

Elizabeth and Essex, London, 1928, in which Bacon is very much a Mephistopheles to Essex's Faustus. Another rehabilitation, this time a Marxist one, has taken place quite recently. Christopher Hill, in *Intellectual Origins of the English Revolution*, Oxford, paperback edition 1980, Chapter 3, has brought Bacon back as the great champion of intellectual work, Puritan freedoms and bourgeois science. Bacon's separation of science from religion, he writes, 'so vital for the advance of science, was in the best Protestant tradition' (p. 92).

One must halt at this point, where studies of Bacon become oceanic in number (there are 873 entries for the period 1926–66 in *Francis Bacon*, by J. Kemp Houck, *Elizabethan Bibliographies: Supplements*, Volume 15, London, 1968). One way of reading out into Bacon's many interests and polymath learning is to consult *Essential Articles for the Study of Francis Bacon*, ed. Brian Vickers, Hamden, Connecticut, 1968 (and London, 1972). This reprints fourteen essays and extracts from books, among them the papers by Anne Righter and R. S. Crane. A more recent compilation, this time of pieces specially written for the collection, is 'The Legacy of Francis Bacon', an issue of *Studies in the Literary Imagination*, IV (April 1971), which contains a further ten essays.

Facsimile of the title-page of the third edition (1625)

THE
ESSAYES
OR
COVNSELS,
CIVILL AND
MORALL,
OF
FRANCIS LO. *VERVLAM,*
VISCOVNT St. ALBAN.

Newly enlarged.

LONDON,
Printed by IOHN HAVILAND for
HANNA BARRET, and RICHARD
WHITAKER, and are to be fold
at the figne of the Kings head in
Pauls Church-yard. 1 6 2 5.

portions of Natural History to the Prince; and these I dedicate to
your Grace, being of the best fruits that by the good increase which
God gives to my pen and labours I could yield. God lead your Grace
by the hand.

The Epistle Dedicatory

to

The Right Honourable, my very good Lord,

THE DUKE OF BUCKINGHAM[1]

His Grace, Lord High Admiral

of England

Excellent Lord:

Solomon says, *A good name is as a precious ointment*,[2] and I
assure myself such will your Grace's name be with posterity. For
your fortune and merit both have been eminent, and you have
planted things that are like to last. I do now publish my *Essays*,
which of all my other works have been most current, for that as it
seems they come home to men's business and bosoms. I have
enlarged them both in number and weight, so that they are indeed a
new work.[3] I thought it therefore agreeable, to my affection and
obligation to your Grace, to prefix your name before them, both in
English and in Latin. For I do conceive that the Latin volume of them
(being in the universal language) may last as long as books last.[4] My
Instauration I dedicated to the King,[5] my *History of Henry the
Seventh* (which I have now also translated into Latin) and my

---

Text: 1625

1. George Villiers, Duke of Buckingham, was King James's favourite from 1616.
He was assassinated by Felton in 1628. The earlier dedications of the *Essays* are
printed below, pp. 237–40.

2. Ecclesiastes 7.1 (where a good name is *better* than a precious ointment).

3. For a description of earlier editions of the *Essays*, see p. 46. Versions of three
essays are printed below, pp. 241–55.

4. The Latin translations of the *Essays*, some of which were by Bacon himself,
were first published in 1638.

5. i.e. King James I, who died in March 1625. The *Instauratio Magna*, published
in 1620, comprises the *Novum Organum* and a set of preliminaries and plans for the
great philosophical work which Bacon never completed.

portions of Natural History to the Prince:[6] and these I dedicate to your Grace, being of the best fruits that by the good increase which God gives to my pen and labours I could yield. God lead your Grace by the hand.

Your Grace's most obliged and
faithful servant,

Francis St Alban.[7]

6. i.e. Prince Charles, subsequently Charles I. The *History of Henry VII* was first published in 1622. Instalments of the Natural History appeared in 1622–3.
7. Bacon was made Viscount St Albans in 1621.

THE TABLE

1.

Of Truth

What is truth? said jesting Pilate,[1] and would not stay for an answer. Certainly there be that delight in giddiness[2] and count it a bondage to fix a belief, affecting[3] free-will in thinking as well as in acting. And though the sects of philosophers of that kind[4] be gone, yet there remain certain discoursing wits[5] which are of the same veins, though there be not so much blood in them as was in those of the ancients. But it is not only the difficulty and labour which men take in finding out of truth, nor again that when it is found it imposeth upon[6] men's thoughts, that doth bring lies in favour, but a natural though corrupt love of the lie itself. One of the later school of the Grecians[7] examineth the matter and is at a stand to think what should be in it, that men should love lies where neither they make for pleasure, as with poets, nor for advantage, as with the merchant, but for the lie's sake. But I cannot tell. This same truth is a naked and open daylight that doth not show the masques and mummeries and triumphs of the world half so stately and daintily[8] as candle-lights. Truth may perhaps come to the price of a pearl, that showeth best by day; but it will not rise to the price of a diamond or carbuncle, that showeth best in varied lights. A mixture of a lie doth ever add pleasure. Doth any man doubt that if there were taken out of men's minds vain opinions, flattering hopes, false valuations, imaginations as one would, and the like, but it would leave the minds of a number of men poor shrunken things, full of melancholy

Text: 1625

1. In John 18.37–8, Jesus declares that he has come into the world to bear witness to the truth, to which Pilate replies 'What is truth?': *jesting*, or scoffing, is Bacon's addition.

2. Constantly changing their minds.   3. Desiring.

4. Probably the schools of ancient Greek philosophy known as the Sceptics and the New (or third) Academy, which taught that men cannot know truth.

5. Talkative, rambling minds.   6. Restrains.

7. Lucian, Greek satirist of the second century, who in the first lines of his *Lover of Lies* brings in a character asking what it is that makes men so fond of lying that they prefer it to truth for the lie's own sake.   8. Elegantly.

and indisposition, and unpleasing to themselves? One of the Fathers, in great severity, called poesy *vinum daemonum*[9] because it filleth the imagination and yet it is but with the shadow of a lie. But it is not the lie that passeth through the mind but the lie that sinketh in and settleth in it, that doth the hurt, such as we spake of before. But howsoever these things are thus in men's depraved judgements and affections, yet truth, which only doth judge itself, teacheth that the inquiry of truth, which is the love-making or wooing of it, the knowledge of truth, which is the presence of it, and the belief of truth, which is the enjoying of it, is the sovereign good of human nature. The first creature[10] of God in the works of the days was the light of the sense; the last was the light of reason; and his sabbath work ever since is the illumination of his Spirit. First he breathed light upon the face of the matter or chaos; then he breathed light into the face of man; and still he breatheth and inspireth light into the face of his chosen. The poet that beautified the sect that was otherwise inferior to the rest,[11] saith yet excellently well: *It is a pleasure to stand upon the shore and to see ships tossed upon the sea; a pleasure to stand in the window of a castle and to see a battle and the adventures thereof below: but no pleasure is comparable to the standing upon the vantage ground of truth* (a hill not to be commanded,[12] and where the air is always clear and serene), *and to see the errors and wanderings and mists and tempests in the vale below*; so always that this prospect be with pity and not with swelling or pride. Certainly it is heaven upon earth to have a man's mind move in charity, rest in providence, and turn upon the poles of truth.

To pass from theological and philosophical truth to the truth of civil business: it will be acknowledged, even by those that practise it not, that clear and round[13] dealing is the honour of man's nature, and that mixture of falsehood is like alloy in coin of gold and silver, which may make the metal work the better, but it embaseth it. For these winding and crooked courses are the goings of the serpent, which goeth basely upon the belly and not upon the feet. There is no vice that doth so cover a man with shame as to be found false and

---

9. The wine of devils (St Augustine calls poetry the 'wine of error'; St Jerome, the 'food of devils').   10. Created thing (see Genesis 1.3 and 27).
11. The Roman poet Lucretius elaborated the philosophy of Epicurus in his poem, in six books, *On the Nature of Things*. Bacon paraphrases the first ten lines of Book II.   12. Not to be looked down on by others.   13. Straightforward.

perfidious. And therefore Montaigne saith prettily when he in-
quired the reason why the word of the lie should be such a disgrace
and such an odious charge. Saith he, *If it be well weighed, to say that
a man lieth is as much to say as that he is brave towards God and a
coward towards men.*[14] For a lie faces God and shrinks from man.
Surely the wickedness of falsehood and breach of faith cannot
possibly be so highly expressed, as in that it shall be the last peal to
call the judgements of God upon the generations of men; it being
foretold that when Christ cometh, *He shall not find faith upon the
earth.*[15]

14. From 'Of giving the lie', *Essays*, II.18, where Montaigne is quoting *prettily*, or
acutely, from Plutarch.

15. Luke 18.8, where Jesus does not prophesy, but *asks* whether the Son of Man
shall find faith on the earth.

Of Death

Men fear death as children fear to go in the dark; and as that natural fear in children is increased with tales, so is the other.[1] Certainly the contemplation of death as the wages of sin and passage to another world is holy and religious, but the fear of it, as a tribute due unto nature, is weak. Yet in religious meditations there is sometimes mixture of vanity and of superstition. You shall read in some of the friars' books of mortification[2] that a man should think with himself what the pain is if he have but his finger's end pressed or tortured, and thereby imagine what the pains of death are when the whole body is corrupted and dissolved; when many times death passeth with less pain than the torture of a limb, for the most vital parts are not the quickest of sense. And by him that spake only as a philosopher and natural man,[3] it was well said: *Pompa mortis magis terret quam mors ipsa.*[4] Groans and convulsions and a discoloured face, and friends weeping, and blacks[5] and obsequies and the like show death terrible. It is worthy the observing that there is no passion in the mind of man so weak but it mates[6] and masters the fear of death; and therefore death is no such terrible enemy, when a man hath so many attendants about him that can win the combat of him.[7] Revenge triumphs over death, love slights it, honour aspireth to it, grief flieth to it, fear preoccupateth it.[8] Nay, we read, after Otho the emperor had slain himself, pity (which is the tenderest of affections) provoked many to die out of mere compassion to their

---

Texts: MS, 1612, 1625

1. Derived from Lucretius, *On the Nature of Things*, III.87–90.
2. Books about repressing fleshly desires.
3. i.e. a man guided by nature alone (and not knowing the supernatural revelations of Christianity): the *man* is Seneca, and Bacon quotes freely from his *Epistles*, XXIV.14.
4. The trappings of death terrify us more than death itself.
5. Mourning garments.   6. Overpowers.   7. From him (i.e. death).
8. Anticipates it (by suicide).

sovereign, and as the truest sort of followers.[9] Nay, Seneca adds niceness[10] and satiety: *Cogita quamdiu eadem feceris; mori velle, non tantum fortis, aut miser, sed etiam fastidiosus potest.*[11] A man would die, though he were neither valiant nor miserable, only upon a weariness to do the same thing so oft over and over. It is no less worthy to observe how little alteration in good spirits the approaches of death make, for they appear to be the same men till the last instant. Augustus Caesar[12] died in a compliment: *Livia, conjugii nostri memor, vive et vale;*[13] Tiberius in dissimulation, as Tacitus saith of him: *Iam Tiberium vires et corpus, non dissimulatio, deserebant;*[14] Vespasian in a jest, sitting upon the stool: *Ut puto deus fio;*[15] Galba with a sentence: *Feri, si ex re sit populi Romani,*[16] holding forth his neck; Septimius Severus in dispatch: *Adeste si quid mihi restat agendum;*[17] and the like. Certainly the Stoics bestowed too much cost upon death,[18] and by their great preparations made it appear more fearful. Better saith he, *Qui finem vitae extremum inter munera ponat naturae.*[19] It is as natural to die as to be born; and to a little infant, perhaps, the one is as painful as the other. He that dies in an earnest pursuit is like one that is wounded in hot blood, who for the time scarce feels the hurt; and therefore a mind fixed and bent upon somewhat that is good doth avert the dolours of death. But above all, believe it, the sweetest canticle is

9. Otho's death is described by Tacitus, *Histories*, II.49.

10. Fastidiousness.

11. Consider how long you have been doing the same things; the desire to die may be felt not only by the brave man or by the wretch, but also by the man wearied with ennui (adapted from Seneca, *Epistles*, LXXVII.6).

12. Augustus, Tiberius, Vespasian, Galba and Septimius Severus were all Roman emperors.

13. Farewell, Livia, remember our married life (Suetonius, *Augustus*, 99).

14. Eventually, bodily strength and vitality failed Tiberius, not his powers of dissimulation (*Annals*, VI.50).

15. While I'm considering, I'm becoming a god (from Suetonius, *Vespasian*, 23). The joke (Bacon's) is in *puto*, meaning both 'I think' and 'I cleanse'.

16. Strike, if it be for the good of the Roman people (from Tacitus, *Histories*, I.41).

17. Make haste, if anything remains for me to do (Dio, *Roman History*, LXXVII.17).

18. This is perhaps true of Seneca, who wrote frequently about the prospect of death, but it is not true of the Stoics generally. They taught that human life was neither good nor bad, but a thing indifferent.

19. Who regards the conclusion of life as one of nature's blessings (Juvenal, *Satires*, X.358).

Nunc dimittis,[20] when a man hath obtained worthy ends and expectations. Death hath this also, that it openeth the gate to good fame, and extinguisheth envy: *Extinctus amabitur idem.*[21]

20. Now let (your servant) depart (in peace) (Luke 2.29).

21. The same man (envied while alive) will be loved once he is dead (Horace, *Epistles*, II.1.14).

3.

Of Unity in Religion

Religion being the chief band of human society, it is a happy thing when itself is well contained within the true band of unity. The quarrels and divisions about religion were evils unknown to the heathen. The reason was, because the religion of the heathen consisted rather in rites and ceremonies than in any constant belief. For you may imagine what kind of faith theirs was, when the chief Doctors[1] and Fathers of their church were the poets. But the true God hath this attribute, that he is a *jealous God*,[2] and therefore his worship and religion will endure no mixture nor partner. We shall therefore speak a few works concerning the unity of the church; what are the fruits thereof, what the bounds, and what the means.

The fruits of unity (next unto the well pleasing of God, which is all in all) are two: the one, towards those that are without the church, the other, towards those that are within. For the former, it is certain that heresies and schisms are of all others the greatest scandals; yea, more than corruption of manners. For as in the natural body a wound or solution of continuity is worse than a corrupt humour, so in the spiritual. So that nothing doth so much keep men out of the church, and drive men out of the church, as breach of unity. And therefore whensoever it cometh to that pass that one saith, *Ecce in deserto*, another saith, *Ecce in penetralibus;*[3] that is, when some men seek Christ in the conventicles of heretics, and others in an outward face of a church, that voice had need continually to sound in men's ears, *Nolite exire – Go not out.* The Doctor of the Gentiles[4] (the propriety[5] of whose vocation drew him to have a special care of those without) saith, *If an heathen come in and hear you speak with several tongues, will he not say that you*

Texts: 1612, 1625

1. Teachers.   2. See Exodus 20.5.
3. Behold he is in the desert . . . Behold he is in the inner rooms (Matthew 24.26).   4. St Paul: the quotation is from 1 Corinthians 14.23.
5. Peculiar nature.

are mad? And certainly it is little better when atheists and profane persons do hear of so many discordant and contrary opinions in religion; it doth avert them from the church, and maketh them *to sit down in the chair of the scorners.*[6] It is but a light thing to be vouched in so serious a matter, but yet it expresseth well the deformity. There is a master of scoffing[7] that in his catalogue of books of a feigned library sets down this title of a book, *The morris dance of heretics.* For indeed every sect of them hath a diverse posture or cringe[8] by themselves, which cannot but move derision in worldlings and depraved politics,[9] who are apt to contemn holy things.

As for the fruit towards those that are within, it is peace, which containeth infinite blessings: it establisheth faith; it kindleth charity; the outward peace of the church distilleth into peace of conscience; and it turneth the labours of writing and reading of controversies into treaties[10] of mortification and devotion.

Concerning the bounds of unity, the true placing of them importeth exceedingly.[11] There appear to be two extremes. For to certain zelants[12] all speech of pacification is odious. *Is it peace, Jehu? What hast thou to do with peace? Turn thee behind me.*[13] Peace is not the matter, but following and party. Contrariwise, certain Laodiceans[14] and lukewarm persons think they may accommodate points of religion by middle ways, and taking part of both, and witty[15] reconcilements, as if they would make an arbitrement between God and man. Both these extremes are to be avoided, which will be done if the league of Christians, penned by our Saviour himself, were in the two cross[16] clauses thereof soundly and plainly expounded: *He that is not with us is against us,*[17] and again, *He that is not against us is with us;*[18] that is, if the points fundamental and of substance in religion were truly discerned and distinguished from points not merely[19] of faith, but of opinion, order, or good intention. This is a thing may seem to many a matter trivial and done already; but if it were done less partially,[20] it would be embraced more generally.

6. See Psalms 1.1.

7. Rabelais: for the fictitious book *La Morisque des Hérétiques,* see *Pantagruel,* II.7.   8. Special trick or posture.   9. Men of affairs.   10. Treatises.

11. Is extremely important.   12. Zealots.   13. See 2 Kings 9.18–19.

14. See Revelation 3.14–16.   15. Ingenious.   16. (At first sight) contradictory.   17. Matthew 12.30.

18. Mark 9.40.   19. Entirely.   20. More impartially.

Of this I may give only this advice, according to my small model.[21] Men ought to take heed of rending God's church by two kinds of controversies. The one is, when the matter of the point controverted is too small and light, not worth the heat and strife about it, kindled only by contradiction. For, as it is noted by one of the Fathers, *Christ's coat indeed had no seam, but the church's vesture was of divers colours;*[22] whereupon he saith, *In veste varietas sit, scissura non sit;*[23] they be two things, unity and uniformity. The other is, when the matter of the point controverted is great, but it is driven to an over-great subtlety and obscurity, so that it becometh a thing rather ingenious than substantial. A man that is of judgement and understanding shall sometimes hear ignorant men differ, and know well within himself that those which so differ mean one thing, and yet they themselves would never agree. And if it come so to pass in that distance of judgement which is between man and man, shall we not think that God above, that knows the heart, doth not discern that frail men in some of their contradictions intend the same thing, and accepteth of both? The nature of such controversies is excellently expressed by St Paul in the warning and precept that he giveth concerning the same, *De vita profanas vocum novitates, et oppositiones falsi nominis scientiae.*[24] Men create oppositions which are not, and put them into new terms so fixed as, whereas the meaning ought to govern the term, the term in effect governeth the meaning. There be also two false peaces or unities: the one, when the peace is grounded but upon an implicit ignorance (for all colours will agree in the dark); the other, when it is pieced up upon a direct admission of contraries in fundamental points. For truth and falsehood in such things are like the iron and clay in the toes of Nebuchadnezzar's image;[25] they may cleave but they will not incorporate.

Concerning the means of procuring unity, men must beware that in the procuring or muniting[26] of religious unity they do not dissolve and deface the laws of charity and of human society. There be two swords amongst Christians, the spiritual and temporal, and

21. Plan.

22. Alluding to Psalms 45.14, where the princess 'in many coloured robes' is led to the king. The Church *Father* is either St Augustine or St Bernard.

23. Let there be variety in the garment, but no rents.

24. Avoid the profane novelties of words and contradictions of what is falsely called knowledge (1 Timothy 6.20).   25. See Daniel 2.31–5.   26. Fortifying.

both have their due office and place in the maintenance of religion. But we may not take up the third sword, which is Mahomet's sword, or like unto it – that is, to propagate religion by wars, or by sanguinary persecutions to force consciences (except it be in cases of overt scandal, blasphemy, or intermixture of practice against the state), much less to nourish seditions, to authorize conspiracies and rebellions, to put the sword into the people's hands, and the like, tending to the subversion of all government, which is the ordinance of God. For this is but to dash the first table against the second,[27] and so to consider men as Christians, as we forget that they are men. Lucretius the poet, when he beheld the act of Agamemnon, that could endure the sacrificing of his own daughter, exclaimed:

Tantum religio potuit suadere malorum.[28]

What would he have said if he had known of the massacre in France,[29] or the powder treason of England?[30] He would have been seven times more Epicure[31] and atheist than he was. For as the temporal sword is to be drawn with great circumspection in cases of religion, so it is a thing monstrous to put it into the hands of the common people. Let that be left unto the Anabaptists[32] and other furies. It was great blasphemy when the devil said, *I will ascend and be like the Highest;*[33] but it is greater blasphemy to personate[34] God, and bring him in saying, *I will descend and be like the prince of darkness.* And what is it better, to make the cause of religion to descend to the cruel and execrable actions of murthering princes, butchery of people, and subversion of states and governments? Surely this is to bring down the Holy Ghost, instead of the likeness of a dove, in the shape of a vulture or raven; and to set out of the bark of a Christian church a flag of a bark of pirates and assassins. Therefore it is most necessary that the church by doctrine and decree, princes by their sword, and all learnings (both Christian and

27. i.e. to make the first half of the Ten Commandments, duty towards God, contradict the second half, duty towards men. The Commandments were twice written on two tablets of stone (see Exodus 20.1–17, 32.15–19, and 34.1 and 29).

28. So powerfully could religion prompt a man to evil deeds (*On the Nature of Things*, I.101).

29. The massacre of Protestants in Paris on St Bartholomew's Day, 1572.

30. The Gunpowder Plot of November 1605.   31. Epicurean.

32. Protestant sectarians who had radical views on the equality of men, and whose history had been violent.   33. Isaiah 14.14.   34. Give a stage-part to.

moral) as by their Mercury rod,[35] do damn and send to hell for ever
those facts[36] and opinions tending to the support of the same, as
hath been already in good part done. Surely in counsels concerning
religion, that counsel of the Apostle would be prefixed, *Ira hominis
non implet justitiam Dei.*[37] And it was a notable observation of a
wise Father,[38] and no less ingenuously confessed, that *those which
held and persuaded pressure of consciences, were commonly
interessed*[39] *therein themselves for their own ends.*

35. The Caduceus was the rod with which Mercury, messenger of the gods and
himself a god of learning, sent souls down to hell.   36. Deeds.
37. The anger of man does not fulfil the justice of God (James 1.20).
38. Perhaps St Cyprian: the quotation has not been traced.   39. Interested.

4.
Of Revenge

Revenge is a kind of wild justice, which the more man's nature runs to, the more ought law to weed it out. For as for the first wrong, it doth but offend the law; but the revenge of that wrong putteth the law out of office. Certainly, in taking revenge a man is but even with his enemy, but in passing it over he is superior, for it is a prince's part to pardon. And Solomon, I am sure, saith, *It is the glory of a man to pass by an offence.*[1] That which is past is gone and irrevocable, and wise men have enough to do with things present and to come: therefore they do but trifle with themselves that labour in past matters. There is no man doth a wrong for the wrong's sake, but thereby to purchase himself profit or pleasure or honour or the like. Therefore why should I be angry with a man for loving himself better than me? And if any man should do wrong merely out of ill nature, why, yet it is but like the thorn or briar, which prick and scratch, because they can do no other. The most tolerable sort of revenge is for those wrongs which there is no law to remedy: but then let a man take heed the revenge be such as there is no law to punish; else a man's enemy is still beforehand, and it is two for one. Some, when they take revenge, are desirous the party should know whence it cometh. This is the more generous, for the delight seemeth to be not so much in doing the hurt as in making the party repent. But base and crafty cowards are like the arrow that flieth in the dark.[2] Cosmus, Duke of Florence,[3] had a desperate saying against perfidious or neglecting friends, as if those wrongs were unpardonable: *You shall read* (saith he) *that we are commanded to forgive our enemies; but you never read that we are commanded to forgive our friends.* But yet the spirit of Job was in a better tune: *Shall we* (saith he) *take good at God's hands, and not be*

Text: 1625

1. From Proverbs 19.11.   2. See Psalms 91.5.
3. Cosimo de' Medici, d. 1574: the saying has not been traced.

content to take evil also?[4] And so of friends in a proportion.[5] This is certain, that a man that studieth revenge keeps his own wounds green, which otherwise would heal and do well. Public revenges are for the most part fortunate: as that for the death of Caesar, for the death of Pertinax, for the death of Henry the Third of France,[6] and many more. But in private revenges it is not so. Nay rather, vindicative persons live the life of witches, who, as they are mischievous, so end they infortunate.[7]

4. Job 2.10.

5. To a proportionate extent (i.e. God may treat us as he will: friends have less power to do us good, and less right to do us harm).

6. Augustus Caesar, Septimius Severus and Henry IV of France all prospered, and proved to be good rulers, after they had taken *public revenges* for the murders of, respectively, Julius Caesar, Pertinax and Henry III.   7. Unfortunate.

5.

Of Adversity

It was an high[1] speech of Seneca (after the manner of the Stoics), that *the good things which belong to prosperity are to be wished, but the good things that belong to adversity are to be admired.*[2] *Bona rerum secundarum optabilia, adversarum mirabilia.* Certainly if miracles be the command over nature, they appear most in adversity.[3] It is yet a higher speech of his than the other (much too high for a heathen): *It is true greatness to have in one the frailty of a man and the security[4] of a god. Vere magnum, habere fragilitatem hominis, securitatem dei.*[5] This would have done better in poesy, where transcendencies[6] are more allowed. And the poets indeed have been busy with it, for it is in effect the thing which is figured in that strange fiction of the ancient poets, which seemeth not to be without mystery; nay, and to have some approach to the state of a Christian: that *Hercules, when he went to unbind Prometheus* (by whom human nature is represented), *sailed the length of the great ocean in an earthen pot or pitcher;*[7] lively describing Christian resolution, that saileth in the frail bark of the flesh thorough[8] the waves of the world. But to speak in a mean.[9] The virtue of prosperity is temperance; the virtue of adversity is fortitude, which in morals is the more heroical virtue. Prosperity is the blessing of the Old

Text: 1625

1. Noble: the speech is from *Epistles*, LXVI.29.   2. Wondered at.
3. If miracles mean command over nature, then Seneca is right, for they appear most in times of adversity when men control their natures.
4. Freedom from care.   5. From Seneca, *Epistles*, LIII.12.
6. Elevated (or exaggerated) thoughts and language.
7. Prometheus, having stolen fire from the gods for mankind, was chained to a rock, where each day an eagle tore at his liver until Hercules killed the bird and freed him. The story is in Apollodorus, *The Library*, II.5.11. For the *earthen pot*, not in Apollodorus, see R. S. Peterson, *Imitation and Praise in the Poems of Ben Jonson*, New Haven and London, 1981, pp. 131–3. In *The Wisdom of the Ancients*, Bacon explains the hidden meaning of the story like this: 'The voyage of Hercules especially, sailing in a pitcher to set Prometheus free, seems to present an image of God the Word [Christ] hastening in the frail vessel of the flesh to redeem the human race'. See below, p. 276.   8. Through.   9. In a moderate way.

Testament; adversity is the blessing of the New,[10] which carrieth
the greater benediction and the clearer revelation of God's favour.
Yet even in the Old Testament, if you listen to David's harp, you
shall hear as many hearse-like airs as carols; and the pencil of the
Holy Ghost hath laboured more in describing the afflictions of Job
than the felicities of Solomon. Prosperity is not without many fears
and distastes,[11] and adversity is not without comforts and hopes.
We see in needleworks and embroideries, it is more pleasing to have
a lively work upon a sad and solemn ground, than to have a dark and
melancholy work upon a lightsome ground: judge therefore of the
pleasure of the heart by the pleasure of the eye. Certainly virtue is
like precious odours, most fragrant when they are incensed or
crushed; for prosperity doth best discover[12] vice, but adversity doth
best discover virtue.

10. Probably a reference to the Beatitude, 'Blessed are they who mourn' (Matthew
5.4).   11. Annoyances.   12. Reveal.

6.

Of Simulation and Dissimulation

Dissimulation is but a faint kind of policy or wisdom, for it asketh a strong wit[1] and a strong heart to know when to tell truth, and to do it. Therefore it is the weaker sort of politics[2] that are the great dissemblers.

Tacitus saith, *Livia sorted well with[3] the arts of her husband and dissimulation of her son,[4]* attributing arts or policy to Augustus, and dissimulation to Tiberius. And again, when Mucianus encourageth Vespasian to take arms against Vitellius, he saith, *We rise not against the piercing judgement of Augustus, nor the extreme caution or closeness of Tiberius.[5]* These properties of arts or policy, and dissimulation or closeness, are indeed habits and faculties several,[6] and to be distinguished. For if a man have that penetration of judgement as he can discern what things are to be laid open, and what to be secreted, and what to be showed at half-lights, and to whom, and when (which indeed are arts of state and arts of life, as Tacitus well calleth them[7]), to him a habit of dissimulation is a hindrance and a poorness.[8] But if a man cannot obtain to that judgement, then it is left to him, generally, to be close, and a dissembler. For where a man cannot choose or vary in particulars,[9] there it is good to take the safest and wariest way in general, like the going softly[10] by one that cannot well see. Certainly the ablest men that ever were have had all an openness and frankness of dealing, and a name of certainty and veracity. But then they were like horses well managed,[11] for they could tell passing well when to stop or turn: and at such times when they thought the case indeed required dissimulation, if then they used it, it came to pass that the former

Text: 1625

1. Understanding.   2. Politicians.
3. Accorded well with *or* was a match for.   4. *Annals*, V.1.
5. Tacitus, *Histories*, II.76.   6. Distinct abilities.
7. Bacon is probably recalling both *Annals*, III.70, and *Agricola*, 39.
8. Disadvantage.   9. To suit particular cases.   10. Slowly.
11. Trained.

opinion spread abroad of their good faith and clearness of dealing made them almost invisible.

There be three degrees of this hiding and veiling of a man's self. The first: closeness, reservation, and secrecy, when a man leaveth himself without observation or without hold to be taken what he is. The second: dissimulation, in the negative, when a man lets fall signs and arguments that he is not that he is. And the third: simulation, in the affirmative, when a man industriously[12] and expressly feigns and pretends to be that he is not.

For the first of these, secrecy, it is indeed the virtue of a confessor. And assuredly the secret man heareth many confessions – for who will open himself to a blab or a babbler? But if a man be thought secret, it inviteth discovery,[13] as the more close air sucketh in the more open.[14] And as in confession the revealing is not for worldly use, but for the ease of a man's heart, so secret men come to the knowledge of many things in that kind,[15] while men rather discharge their minds than impart their minds. In few words, mysteries are due to secrecy.[16] Besides (to say truth) nakedness is uncomely, as well in mind as body; and it addeth no small reverence to men's manners and actions, if they be not altogether open. As for talkers and futile persons,[17] they are commonly vain and credulous withal. For he that talketh what he knoweth, will also talk what he knoweth not. Therefore set it down, that *an habit of secrecy is both politic and moral.* And in this part it is good that a man's face give his tongue leave to speak.[18] For the discovery of a man's self by the tracts of his countenance[19] is a great weakness and betraying, by how much it is many times more marked and believed than a man's words.

For the second, which is dissimulation, it followeth many times upon secrecy by a necessity; so that he that will be secret must be a dissembler in some degree. For men are too cunning to suffer a man to keep an indifferent carriage[20] between both, and to be secret, without swaying the balance on either side. They will so beset a man with questions, and draw him on, and pick it out of him, that,

12. On purpose.   13. Disclosures.

14. In the same way that warm, rarified air in a room draws in colder and denser air entering from outside.   15. In the same way.

16. i.e. a man who can hold his tongue is entitled to be entrusted with secrets.

17. Blabbers.

18. i.e. does not contradict what he has said, nor give away what he is about to say.

19. By the expressions on his face.   20. Impartial behaviour.

without an absurd silence, he must show an inclination one way; or if he do not, they will gather as much by his silence as by his speech. As for equivocations, or oraculous[21] speeches, they cannot hold out long. So that no man can be secret, except he give himself a little scope of dissimulation, which is, as it were, but the skirts or train of secrecy.

But for the third degree, which is simulation and false profession, that I hold more culpable, and less politic, except it be in great and rare matters. And therefore a general custom of simulation (which is this last degree) is a vice rising either of a natural falseness or fearfulness, or of a mind that hath some main faults, which because a man must needs disguise, it maketh him practise simulation in other things, lest his hand should be out of ure.[22]

The great advantages of simulation and dissimulation are three. First, to lay asleep opposition, and to surprise. For where a man's intentions are published, it is an alarum to call up all that are against them. The second is, to reserve to a man's self a fair retreat. For if a man engage himself by a manifest declaration, he must go through or take a fall. The third is, the better to discover the mind of another. For to him that opens himself men will hardly show themselves adverse, but will (fair)[23] let him go on, and turn their freedom of speech to freedom of thought. And therefore it is a good shrewd proverb of the Spaniard, *Tell a lie and find a troth*; as if there were no way of discovery but by simulation. There be also three disadvantages, to set it even. The first, that simulation and dissimulation commonly carry with them a show of fearfulness, which in any business doth spoil the feathers of round flying up to the mark.[24] The second, that it puzzleth and perplexeth the conceits[25] of many that perhaps would otherwise co-operate with him, and makes a man walk almost alone to his own ends. The third and greatest is, that it depriveth a man of one of the most principal instruments for action, which is trust and belief. The best composition and temperature[26] is to have openness in fame and opinion,[27] secrecy in habit, dissimulation in seasonable use, and a power to feign, if there be no remedy.

21. Ambiguous (as from an oracle).   22. Practice.   23. Simply.
24. Prevents the arrow from flying directly to the target.
25. Thoughts.   26. Temperament.
27. To have a reputation for frankness.

7

Of Parents and Children

The joys of parents are secret, and so are their griefs and fears: they cannot utter the one, nor they will not utter the other. Children sweeten labours, but they make misfortunes more bitter: they increase the cares of life, but they mitigate the remembrance of death. The perpetuity by generation is common to beasts, but memory,[1] merit, and noble works are proper to men. And surely a man shall see the noblest works and foundations have proceeded from childless men, which have sought to express the images of their minds, where those of their bodies have failed. So the care of posterity is most in them that have no posterity. They that are the first raisers of their houses are most indulgent towards their children, beholding them as the continuance not only of their kind but of their work; and so both children and creatures.[2]

The difference in affection of parents towards their several children is many times unequal, and sometimes unworthy, especially in the mother. As Solomon saith, *A wise son rejoiceth the father, but an ungracious son shames the mother*.[3] A man shall see, where there is a house full of children, one or two of the eldest respected,[4] and the youngest made wantons,[5] but in the midst some that are as it were forgotten, who many times nevertheless prove the best. The illiberality of parents in allowance towards their children is an harmful error, makes them base, acquaints them with shifts, makes them sort[6] with mean company, and makes them surfeit more when they come to plenty. And therefore the proof[7] is best when men

---

Texts: MS, 1612, 1625

1. Being remembered.   2. Created objects.
3. Proverbs 10.1. Elsewhere Bacon explains the verse in this way: 'a wise and prudent son is of most comfort to the father, who knows the value of virtue better than the mother . . . But the mother has most sorrow and discomfort at the ill fortune of her son, both because the affection of a mother is more gentle and tender, and because she is conscious perhaps that she has spoiled and corrupted him by her indulgence' (*Works*, V.40).
4. Favoured.   5. Spoiled.   6. Associate.   7. Outcome.

keep their authority towards their children, but not their purse. Men have a foolish manner (both parents and schoolmasters and servants) in creating and breeding an emulation between brothers during childhood, which many times sorteth to[8] discord when they are men, and disturbeth families. The Italians make little difference between children and nephews or near kinsfolks; but so they be of the lump, they care not though they pass not through their own body. And, to say truth, in nature it is much a like matter, insomuch that we see a nephew sometimes resembleth an uncle or a kinsman more than his own parent, as the blood happens. Let parents choose betimes the vocations and courses they mean their children should take, for then they are most flexible. And let them not too much apply[9] themselves to the disposition of their children, as thinking they will take best to that which they have most mind to. It is true that if the affection[10] or aptness of the children be extraordinary, then it is good not to cross it: but generally the precept is good, *Optimum elige, suave et facile illud faciet consuetudo.*[11] Younger brothers are commonly fortunate, but seldom or never where the elder are disinherited.

---

8. Results in.   9. Accommodate.   10. Inclination.
11. Choose what is best, and habit will make it pleasant and easy (a saying ascribed to the followers of Pythagoras, in Plutarch, *On Exile*, 8 (*Moralia*, 602B)).

8.

Of Marriage and Single Life

He that hath wife and children hath given hostages to fortune,[1] for they are impediments to great enterprises, either of virtue or mischief. Certainly the best works, and of greatest merit for the public, have proceeded from the unmarried or childless men, which both in affection and means have married and endowed the public. Yet it were great reason that those that have children should have greatest care of future times, unto which they know they must transmit their dearest pledges. Some there are who, though they lead a single life, yet their thoughts do end with themselves, and account future times impertinences.[2] Nay, there are some other that account wife and children but as bills of charges. Nay more, there are some foolish rich covetous men that take a pride in having no children, because they may be thought so much the richer. For perhaps they have heard some talk, *Such an one is a great rich man*, and another except to it, *Yea, but he hath a great charge of children*, as if it were an abatement to his riches. But the most ordinary cause of a single life is liberty, especially in certain self-pleasing and humorous[3] minds, which are so sensible of every restraint as they will go near to think their girdles and garters to be bonds and shackles. Unmarried men are best friends, best masters, best servants; but not always best subjects, for they are light[4] to run away; and almost all fugitives are of that condition. A single life doth well with churchmen, for charity will hardly water the ground where it must first fill a pool. It is indifferent[5] for judges and magistrates, for if they be facile[6] and corrupt, you shall have a servant five times

Texts: MS, 1612, 1625

1. i.e. has placed himself at a disadvantage, since he must do nothing which may jeopardize the well-being of his wife and children (the hostages who prosper or suffer according to his good or bad fortunes).

2. Things which do not concern them.

3. Eccentric, guided by their own fancy or humour.

4. Ready *or* unencumbered.   5. Unimportant either way.

6. Easily manipulated or got at.

worse than a wife. For soldiers, I find the generals commonly in
their hortatives[7] put men in mind of their wives and children; and I
think the despising of marriage amongst the Turks maketh the
vulgar[8] soldier more base. Certainly wife and children are a kind of
discipline of humanity; and single men, though they be many times
more charitable, because their means are less exhaust,[9] yet, on the
other side, they are more cruel and hard-hearted (good to make
severe inquisitors), because their tenderness is not so oft called
upon. Grave natures, led by custom, and therefore constant, are
commonly loving husbands, as was said of Ulysses, *Vetulam suam
praetulit immortalitati.*[10] Chaste women are often proud and forward, as presuming upon the merit of their chastity. It is one of the
best bonds both of chastity and obedience in the wife if she think her
husband wise, which she will never do if she find him jealous. Wives
are young men's mistresses, companions for middle age, and old
men's nurses. So as a man may have a quarrel to marry[11] when he
will. But yet he was reputed one of the wise men[12] that made answer
to the question, when a man should marry: *A young man not yet,
an elder man not at all.* It is often seen that bad husbands have very
good wives; whether it be that it raiseth the price of their husband's
kindness when it comes, or that the wives take a pride in their
patience. But this never fails if the bad husbands were of their own
choosing, against their friends' consent; for then they will be sure to
make good their own folly.

7. Exhortations.   8. Common.   9. Exhausted.
10. He preferred his old wife to immortality (from Cicero, *On the Orator*, I.44):
i.e. Ulysses preferred to return home to Ithaca and his wife Penelope rather than stay
with the goddess Calypso, who offered him immortality.
11. A reason or pretext for marrying.
12. Thales of Miletus, one of the Seven Sages of ancient Greece. He excused
himself to his mother for not marrying by saying at first that he was too young, and
afterwards that he was too old (see Plutarch, *Table-Talk*, III.6.3. (*Moralia*, 654c)).

9.

Of Envy

There be none of the affections which have been noted to fascinate or bewitch, but love and envy. They both have[1] vehement wishes; they frame themselves readily into imaginations and suggestions; and they come easily into the eye, especially upon the presence of the objects: which are the points that conduce to fascination,[2] if any such thing there be. We see likewise the Scripture calleth envy an *evil eye*,[3] and the astrologers call the evil influences[4] of the stars *evil aspects*,[5] so that still there seemeth to be acknowledged, in the act of envy, an ejaculation[6] or irradiation of the eye. Nay, some have been so curious[7] as to note that the times when the stroke or percussion of an envious eye doth most hurt are when the party envied is beheld in glory or triumph, for that sets an edge upon envy: and besides, at such times the spirits of the person envied do come forth most into the outward parts, and so meet the blow.

But leaving these curiosities[8] (though not unworthy to be thought on in fit place), we will handle what persons are apt to envy others; what persons are most subject to be envied themselves; and what is the difference between public and private envy.

A man that hath no virtue in himself ever envieth virtue in others. For men's minds will either feed upon their own good or upon others' evil; and who wanteth the one will prey upon the other; and whoso is out of hope to attain to another's virtue will seek to come at even hand by depressing another's fortune.

A man that is busy and inquisitive is commonly envious. For to know much of other men's matters cannot be because all that ado

---

Text: 1625

1. Create.
2. Bacon defines *fascination* as 'the power and act of imagination, intensive upon other bodies than the body of the imaginant' (*Works*, III.381).
3. See Mark 7.21–3.   4. Power over men's actions.
5. An *aspect* is a configuration of stars in the heavens, here taken to mean how the stars look down upon the earth and men.   6. Emission.
7. Carefully observant.   8. Minutiae, subtleties.

may concern his own estate:[9] therefore it must needs be that he taketh a kind of play-pleasure[10] in looking upon the fortunes of others. Neither can he that mindeth but his own business find much matter for envy. For envy is a gadding passion, and walketh the streets, and doth not keep home: *Non est curiosus, quin idem sit malevolus.*[11]

Men of noble birth are noted to be envious towards new men when they rise. For the distance[12] is altered, and it is like a deceit of the eye, that when others come on they think themselves go back.

Deformed persons and eunuchs and old men and bastards are envious. For he that cannot possibly mend his own case will do what he can to impair another's: except these defects light upon a very brave and heroical nature, which thinketh to make his natural wants[13] part of his honour, in that it should be said that an eunuch or a lame man did such great matters; affecting[14] the honour of a miracle, as it was in[15] Narses the eunuch, and Agesilaus and Tamberlanes, that were lame men.[16]

The same is the case of men that rise after calamities and misfortunes. For they are as men fallen out with the times, and think other men's harms a redemption of their own sufferings.

They that desire to excel in too many matters, out of levity and vainglory, are ever envious. For they cannot want work, it being impossible but many in some one of those things should surpass them. Which was the character of Hadrian the Emperor,[17] that mortally envied poets and painters and artificers in works wherein he had a vein[18] to excel.

Lastly, near kinsfolks and fellows in office and those that have been bred together are more apt to envy their equals when they are raised. For it doth upbraid unto them their own fortunes, and pointeth at them, and cometh oftener into their remembrance, and

9. Affairs.   10. The pleasure felt from seeing a play.

11. No one is inquisitive without being malevolent as well (Plautus, *Stichus*, I.3.54).   12. Distance in social rank.   13. Defects.   14. Striving after.

15. As was the case with.

16. Narses was the Byzantine general who defeated the Goths and governed Italy until A.D.567. Agesilaus, king of Sparta from 398 to 361 B.C., inflicted heavy defeats on the Persians. Tamerlane, or Timur the Lame, d. 1405, conquered huge areas of Asia.

17. Hadrian, Roman emperor from 117 to 138, is said to have designed a temple and then banished an architect who dared to criticize his plans.

18. Disposition.

incurreth likewise more into the note of others;[19] and envy ever redoubleth from speech and fame. Cain's envy was the more vile and malignant towards his brother Abel, because when his sacrifice was better accepted there was nobody to look on.[20] Thus much for those that are apt to envy.

Concerning those that are more or less subject to envy. First, persons of eminent virtue, when they are advanced, are less envied. For their fortune seemeth but due unto them, and no man envieth the payment of a debt, but rewards and liberality rather. Again, envy is ever joined with the comparing of a man's self, and where there is no comparison, no envy; and therefore kings are not envied but by kings. Nevertheless it is to be noted that unworthy persons are most envied at their first coming in, and afterwards overcome it better; whereas, contrariwise, persons of worth and merit are most envied when their fortune continueth long. For by that time, though their virtue be the same, yet it hath not the same lustre, for fresh men grow up that darken it.

Persons of noble blood are less envied in their rising, for it seemeth but right done to their birth. Besides, there seemeth not much added to their fortune; and envy is as the sunbeams, that beat hotter upon a bank or steep rising ground than upon a flat. And for the same reason those that are advanced by degrees are less envied than those that are advanced suddenly and *per saltum*.[21]

Those that have joined with their honour great travails, cares, or perils are less subject to envy. For men think that they earn their honours hardly, and pity them sometimes; and pity ever healeth envy. Wherefore you shall observe that the more deep and sober sort of politic persons, in their greatness, are ever bemoaning themselves what a life they lead, chanting a *quanta patimur*.[22] Not that they feel it so, but only to abate the edge of envy. But this is to be understood of business that is laid upon men, and not such as they call unto themselves. For nothing increaseth envy more than an unnecessary and ambitious engrossing of business. And nothing doth extinguish envy more than for a great person to preserve all other inferior officers in their full rights and pre-eminences of their places. For by that means there be so many screens between him and envy.

19. Also comes more to the notice of others.
20. See Genesis 4.1–15.   21. At a bound.
22. How many things we suffer!

Above all, those are most subject to envy, which carry the greatness of their fortunes in an insolent and proud manner, being never well but while they are showing how great they are, either by outward pomp, or by triumphing over all opposition or competition. Whereas wise men will rather do sacrifice to envy, in suffering themselves sometimes of purpose[23] to be crossed and overborne in things that do not much concern them. Notwithstanding, so much is true, that the carriage of greatness in a plain and open manner (so it be without arrogancy and vainglory) doth draw less envy than if it be in a more crafty and cunning fashion. For in that course a man doth but disavow fortune,[24] and seemeth to be conscious of his own want in worth, and doth but teach others to envy him.

Lastly, to conclude this part: as we said in the beginning that the act of envy had somewhat in it of witchcraft, so there is no other cure of envy but the cure of witchcraft; and that is, to remove the *lot*[25] (as they call it) and to lay it upon another. For which purpose, the wiser sort of great persons bring in ever upon the stage somebody upon whom to derive[26] the envy that would come upon themselves; sometimes upon ministers and servants, sometimes upon colleagues and associates, and the like; and for that turn there are never wanting some persons of violent and undertaking[27] natures, who, so they may have power and business, will take it at any cost.

Now, to speak of public envy. There is yet some good in public envy, whereas in private there is none. For public envy is as an ostracism, that eclipseth men when they grow too great. And therefore it is a bridle also to great ones to keep them within bounds.

This envy, being in the Latin word *invidia*, goeth in the modern languages by the name of *discontentment*, of which we shall speak in handling sedition. It is a disease in a state like to infection. For as infection spreadeth upon that which is sound, and tainteth it, so when envy is gotten once into a state, it traduceth even the best actions thereof, and turneth them into an ill odour. And therefore there is little won by intermingling of plausible[28] actions. For that doth argue but a weakness and fear of envy, which hurteth so much the more; as it is likewise usual in infections, which, if you fear them, you call them upon you.

23. Deliberately.
24. i.e. he admits that fortune is to blame for having used him better than he deserved.   25. Spell.   26. Divert.   27. Enterprising.
28. Praiseworthy.

This public envy seemeth to beat chiefly upon principal officers or ministers, rather than upon kings and estates[29] themselves. But this is a sure rule, that if the envy upon the minister be great, when the cause of it in him is small, or if the envy be general in a manner upon all the ministers of an estate, then the envy (though hidden) is truly upon the state itself. And so much of public envy or discontentment, and the difference thereof from private envy, which was handled in the first place.

We will add this in general, touching the affection of envy, that of all other affections it is the most importune[30] and continual. For of other affections there is occasion given but now and then. And therefore it was well said, *Invidia festos dies non agit*,[31] for it is ever working upon some or other. And it is also noted that love and envy do make a man pine, which other affections do not, because they are not so continual. It is also the vilest affection, and the most depraved, for which cause it is the proper attribute of the devil, who is called *the envious man, that soweth tares amongst the wheat by night*;[32] as it always cometh to pass that envy worketh subtly and in the dark, and to the prejudice of good things, such as is the wheat.

29. States.   30. Importunate.   31. Envy keeps no holidays.
32. Matthew 13.25. The text says nothing of an *envious man*, simply that 'his enemy came and sowed weeds among the wheat'. The enemy is identified as the devil in 13.37–9.

10.

Of Love

The stage is more beholding[1] to love than the life of man. For as to the stage, love is ever matter of comedies and now and then of tragedies; but in life it doth much mischief, sometimes like a siren, sometimes like a fury. You may observe that amongst all the great and worthy persons (whereof the memory remaineth, either ancient or recent) there is not one that hath been transported to the mad degree of love; which shows that great spirits and great business do keep out this weak passion. You must except, nevertheless, Marcus Antonius,[2] the half-partner of the empire of Rome, and Appius Claudius,[3] the decemvir and lawgiver: whereof the former was indeed a voluptuous man and inordinate, but the latter was an austere and wise man. And therefore it seems (though rarely) that love can find entrance not only into an open heart, but also into a heart well fortified, if watch be not well kept. It is a poor saying of Epicurus, *Satis magnum alter alteri theatrum sumus:*[4] as if man, made for the contemplation of heaven and all noble objects, should do nothing but kneel before a little idol, and make himself subject, though not of the mouth (as beasts are), yet of the eye, which was given him for higher purposes. It is a strange thing to note the excess of this passion and how it braves[5] the nature and value of things, by this: that the speaking in a perpetual hyperbole is comely in nothing but in love. Neither is it merely in the phrase; for whereas it hath been well said[6] that the arch-flatterer, with whom all the petty flatterers have intelligence,[7] is a man's self, certainly

---

Texts: 1612, 1625

1. Indebted.   2. Mark Antony loved Cleopatra.
3. According to Livy, Virginia, the daughter of a commoner, was killed by her father to save her from the designs of Appius Claudius, one of the Board of Ten (*decemviri*) which had been elected to draw up a code of laws for Rome.
4. Each of us is enough of an audience for the other (Seneca, *Epistles*, VII.11).
5. Insultingly disregards.
6. See Plutarch, *How to tell a Flatterer from a Friend*, 1 (*Moralia*, 48E–F).
7. Have an understanding.

the lover is more.[8] For there was never proud man thought so absurdly well of himself as the lover doth of the person loved: and therefore it was well said, *That it is impossible to love and to be wise*.[9] Neither doth this weakness appear to others only, and not to the party loved, but to the loved most of all, except the love be reciproque.[10] For it is a true rule that love is ever rewarded either with the reciproque[11] or with an inward and secret contempt. By how much the more men ought to beware of this passion, which loseth not only other things, but itself. As for the other losses, the poet's relation doth well figure them: that he that preferred Helena quitted the gifts of Juno and Pallas.[12] For whosoever esteemeth too much of amorous affection quitteth both riches and wisdom. This passion hath his floods in the very times of weakness, which are great prosperity and great adversity (though this latter hath been less observed); both which times kindle love and make it more fervent, and therefore show it to be the child of folly. They do best who, if they cannot but admit love, yet make it keep quarter,[13] and sever it wholly from their serious affairs and actions of life; for if it check[14] once with business, it troubleth men's fortunes, and maketh men that they can no ways be true to their own ends. I know not how, but martial men are given to love: I think it is but as they are given to wine; for perils commonly ask to be paid in pleasures. There is in man's nature a secret inclination and motion towards love of others, which, if it be not spent upon some one or a few, doth naturally spread itself towards many, and maketh men become humane and charitable; as it is seen sometime in friars. Nuptial love maketh mankind; friendly love perfecteth it; but wanton love corrupteth and embaseth it.

---

8. i.e. a lover flatters one even more than one flatters oneself.

9. From Publilius Syrus, *Sententiae*, 15.   10. Mutual.

11. Reciprocal feeling.

12. The goddesses Juno, Venus and Pallas Athene (or Minerva, goddess of wisdom) asked Paris, prince of Troy, to decide which of them was the most beautiful. Juno offered him empire, Pallas military glory, and Venus the most beautiful woman in the world (Helen of Troy). Paris's choice of Venus, and Helen, was the start of the Trojan War.   13. Keep its proper place.   14. Interfere.

11.

Of Great Place[1]

Men in great places are thrice servants: servants of the sovereign or
state, servants of fame,[2] and servants of business. So as they have no
freedom, neither in their persons nor in their actions nor in their
times. It is a strange desire to seek power and to lose liberty; or to
seek power over others and to lose power over a man's self. The
rising unto place is laborious, and by pains men come to greater
pains; and it is sometimes base, and by indignities men come to
dignities. The standing is slippery, and the regress is either a
downfall or at least an eclipse, which is a melancholy thing. *Cum
non sis qui fueris, non esse cur velis vivere.*[3] Nay, retire men cannot
when they would; neither will they when it were reason,[4] but are
impatient of privateness,[5] even in age and sickness, which require
the shadow:[6] like old townsmen that will be still sitting at their
street door though thereby they offer age to scorn. Certainly great
persons had need to borrow other men's opinions to think themselves happy, for if they judge by their own feeling they cannot find
it: but if they think with themselves what other men think of them,
and that other men would fain be as they are, then they are happy as
it were by report, when perhaps they find the contrary within. For
they are the first that find their own griefs, though they be the last
that find their own faults. Certainly men in great fortunes are
strangers to themselves, and while they are in the puzzle of business
they have no time to tend their health, either of body or mind. *Illi
mors gravis incubat, qui notus nimis omnibus, ignotus moritur
sibi.*[7] In place there is licence to do good and evil, whereof the latter

Texts: MS, 1612, 1625

1. High office.   2. Public opinion.

3. When you are no longer what you were, there is no reason for wishing to live
(Cicero, *Letters to Friends*, VII.3.4).

4. Reasonable.   5. Private life.

6. i.e. the shade of retirement rather than the sunlight of publicity.

7. Death lies heavily on the man who, too well known to others, dies a stranger to
himself (Seneca, *Thyestes*, 401–3).

is a curse; for in evil the best condition is not to will, the second not to can.[8] But power to do good is the true and lawful end of aspiring. For good thoughts, though God accept them, yet towards men are little better than good dreams except they be put in act, and that cannot be without power and place as the vantage and commanding ground. Merit and good works is the end of man's motion, and conscience[9] of the same is the accomplishment of man's rest. For if a man can be partaker of God's theatre,[10] he shall likewise be partaker of God's rest. *Et conversus Deus, ut aspiceret opera quae fecerunt manus suae, vidit quod omnia essent bona nimis;*[11] and then the sabbath. In the discharge of thy place set before thee the best examples, for imitation is a globe of precepts.[12] And after a time set before thee thine own example, and examine thyself strictly whether thou didst not best at first. Neglect not also the examples of those that have carried themselves ill in the same place; not to set off thyself by taxing[13] their memory, but to direct thyself what to avoid. Reform therefore without bravery or scandal[14] of former times and persons, but yet set it down to thyself as well to create good precedents as to follow them. Reduce[15] things to the first institution, and observe wherein and how they have degenerate,[16] but yet ask counsel of both times: of the ancient time, what is best; and of the latter time, what is fittest. Seek to make thy course regular, that men may know beforehand what they may expect; but be not too positive and peremptory; and express thyself well[17] when thou digressest from thy rule. Preserve the right of thy place, but stir not questions of jurisdiction, and rather assume thy right in silence and *de facto* than voice it with claims and challenges. Preserve likewise the rights of inferior places, and think it more honour to direct in chief than to be busy in all. Embrace and invite helps and advices touching the execution of thy place, and do not drive away such as bring thee information, as meddlers, but accept of them in good part. The vices of authority are chiefly four: delays,

8. Be able.   9. Consciousness.

10. If a man can look back upon the spectacle of good works he has performed, as God did.

11. And God turned to look upon the works which his hands had made, and he saw that they were all very good (from Genesis 1.31).

12. Is (as valuable as) a whole mass of rules.   13. Finding fault with.

14. Ostentation or defamation.   15. Return.   16. Degenerated.

17. Explain your reasons clearly.

corruption, roughness and facility.[18] For delays: give easy access;
keep times appointed; go through with that which is in hand; and
interlace not business[19] but of necessity. For corruption: do not only
bind thine own hands or thy servants' hands from taking, but bind
the hands of suitors also from offering. For integrity used, doth the
one; but integrity professed, and with a manifest detestation of
bribery, doth the other. And avoid not only the fault but the
suspicion. Whosoever is found variable, and changeth manifestly
without manifest cause, giveth suspicion of corruption. Therefore
always when thou changest thine opinion or course, profess it
plainly and declare it together with the reasons that move thee to
change; and do not think to steal it.[20] A servant or a favourite, if he
be inward,[21] and no other apparent cause of esteem, is commonly
thought but a by-way to close[22] corruption. For roughness, it is a
needless cause of discontent: severity breedeth fear, but roughness
breedeth hate. Even reproofs from authority ought to be grave, and
not taunting. As for facility, it is worse than bribery. For bribes
come but now and then; but if importunity or idle respects[23] lead a
man, he shall never be without.[24] As Solomon saith: *To respect
persons*[25] *is not good, for such a man will transgress for a piece of
bread.*[26] It is most true that was anciently spoken, *A place showeth
the man.*[27] And it showeth some to the better, and some to the
worse. *Omnium consensu capax imperii, nisi imperasset,* saith
Tacitus of Galba;[28] but of Vespasian he saith, *Solus imperantium
Vespasianus mutatus in melius;*[29] though the one was meant of
sufficiency,[30] the other of manners and affection.[31] It is an assured
sign of a worthy and generous spirit, whom honour amends. For
honour is, or should be, the place of virtue; and as in nature things
move violently to their place, and calmly in their place, so virtue in
ambition is violent, in authority settled and calm. All rising to great

18. Over-readiness to give way.
19. Do not mix different matters of business.
20. Do it by stealth.   21. Intimate.   22. Secret.
23. Trivial preferences.   24. Never rise above them.
25. To favour individuals.   26. Proverbs 28.21.
27. A saying attributed to, among others, Solon and Pittacus (two of the Seven
Sages of Greece).
28. Everyone would have thought him fit for empire – had he never been emperor
(*Histories*, I.49).
29. Vespasian was the only emperor who was changed for the better by empire
(*Histories*, I.50).   30. Administrative ability.   31. Morals and disposition.

place is by a winding stair; and if there be factions, it is good to side[32] a man's self whilst he is in the rising, and to balance himself when he is placed. Use the memory of thy predecessor fairly and tenderly; for if thou dost not, it is a debt will sure be paid when thou art gone. If thou have colleagues, respect them, and rather call them when they look not for it, than exclude them when they have reason to look to be called. Be not too sensible[33] or too remembering of thy place in conversation and private answers to suitors; but let it rather be said, *When he sits in place, he is another man.*

32. To take sides with.   33. Sensitive.

12.

Of Boldness

It[1] is a trivial grammar-school text, but yet worthy a wise man's consideration. Question was asked of Demosthenes,[2] *What was the chief part of an orator?* He answered, *Action.*[3] What next? *Action.* What next again? *Action.* He said it that knew it best, and had by nature himself no advantage in that he commended.[4] A strange thing, that that part of an orator which is but superficial, and rather the virtue of a player, should be placed so high above those other noble parts of invention,[5] elocution and the rest – nay, almost alone, as if it were all in all. But the reason is plain. There is in human nature generally more of the fool than of the wise; and therefore those faculties by which the foolish part of men's minds is taken are most potent. Wonderful like is the case of boldness in civil business. What first? *Boldness.* What second and third? *Boldness.* And yet boldness is a child of ignorance and baseness, far inferior to other parts. But nevertheless it doth fascinate[6] and bind hand and foot those that are either shallow in judgement or weak in courage, which are the greatest part; yea, and prevaileth with wise men at weak times. Therefore we see it hath done wonders in popular states,[7] but with senates and princes less; and more ever upon the first entrance of bold persons into action than soon after, for boldness is an ill keeper of promise. Surely, as there are mountebanks for the natural body, so are there mountebanks for the politic body:[8] men that undertake great cures, and perhaps have been lucky in two or three experiments, but want the grounds[9] of science, and therefore cannot hold out. Nay, you shall see a bold fellow many

Text: 1625

1. The following story.
2. Greek orator, d. 322 B.C. Cicero gives an account of his replies in *On the Orator*, III.56, and *Brutus*, XXXVIII.
3. Delivery (i.e. facial expressions, gestures and way of speaking).
4. Demosthenes had at first to overcome an impediment in his speech.
5. Choice of topics or arguments (for the speech).   6. See Essay 9, note 2.
7. Democracies.   8. Body of the state.   9. Fundamentals.

times do Mahomet's miracle. Mahomet made the people believe
that he would call an hill to him, and from the top of it offer up his
prayers for the observers of his law. The people assembled;
Mahomet called the hill to come to him, again and again; and when
the hill stood still, he was never a whit abashed, but said, *If the hill
will not come to Mahomet, Mahomet will go to the hill.* So these
men, when they have promised great matters and failed most
shamefully, yet (if they have the perfection of boldness) they will
but slight it over, and make a turn,[10] and no more ado. Certainly to
men of great judgement, bold persons are a sport to behold; nay, and
to the vulgar also, boldness hath somewhat of the ridiculous. For
if absurdity be the subject of laughter, doubt you not but great
boldness is seldom without some absurdity. Especially it is a sport to
see, when a bold fellow is out of countenance, for that puts his face
into a most shrunken and wooden posture: as needs it must, for in
bashfulness the spirits do a little go and come;[11] but with bold men,
upon like occasion, they stand at a stay,[12] like a stale at chess, where
it is no mate but yet the game cannot stir.[13] But this last were fitter
for a satire than for a serious observation. This is well to be weighed,
that boldness is ever blind; for it seeth not dangers and inconveniences. Therefore it is ill in counsel, good in execution: so that the
right use of bold persons is that they never command in chief, but be
seconds and under the direction of others. For in counsel it is good to
see dangers, and in execution not to see them, except they be very
great.

10. Make light of it, and do a volte-face.
11. i.e. with the result that the expressions change.
12. The expressions become fixed and wooden.
13. i.e. the bold man out of countenance is like a king in a game of chess when a
stalemate leaves him unbeaten but also unable to do anything.

13.

Of Goodness and
Goodness of Nature

I take goodness in this sense, the affecting[1] of the weal of men,
which is that the Grecians call *philanthropia*; and the word *humanity* (as it is used) is a little too light to express it. Goodness I call the
habit, and goodness of nature the inclination. This of all virtues and
dignities of the mind is the greatest, being the character of the
Deity; and without it man is a busy, mischievous, wretched thing,
no better than a kind of vermin. Goodness answers[2] to the theological virtue charity, and admits no excess, but error. The desire of
power in excess caused the angels to fall; the desire of knowledge in
excess caused man to fall: but in clarity there is no excess, neither
can angel or man come in danger by it. The inclination to goodness
is imprinted deeply in the nature of man, insomuch that if it issue
not towards men, it will take unto other living creatures: as it is seen
in the Turks, a cruel people, who nevertheless are kind to beasts and
give alms to dogs and birds; insomuch, as Busbechius[3] reporteth, a
Christian boy in Constantinople had like to have been stoned for
gagging in a waggishness a long-billed fowl. Errors indeed in this
virtue of goodness or charity may be committed. The Italians have
an ungracious proverb, *Tanto buon che val niente: So good, that he
is good for nothing.* And one of the doctors[4] of Italy, Nicholas
Machiavel, had the confidence to put in writing, almost in plain
terms, that *the Christian faith had given up good men in prey to*

Texts: MS, 1612, 1625

1. Desiring.   2. Corresponds.

3. Flemish scholar and ambassador to the Turks, d. 1592. Bacon's version of the
incident differs from Busbequius' in several details: in the original, it was a Venetian
goldsmith, not a Christian boy, the bird was a short-billed fowl with a huge gape, and
there was no mention of stoning. In the Latin version of the essay, Bacon follows
Busbequius more exactly.

4. Teachers. Machiavelli, d. 1527, is famous as the author of *The Prince*.

those that are tyrannical and unjust.[5] Which he spake, because indeed there was never law or sect or opinion did so much magnify goodness as the Christian religion doth. Therefore, to avoid the scandal and the danger both, it is good to take knowledge of the errors of an habit so excellent. Seek the good of other men, but be not in bondage to their faces or fancies, for that is but facility[6] or softness, which taketh an honest mind prisoner. Neither give thou Aesop's cock a gem, who would be better pleased and happier if he had had a barley-corn.[7] The example of God teacheth the lesson truly: *He sendeth his rain and maketh his sun to shine upon the just and unjust;*[8] but he doth not rain wealth nor shine honour and virtues upon men equally. Common benefits are to be communicate[9] with all, but peculiar benefits with choice. And beware how in making the portraiture thou breakest the pattern: for divinity maketh the love of ourselves the pattern, the love of our neighbours but the portraiture. *Sell all thou hast, and give it to the poor, and follow me;*[10] but sell not all thou hast, except thou come and follow me; that is, except thou have a vocation wherein thou mayest do as much good with little means as with great, for otherwise in feeding the streams thou driest the fountain. Neither is there only a habit of goodness, directed by right reason; but there is in some men, even in nature, a disposition towards it, as on the other side there is a natural malignity. For there be that in their nature do not affect[11] the good of others. The lighter sort of malignity turneth but to a crossness[12] or frowardness or aptness to oppose or difficilness[13] or the like; but the deeper sort, to envy and mere mischief. Such men in other men's calamities are, as it were, in season,[14] and are ever on the loading part:[15] not so good as the dogs that licked Lazarus' sores,[16] but like flies that are still buzzing upon anything that is raw; *misanthropi*,[17] that make it their practice to

---

5. In his *Discourses*, II.2, Machiavelli says that emphasis on humility and unworldliness makes Christians weak and effeminate, and leaves them prey to the wicked. But then he goes on to say – and Bacon is silent about this – that such a view of Christian teaching is erroneous because in fact it permits men to love and honour their country and defend themselves.

6. Complaisance.   7. See Phaedrus, *Fables*, III.12.   8. Matthew 5.45.

9. Shared.   10. Mark 10.21.   11. Desire.   12. Contrariness.

13. Harshness (in being difficult to deal with).   14. At their happiest.

15. Always take the side which adds burdens (to men already weighed down with misfortune).   16. See Luke 16.19–21.   17. Misanthropes.

bring men to the bough,[18] and yet have never a tree for the purpose in their gardens, as Timon had.[19] Such dispositions are the very errors of human nature, and yet they are the fittest timber to make great politics[20] of; like to knee-timber,[21] that is good for ships that are ordained to be tossed, but not for building houses that shall stand firm. The parts and signs of goodness are many. If a man be gracious and courteous to strangers, it shows he is a citizen of the world, and that his heart is no island cut off from other lands, but a continent that joins to them. If he be compassionate towards the afflictions of others, it shows that his heart is like the noble tree that is wounded itself when it gives the balm.[22] If he easily pardons and remits offences, it shows that his mind is planted above injuries, so that he cannot be shot. If he be thankful for small benefits, it shows that he weighs men's minds, and not their trash. But above all, if he have St Paul's perfection, that he would wish to be an *anathema* from Christ for the salvation of his brethren,[23] it shows much of a divine nature, and a kind of conformity with Christ himself.

18. i.e. to hang themselves.

19. Timon of Athens, known as the Misanthrope, announced that since he was going to cut down a tree in his garden on which many had hanged themselves, would-be suicides should use it at once. 20. Politicians.

21. Timber grown crooked.

22. When cut open the frankincense tree exudes an aromatic resin.

23. In Romans 9.3, St Paul writes: 'For I could wish that I myself were accursed and cut off from Christ for the sake of my brethren, my kinsmen by race.'

14.

Of Nobility

We will speak of nobility first as a portion of an estate,[1] then as a condition of particular persons. A monarchy where there is no nobility at all is ever a pure and absolute tyranny, as that of the Turks. For nobility attempers sovereignty, and draws the eyes of the people somewhat aside from the line royal. But for democracies, they need it not, and they are commonly more quiet and less subject to sedition than where there are stirps[2] of nobles. For men's eyes are upon the business and not upon the persons; or, if upon the persons, it is for the business' sake, as fittest, and not for flags and pedigree. We see the Switzers last well, notwithstanding their diversity of religion and of cantons; for utility is their bond, and not respects.[3] The United Provinces of the Low Countries in their government excel; for where there is an equality, the consultations are more indifferent,[4] and the payments and tributes more cheerful. A great and potent nobility addeth majesty to a monarch, but diminisheth power; and putteth life and spirit into the people, but presseth[5] their fortune. It is well when nobles are not too great for sovereignty, nor for justice, and yet maintained in that height as[6] the insolency of inferiors may be broken upon them before it come on too fast upon the majesty of kings. A numerous nobility causeth poverty and inconvenience in a state, for it is a surcharge of expense; and besides, it being of necessity that many of the nobility fall in time to be weak in fortune, it maketh a kind of disproportion between honour and means.

As for nobility in particular persons, it is a reverend thing to see an ancient castle or building not in decay, or to see a fair timber-tree sound and perfect: how much more to behold an ancient noble family which hath stood against the waves and weathers of time. For new nobility is but the act of power, but ancient nobility is the act

Texts: MS, 1612, 1625

1. A state.   2. Families.   3. Regard for rank.   4. Impartial.
5. Depresses.   6. At such a height that.

of time. Those that are first raised to nobility are commonly more virtuous[7] but less innocent than their descendants – for there is rarely any rising but by a commixture of good and evil arts. But it is reason[8] the memory of their virtues remain to their posterity, and their faults die with themselves. Nobility of birth commonly abateth industry, and he that is not industrious envieth him that is. Besides, noble persons cannot go much higher, and he that standeth at a stay[9] when others rise can hardly avoid motions[10] of envy. On the other side, nobility extinguisheth the passive envy from others towards them, because they are in possession of honour.[11] Certainly kings that have able men of their nobility shall find ease in employing them, and a better slide[12] in their business; for people naturally bend to them as born in some sort to command.

7. Possess more excellent qualities (i.e. not only moral virtues).
8. It is reasonable that.   9. Who is at a standstill.   10. Feelings.
11. i.e. if a man is born to a title, the latent envy which might be aroused in men of lesser rank is extinguished; but envy *is* kindled, in men who fail to rise, towards those who gain such titles instead of inheriting them.   12. A smoother passage.

15.

Of Seditions and Troubles

Shepherds of people had need know the calendars[1] of tempests in
state; which are commonly greatest when things grow to equality,
as natural tempests are greatest about the *equinoctia*.[2] And as there
are certain hollow blasts of wind and secret swellings of seas before a
tempest, so are there in states:

> *Ille etiam caecos instare tumultus*
> *Saepe monet, fraudesque et operta tumescere bella.*[3]

Libels and licentious discourses against the state, when they are
frequent and open, and (in like sort) false news, often running up
and down to the disadvantage of the state, and hastily embraced, are
amongst the signs of troubles. Virgil, giving the pedigree of Fame,
saith, *She was sister to the giants:*

> *Illam Terra parens, ira irritata deorum,*
> *Extremam (ut perhibent) Coeo Enceladoque sororem*
> *Progenuit.*[4]

As if fames were the relics of seditions past; but they are no less
indeed the preludes of seditions to come. Howsoever, he noteth it
right that seditious tumults and seditious fames differ no more but
as brother and sister, masculine and feminine; especially if it come
to that, that the best actions of a state, and the most plausible,[5] and
which ought to give greatest contentment, are taken in ill sense and
traduced. For that shows the envy great, as Tacitus saith, *Conflata
magna invidia, seu bene seu male gesta premunt.*[6] Neither doth it
follow that because these fames are a sign of troubles, that the

Texts: MS, 1625

1. Accurate predictions.   2. Equinoxes.
3. He (the sun) also often warns us that dark uprisings threaten, that treachery
and hidden wars are swelling to a head (Virgil, *Georgics*, I.464–5).
4. The story goes that Mother Earth, provoked to anger against the gods, gave
birth to her (Fame), as youngest sister to (the giants) Coeus and Enceladus (*Aeneid*,
IV.178–80).   5. Praiseworthy.
6. Once envy has been aroused, good actions are disparaged as much as bad ones
(from *Histories*, I.7).

suppressing of them with too much severity should be a remedy of troubles. For the despising of them many times checks them best, and the going about to stop them doth but make a wonder long-lived. Also that kind of obedience which Tacitus speaketh of is to be held suspected: *Erant in officio, sed tamen qui mallent mandata imperantium interpretari, quam exequi.*[7] Disputing, excusing, cavilling upon mandates[8] and directions, is a kind of shaking off the yoke, and assay of disobedience; especially if in those disputings they which are for the direction speak fearfully and tenderly,[9] and those that are against it, audaciously.

Also, as Machiavel noteth well, when princes, that ought to be common parents, make themselves as a party and lean to a side, it is as a boat that is overthrown by uneven weight on the one side:[10] as was well seen in the time of Henry the Third of France; for first himself entered league for the extirpation of the Protestants,[11] and presently after the same league was turned upon himself. For when the authority of princes is made but an accessary to a cause, and that there be other bands that tie faster than the band of sovereignty, kings begin to be put almost out of possession.

Also, when discords and quarrels and factions are carried openly and audaciously, it is a sign the reverence of government is lost. For the motions of the greatest persons in a government ought to be as the motions of the planets under *primum mobile*, according to the old opinion:[12] which is that every of them is carried swiftly by the highest motion, and softly in their own motion. And therefore, when great ones in their own particular motion move violently and, as Tacitus expresseth it well, *liberius quam ut imperantium meminissent,*[13] it is a sign the orbs are out of frame.[14] For reverence

7. They remained outwardly loyal, but yet they would sooner question the orders of their commanders than obey them (from *Histories*, II.39).   8. Orders.

9. Too gently.   10. See Machiavelli, *Discourses*, III.27.

11. The Holy League was formed in France in 1575 to defend the Catholic faith and to crush the Protestants. Henry III at first gave it his support, but eventually he broke with it (causing its leader Henry de Guise to be assassinated). For this he was driven out of Paris in 1588.

12. i.e. the theory (known as the Ptolemaic System) that the earth was enclosed within a set of nine massive crystalline spheres, each fitting tightly with and moved by the sphere above it. Another sphere around these, the *primum mobile*, was supposed to revolve round the earth in twenty-four hours, and to communicate its motion to the lower heavens, or spheres, which contained the planets.

13. More freely than was compatible with respect for their rulers (from *Annals*, III.4).   14. Disordered.

is that wherewith princes are girt from God, who threateneth the
dissolving thereof: *Solvam cingula regum.*[15]

So when any of the four pillars of government are mainly[16]
shaken or weakened (which are religion, justice, counsel and treasure), men had need to pray for fair weather. But let us pass from
this part of[17] predictions (concerning which, nevertheless, more
light may be taken from that which followeth), and let us speak first
of the materials of seditions; then of the motives of them; and
thirdly of the remedies.

Concerning the materials of seditions. It is a thing well to be
considered, for the surest way to prevent seditions (if the times do
bear[18] it) is to take away the matter of them. For if there be fuel
prepared, it is hard to tell whence the spark shall come that shall set
it on fire. The matter of seditions is of two kinds; much poverty and
much discontentment. It is certain, so many overthrown estates, so
many votes for troubles. Lucan noteth well the state of Rome before
the civil war:

> *Hinc usura vorax, rapidumque in tempore foenus,*
> *Hinc concussa fides, et multis utile bellum.*[19]

This same *multis utile bellum*[20] is an assured and infallible sign of
a state disposed to seditions and troubles. And if this poverty and
broken estate in the better sort be joined with a want and necessity
in the mean people, the danger is imminent and great. For the
rebellions of the belly are the worst. As for discontentments, they
are in the politic body[21] like to humours in the natural, which are apt
to gather a preternatural heat and to inflame. And let no prince
measure the danger of them by this, whether they be just or unjust;
for that were to imagine people to be too reasonable, who do often
spurn at their own good: nor yet by this, whether the griefs
whereupon they rise be in fact great or small; for they are the most
dangerous discontentments where the fear is greater than the
feeling. *Dolendi modus, timendi non item.*[22] Besides, in great

---

15. I will loosen the girdles of kings (Isaiah 45.1).   16. Greatly.
17. Part of the subject of.   18. Permit.
19. Hence came devouring usury and interest greedy of the reckoning day; hence
was credit shaken and war profitable to many (*The Civil War*, I.181–2).
20. Profit in war for many.   21. Body of the state.
22. There is a limit to suffering but no limit to fear (Pliny, *Letters*, VIII.17.6).

oppressions, the same things that provoke the patience do withal mate[23] the courage; but in fears it is not so. Neither let any prince or state be secure[24] concerning discontentments, because they have been often, or have been long, and yet no peril hath ensued. For as it is true that every vapour or fume doth not turn into a storm, so it is nevertheless true that storms, though they blow over divers times, yet may fall at last: and, as the Spanish proverb noteth well, *The cord breaketh at the last by the weakest pull.*

The causes and motives of seditions are: innovation in religion, taxes, alteration of laws and customs, breaking of privileges, general oppression, advancement of unworthy persons, strangers, dearths, disbanded soldiers, factions grown desperate, and whatsoever in offending people joineth and knitteth them in a common cause.

For the remedies, there may be some general preservatives, whereof we will speak: as for the just[25] cure, it must answer to the particular disease, and so be left to counsel rather than rule.

The first remedy or prevention is to remove by all means possible that material cause of sedition whereof we spake, which is want and poverty in the estate.[26] To which purpose serveth the opening and well-balancing of trade; the cherishing of manufactures; the banishing of idleness; the repressing of waste and excess by sumptuary laws; the improvement and husbanding of the soil; the regulating of prices of things vendible; the moderating of taxes and tributes; and the like. Generally, it is to be foreseen that the population of a kingdom (especially if it be not mown down by wars) do not exceed the stock[27] of the kingdom which should maintain them. Neither is the population to be reckoned only by number: for a smaller number, that spend more and earn less, do wear out an estate sooner than a greater number that live lower and gather more. Therefore the multiplying of nobility and other degrees of quality, in an over-proportion to the common people, doth speedily bring a state to necessity; and so doth likewise an overgrown clergy, for they bring nothing to the stock; and in like manner when more are bred scholars than preferments can take off.

It is likewise to be remembered that, forasmuch as the increase of any estate must be upon[28] the foreigner (for whatsoever is somewhere gotten is somewhere lost), there be but three things which

23. Overwhelm.   24. Feel free from care.   25. Exact *or* proper.
26. State.   27. Resources (produce and capital).   28. At the expense of.

one nation selleth unto another: the commodity as nature yieldeth it, the manufacture, and the vecture or carriage. So that if these three wheels go, wealth will flow as in a spring tide. And it cometh many times to pass, that *materiam superabit opus*;[29] that the work and carriage is more worth than the material, and enricheth a state more; as is notably seen in the Low-Countrymen, who have the best mines above ground in the world.

Above all things, good policy is to be used, that the treasure and monies in a state be not gathered into few hands. For otherwise a state may have a great stock, and yet starve: and money is like muck, not good except it be spread. This is done chiefly by suppressing, or at the least keeping a strait hand upon the devouring trades of usury, engrossing,[30] great pasturages,[31] and the like.

For removing discontentments, or at least the danger of them. There is in every state (as we know) two portions of subjects, the noblesse and the commonalty. When one of these is discontent,[32] the danger is not great: for common people are of slow motion if they be not excited by the greater sort; and the greater sort are of small strength except the multitude be apt and ready to move of themselves. Then is the danger, when the greater sort do but wait for the troubling of the waters amongst the meaner, that then they may declare themselves. The poets feign that the rest of the gods would have bound Jupiter; which he hearing of, by the counsel of Pallas sent for Briareus, with his hundred hands, to come in to his aid.[33] An emblem, no doubt, to show how safe it is for monarchs to make sure of the good will of common people.

To give moderate liberty for griefs and discontentments to evaporate (so it be without too great insolency or bravery[34]) is a safe way. For he that turneth the humours back, and maketh the wound bleed inwards, endangereth malign ulcers and pernicious impostumations.[35]

The part of Epimetheus mought[36] well become Prometheus, in the case of discontentments, for there is not a better provision

29. The workmanship will surpass the material (Ovid, *Metamorphoses*, II.5).
30. Monopolies.   31. Arable lands converted to pasture.
32. Discontented.

33. The monster Briareus helped Zeus (or Jupiter) to put down the rebellion of the gods. According to Homer, however, it was the goddess Thetis, not Pallas Athene, who advised Zeus to send for him.   34. Boastful defiance.   35. Abscesses.
36. Might.

against them.[37] Epimetheus, when griefs and evils flew abroad, at last shut the lid, and kept hope in the bottom of the vessel. Certainly the politic and artificial[38] nourishing and entertaining of hopes, and carrying men from hopes to hopes, is one of the best antidotes against the poison of discontentments. And it is a certain sign of a wise government and proceeding when it can hold men's hearts by hopes, when it cannot by satisfaction; and when it can handle things in such manner as no evil shall appear so peremptory but that it hath some outlet of hope: which is the less hard to do, because both particular persons and factions are apt enough to flatter themselves, or at least to brave[39] that which they believe not.

Also, the foresight and prevention that there be no likely or fit head whereunto discontented persons may resort, and under whom they may join, is a known but an excellent point of caution. I understand a fit head to be one that hath greatness and reputation, that hath confidence with the discontented party and upon whom they turn their eyes, and that is thought discontented in his own particular.[40] Which kind of persons are either to be won and reconciled to the state, and that in a fast[41] and true manner, or to be fronted[42] with some other of the same party that may oppose them, and so divide the reputation. Generally, the dividing and breaking of all factions and combinations that are adverse to the state, and setting them at distance or at least distrust amongst themselves, is not one of the worst remedies. For it is a desperate case if those that hold with the proceeding of the state be full of discord and faction, and those that are against it be entire and united.

I have noted that some witty[43] and sharp speeches which have fallen from princes have given fire to seditions. Caesar did himself infinite hurt in that speech, *Sulla nescivit litteras, non potuit dictare*,[44] for it did utterly cut off that hope which men had entertained, that he would at one time or other give over his

---

37. Epimetheus opened the box which Pandora offered him, and which his brother Prometheus had earlier declined. In *The Wisdom of the Ancients* Bacon says that the brothers represent the two conditions of life: 'The followers of Epimetheus are the improvident, who take no care for the future', while those of Prometheus are 'the wise and fore-thoughtful class of men'. See below, p. 274.

38. Safe and skilful.   39. Make a bold show of.   40. Private interest.

41. Firm.   42. Confronted.   43. Ingenious.

44. Sulla was ignorant of letters, and so could not dictate (Suetonius, *Julius Caesar*, 77): there is a play on *dictare*, meaning 'to dictate or write letters' but also 'to be a dictator'.

dictatorship. Galba undid himself by that speech, *Legi a se militem, non emi,*[45] for it put the soldiers out of hope of the donative. Probus likewise by that speech, *Si vixero, non opus erit amplius Romano imperio militibus,*[46] a speech of great despair for the soldiers. And many the like. Surely princes had need in tender[47] matters and ticklish times to beware what they say, especially in these short speeches, which fly abroad like darts and are thought to be shot out of their secret intentions. For as for large discourses, they are flat[48] things, and not so much noted.

Lastly, let princes, against all events, not be without some great person, one or rather more, of military valour, near unto them, for the repressing of seditions in their beginnings. For without that, there useth to be[49] more trepidation in court upon the first breaking out of troubles than were fit. And the state runneth the danger of that which Tacitus saith: *Atque is habitus animorum fuit, ut pessimum facinus auderent pauci, plures vellent, omnes paterentur.*[50] But let such military persons be assured[51] and well reputed of, rather than factious and popular,[52] holding also good correspondence with the other great men in the state; or else the remedy is worse than the disease.

45. That his soldiers were levied, not bought (Tacitus, *Histories*, I.5).
46. If I live, the Roman empire will have no further need of soldiers (from Vopiscus, *Probus*, 20).   47. Delicate.   48. Dull.
49. There is customarily.
50. And such was the state of feeling that this execrable deed was attempted by a few, desired by more, and tolerated by all (*Histories*, I.28).
51. Trustworthy.   52. Out to curry favour with the people.

16.

Of Atheism

I had rather believe all the fables in the Legend,[1] and the Talmud,[2] and the Alcoran,[3] than that this universal frame is without a mind.[4] And therefore God never wrought miracle to convince[5] atheism, because his ordinary works convince it. It is true that a little philosophy inclineth man's mind to atheism, but depth in philosophy bringeth men's minds about to religion: for while the mind of man looketh upon second causes scattered, it may sometimes rest in them, and go no further; but when it beholdeth the chain of them, confederate and linked together, it must needs fly to Providence and Deity.[6] Nay, even that school which is most accused of atheism doth most demonstrate religion; that is, the school of Leucippus and Democritus and Epicurus.[7] For it is a thousand times more credible that four mutable elements and one immutable fifth essence,[8] duly and eternally placed, need no God, than that an army of infinite small portions or seeds[9] unplaced should have produced this order and beauty without a divine marshal. The Scripture saith, *The fool hath said in his heart, there is no God;*[10] it is not said, *The fool hath thought in his heart:* so as he rather saith it by rote to himself, as

Texts: MS, 1612, 1625

1. The Golden Legend, a thirteenth-century collection of saints' lives written by Jacobus de Voragine. It includes the most far-fetched of stories.

2. Compilation of Jewish laws.

3. The Koran, sacred book of the Mohammedans.

4. In Bacon's day, an atheist was not necessarily someone who denied the existence of God, but someone who identified the creative principles of the universe with God.   5. Refute.

6. In *The Advancement of Learning*, I.1.3, Bacon writes that it is certain 'that God worketh nothing but by second causes'. God is the First Cause, as a man will realize if he traces through any sequence, or *chain*, of second causes (as opposed to regarding them as *scattered* or unrelated).

7. Philosophers of the fifth and fourth centuries B.C. who held that the universe was formed from atoms coming together by chance, not by the will of a creator.

8. Aristotle, in contradiction of the atomic theory, taught that the earth was made up of four mutable elements (earth, water, air and fire) and that the heavens were composed of a fifth, unchangeable element, the quintessence.   9. Atoms.

10. Psalms 14.1 and 53.1.

that[11] he would have, than that he can throughly[12] believe it or be persuaded of it. For none deny there is a God but those for whom it maketh[13] that there were no God. It appeareth in nothing more, that atheism is rather in the lip than in the heart of man, than by this: that atheists will ever be talking of that their opinion, as if they fainted in it within themselves and would be glad to be strengthened by the consent of others. Nay more, you shall have atheists strive to get disciples, as it fareth with other sects. And, which is most of all, you shall have of them[14] that will suffer for atheism and not recant; whereas if they did truly think that there were no such thing as God, why should they trouble themselves? Epicurus is charged that he did dissemble for his credit's sake when he affirmed there were blessed natures, but such as enjoyed themselves without having respect to the government of the world. Wherein they say he did temporize, though in secret he thought there was no God. But certainly he is traduced, for his words are noble and divine: *Non deos vulgi negare profanum, sed vulgi opiniones diis applicare profanum.*[15] Plato could have said no more. And although he had the confidence to deny the administration, he had not the power to deny the nature. The Indians of the West have names for their particular gods, though they have no name for God: as if the heathens should have had the names Jupiter, Apollo, Mars, etc., but not the word *Deus*[16] – which shows that even those barbarous people have the notion, though they have not the latitude and extent of it. So that against atheists the very savages take part with the very subtlest philosophers. The contemplative atheist is rare: a Diagoras,[17] a Bion,[18] a Lucian[19] perhaps, and some others; and yet they seem to be more than they are, for that all that impugn a received religion or superstition are by the adverse part branded with the name of atheists. But the great atheists indeed are hypocrites, which are ever handling holy things, but without feeling; so as they must needs be cauterized in the end. The causes of atheism

11. That which.   12. Thoroughly.

13. It seems to be an advantage to believe.   14. Some of them.

15. It is not profane to deny the existence of the gods of the people: the profanity is in attributing to the gods what the people believe of them (Diogenes Laertius, *Lives of Eminent Philosophers*, X.123).   16. God.

17. Greek poet, fifth century B.C. Renowned for his atheism, he fled from Athens to avoid being punished for his impieties.

18. Greek philosopher, third century B.C.

19. Greek satirist, second century A.D.

are, divisions in religion, if they be many, for any one main division addeth zeal to both sides, but many divisions introduce atheism. Another is scandal of priests, when it is come to that which St Bernard[20] saith, *Non est iam dicere, ut populus sic sacerdos; quia nec sic populus ut sacerdos.*[21] A third is custom of profane scoffing in holy matters, which doth by little and little deface the reverence of religion. And lastly, learned times, specially with peace and prosperity, for troubles and adversities do more bow men's minds to religion. They that deny a God destroy man's nobility, for certainly man is of kin to the beasts by his body, and if he be not of kin to God by his spirit, he is a base and ignoble creature. It destroys likewise magnanimity, and the raising of human nature. For take an example of a dog, and mark what a generosity and courage he will put on when he finds himself maintained[22] by a man, who to him is in stead of a god, or *melior natura;*[23] which courage is manifestly such as that creature, without that confidence of a better nature than his own, could never attain. So man, when he resteth and assureth himself upon divine protection and favour, gathereth a force and faith which human nature in itself could not obtain. Therefore, as atheism is in all respects hateful, so in this, that it depriveth human nature of the means to exalt itself above human frailty. As it is in particular persons, so it is in nations. Never was there such a state for magnanimity as Rome: of this state hear what Cicero saith: *Quam volumus licet, patres conscripti, nos amemus, tamen nec numero Hispanos, nec robore Gallos, nec calliditate Poenos, nec artibus Graecos, nec denique hoc ipso huius gentis et terrae domestico nativoque sensu Italos ipsos et Latinos; sed pietate, ac religione, atque hac una sapientia, quod deorum immortalium numine omnia regi gubernarique perspeximus, omnes gentes nationesque superavimus.*[24]

20. French abbot, d. 1153.

21. One can no longer say 'as the people are, so is the priest', but rather 'as the people are, so the priest is not' (i.e. because the people are better than the priests).

22. Supported.   23. A better nature (from Ovid, *Metamorphoses*, I.21).

24. We may admire ourselves as much as we please, Senators, yet we cannot match the Spaniards in number, nor the Gauls in bodily strength, nor the Carthaginians in cunning, nor the Greeks in art, nor indeed our own Italians and Latins in the homebred and native good sense characteristic of this land and nation. But in our piety, and in our religion, and in our recognition of the one great truth that all things are ruled and ordered by the divine will of the immortal gods – in these things we have surpassed all peoples and nations (*A Speech Concerning the Response of the Soothsayers*, IX.19).

17.

Of Superstition

It were better to have no opinion of God at all than such an opinion as is unworthy of him: for the one is unbelief, the other is contumely; and certainly superstition is the reproach of the Deity. Plutarch saith well to that purpose: *Surely* (saith he) *I had rather a great deal men should say there was no such man at all as Plutarch than that they should say that there was one Plutarch that would eat his children as soon as they were born*,[1] as the poets speak of Saturn.[2] And as the contumely is greater towards God, so the danger is greater towards men. Atheism leaves a man to sense, to philosophy, to natural piety,[3] to laws, to reputation; all which may be guides to an outward moral virtue, though religion were not; but superstition dismounts all these and erecteth an absolute monarchy in the minds of men. Therefore atheism did never perturb states, for it makes men wary of themselves, as looking no further: and we see the times inclined to atheism (as the time of Augustus Caesar) were civil[4] times. But superstition hath been the confusion of many states, and bringeth in a new *primum mobile*[5] that ravisheth all the spheres of government. The master of superstition is the people, and in all superstition wise men follow fools, and arguments are fitted to practice, in a reversed order. It was gravely said by some of the prelates in the Council of Trent,[6] where the doctrine of the Schoolmen[7] bare great sway, *that the Schoolmen were like astronomers, which did feign eccentrics and epicycles, and such engines of orbs, to save the phenomena, though they knew there were no*

Texts: MS, 1612, 1625

1. Derived from *Superstition*, 10 (*Moralia*, 169–70), where Saturn is not mentioned.

2. Saturn, one of the most ancient of the gods, was said to have eaten all his children except Jupiter, for whom a stone was substituted.

3. Affection.　　　4. Orderly, free from turmoil.　　　5. See Essay 15, note 12.

6. Religious conference convened in 1545 to oppose Protestant doctrines and settle disputed Catholic ones.

7. Medieval philosophers and teachers in the universities who sought to regulate the doctrines of the Christian Church according to the rules of Aristotelian logic.

such things;[8] and in like manner, that the Schoolmen had framed a number of subtle and intricate axioms and theorems to save the practice of the church. The causes of superstition are: pleasing and sensual rites and ceremonies; excess of outward and pharisaical holiness; over-great reverence of traditions, which cannot but load[9] the church; the stratagems of prelates for their own ambition and lucre; the favouring too much of good intentions, which openeth the gate to conceits and novelties; the taking an aim at divine matters by human, which cannot but breed mixture of imaginations;[10] and lastly, barbarous times, especially joined with calamities and disasters. Superstition without a veil is a deformed thing, for, as it addeth deformity to an ape to be so like a man, so the similitude of superstition to religion makes it the more deformed. And as wholesome meat corrupteth to little worms, so good forms and orders corrupt into a number of petty observances. There is a superstition in avoiding superstition, when men think to do best if they go furthest from the superstition formerly received: therefore care would be had[11] that (as it fareth in ill purgings[12]) the good be not taken away with the bad, which commonly is done, when the people is the reformer.

8. As it became obvious that the simple Ptolemaic astronomy (a theory of concentric spheres moving around the earth) could not account for newly observed phenomena, astronomers devised elaborate explanations to make the facts fit the received view (or *save the phenomena*). They claimed, among other things, that the planets moved in eccentric orbits or in epicycles.   9. Overload.

10. Conceptions.   11. Ought to be taken.   12. Purgings of the body.

18.

Of Travel

Travel in the younger sort is a part of education; in the elder, a part of experience. He that travelleth into a country before he hath some entrance into the language, goeth to school and not to travel. That young men travel under some tutor or grave servant, I allow well;[1] so that he be such a one that hath the language and hath been in the country before, whereby he may be able to tell them what things are worthy to be seen in the country where they go, what acquaintances they are to seek, what exercises or discipline[2] the place yieldeth. For else young men shall go hooded,[3] and look abroad little. It is a strange thing that in sea voyages, where there is nothing to be seen but sky and sea, men should make diaries; but in land-travel, wherein so much is to be observed, for the most part they omit it; as if chance were fitter to be registered than observation. Let diaries therefore be brought in use. The things to be seen and observed are: the courts of princes, specially when they give audience to ambassadors; the courts of justice, while they sit and hear causes, and so of consistories ecclesiastic; the churches and monasteries, with the monuments which are therein extant; the walls and fortifications of cities and towns, and so the havens and harbours; antiquities and ruins; libraries; colleges, disputations,[4] and lectures, where any are; shipping and navies; houses and gardens of state and pleasure near great cities; armories; arsenals; magazines[5]; exchanges; burses[6]; warehouses; exercises of horsemanship, fencing, training of soldiers, and the like; comedies, such whereunto the better sort of persons do resort; treasuries of jewels and robes; cabinets and rarities; and, to conclude, whatsoever is memorable in the places where they go. After all which the tutors or servants ought to make diligent inquiry. As for triumphs,[7] masques, feasts, weddings,

Text: 1625

1. I fully approve of.   2. Learning.
3. i.e. with their heads covered up so that they cannot see (as with hawks, in falconry).   4. Academic debates in the universities.   5. Storehouses.
6. Money markets.   7. Magnificent displays.

funerals, capital executions, and such shows, men need not to be put in mind of them; yet are they not to be neglected. If you will have a young man to put his travel into a little room, and in short time to gather much, this you must do. First, as was said, he must have some entrance into the language before he goeth. Then he must have such a servant or tutor as knoweth the country, as was likewise said. Let him carry with him also some card[8] or book describing the country where he travelleth, which will be a good key to his inquiry. Let him keep also a diary. Let him not stay long in one city or town; more or less as the place deserveth, but not long: nay, when he stayeth in one city or town, let him change his lodging from one end and part of the town to another, which is a great adamant[9] of acquaintance. Let him sequester himself from the company of his countrymen, and diet[10] in such places where there is good company of the nation where he travelleth. Let him upon his removes from one place to another procure recommendation to some person of quality residing in the place whither he removeth, that he may use his favour in those things he desireth to see or know. Thus he may abridge his travel with much profit. As for the acquaintance which is to be sought in travel, that which is most of all profitable is acquaintance with the secretaries and employed men of ambassadors, for so in travelling in one country he shall suck the experience of many. Let him also see and visit eminent persons in all kinds which are of great name abroad, that he may be able to tell how the life agreeth with the fame. For quarrels, they are with care and discretion to be avoided. They are commonly for mistresses, healths,[11] place, and words. And let a man beware how he keepeth company with choleric and quarrelsome persons, for they will engage him into their own quarrels. When a traveller returneth home, let him not leave the countries where he hath travelled altogether behind him, but maintain a correspondence by letters with those of his acquaintance which are of most worth. And let his travel appear rather in his discourse than in his apparel or gesture; and in his discourse, let him be rather advised[12] in his answers than forwards to tell stories; and let it appear that he doth not change his country manners for those of foreign parts, but only prick in[13] some flowers of that he hath learned abroad into the customs of his own country.

8. Map.   9. Loadstone (i.e. something which attracts).   10. Eat his meals.
11. Toasts, drinking bouts.   12. Knowledgeable, thoughtful.   13. Plant.

19.

Of Empire

It is a miserable state of mind to have few things to desire and many
things to fear. And yet that commonly is the case of kings, who,
being at the highest, want matter of desire, which makes their minds
more languishing; and have many representations[1] of perils and
shadows, which makes their minds the less clear. And this is one
reason also of that effect which the Scripture speaketh of, *that the
king's heart is inscrutable.*[2] For multitude of jealousies, and lack of
some predominant desire that should marshal and put in order all
the rest, maketh any man's heart hard to find or sound. Hence it
comes likewise that princes many times make themselves desires,
and set their hearts upon toys:[3] sometimes upon a building;
sometimes upon erecting of an order;[4] sometimes upon the advancing of a person; sometimes upon obtaining excellency in some art
or feat of the hand – as Nero for playing on the harp, Domitian for
certainty of the hand with the arrow, Commodus for playing at
fence, Caracalla for driving chariots,[5] and the like. This seemeth
incredible unto those that know not the principle, *that the mind of
man is more cheered and refreshed by profiting in small things than
by standing at a stay[6] in great.* We see also that kings that have been
fortunate conquerors in their first years, it being not possible for
them to go forward infinitely, but that they must have some check
or arrest in their fortunes, turn in their latter years to be superstitious and melancholy; as did Alexander the Great, Diocletian,[7] and
in our memory Charles the Fifth,[8] and others. For he that is used to

---

Texts: MS, 1612, 1625

1. Appearances.   2. Proverbs 25.3.   3. Trivial things.
4. Religious order.
5. Nero, d. A.D. 68, Domitian, d. 96, Commodus, d. 192, and Caracalla, d. 217,
were Roman emperors; all notorious for their great cruelties.   6. Still.
7. Roman emperor, d. 313, said to be the first sovereign to resign his power
voluntarily (he abdicated in 305).
8. German (and Holy Roman) emperor, d. 1558; he abdicated the empire 1556.

go forward, and findeth a stop, falleth out of his own favour and is not the thing he was.

To speak now of the true temper of empire: it is a thing rare and hard to keep, for both temper and distemper consist of contraries. But it is one thing to mingle contraries, another to interchange them.[9] The answer of Apollonius[10] to Vespasian[11] is full of excellent instruction. Vespasian asked him, *What was Nero's overthrow?* He answered: *Nero could touch and tune the harp well; but in government, sometimes he used to wind the pins too high, sometimes to let them down too low.*[12] And certain it is that nothing destroyeth authority so much as the unequal and untimely interchange of power pressed too far, and relaxed too much.

This is true, that the wisdom of all these latter times in princes' affairs is rather fine deliveries and shiftings of[13] dangers and mischiefs when they are near, than solid and grounded courses to keep them aloof. But this is but to try masteries with fortune.[14] And let men beware how they neglect and suffer matter of trouble to be prepared: for no man can forbid the spark nor tell whence it may come. The difficulties in princes' business are many and great, but the greatest difficulty is often in their own mind. For it is common with princes (saith Tacitus) to will contradictories: *Sunt plerumque regum voluntates vehementes, et inter se contrariae.*[15] For it is the solecism[16] of power to think to command the end, and yet not to endure the mean.

Kings have to deal with their neighbours, their wives, their children, their prelates or clergy, their nobles, their second-nobles or gentlemen, their merchants, their commons, and their men of war; and from all these arise dangers, if care and circumspection be not used.

First for their neighbours: there can no general rule be given (the occasions are so variable), save one which ever holdeth. Which is that princes do keep due sentinel that none of their neighbours do

9. i.e. the true *temper* of empire is when the contraries, sovereignty and liberty, are mingled and made whole: *distemper* is when they are alternated or *interchanged*.
10. Pythagorean philosopher and magician of the first century.
11. Roman emperor, 69–79.
12. Philostratus, *Life of Apollonius*, V.28.
13. Tricks and subterfuges for extricating oneself from.
14. Test who is the stronger, fortune or oneself.
15. The desires of kings are mostly vehement, and incompatible with one another (not Tacitus, but from Sallust, *Jugurthine War*, CXIII.1).   16. Great mistake.

overgrow so (by increase of territory, by embracing of trade,[17] by approaches,[18] or the like) as they become more able to annoy them than they were. And this is generally the work of standing councils to foresee and to hinder it. During that triumvirate of kings, King Henry the Eighth of England, Francis the First, King of France, and Charles the Fifth, Emperor, there was such a watch kept, that none of the three could win a palm[19] of ground but the other two would straightways balance it, either by confederation or, if need were, by a war, and would not in any wise take up peace at interest.[20] And the like was done by that league (which Guicciardini saith was the security of Italy) made between Ferdinando, King of Naples, Lorenzius Medices, and Ludovicus Sforza, potentates, the one of Florence, the other of Milan.[21] Neither is the opinion of some of the Schoolmen[22] to be received, *that a war cannot justly be made but upon a precedent injury or provocation.* For there is no question but a just fear of an imminent danger, though there be no blow given, is a lawful cause of a war.

For their wives: there are cruel examples of them. Livia is infamed for the poisoning of her husband; Roxolana, Solyman's wife, was the destruction of that renowned prince, Sultan Mustapha, and otherwise troubled his house and succession;[23] Edward the Second of England his queen[24] had the principal hand in the deposing and murther of her husband. This kind of danger is then to be feared chiefly when the wives have plots for the raising of their own children, or else that they be advoutresses.[25]

For their children: the tragedies likewise of dangers from them have been many. And generally the entering of fathers into suspicion of their children hath been ever unfortunate. The destruction of Mustapha (that we named before) was so fatal to Solyman's line, as the succession of the Turks from Solyman until this day is suspected to be untrue and of strange blood; for that Selymus the

17. By drawing trade to themselves.
18. By approaching the frontier (with an army).   19. A hand's breadth.
20. Would not in any way agree to peace on terms which would cost them dearly later on.   21. See Guicciardini, *History of Italy*, I.
22. See Essay 17, note 7. Bacon is probably thinking of Aquinas in particular.
23. Solyman the Magnificent (or Selymus the First), Sultan of Turkey 1520–66, put his eldest son Mustapha to death at the instigation of his wife, the prince's stepmother, Roxalana. One of her own sons, Bayezid (or Bajazet), rebelled and was executed by Solyman. The Sultan was succeeded by another of her sons, Selymus II, who appeared to have none of Solyman's features or character. See also Essay 44, note 12.   24. Isabella of Anjou, d. 1358.   25. Adultresses.

Second was thought to be supposititious.[26] The destruction of
Crispus, a young prince of rare towardness,[27] by Constantinus the
Great, his father, was in like manner fatal to his house: for both
Constantinus and Constance, his sons, died violent deaths; and
Constantius, his other son, did little better; who died indeed of
sickness, but after that Julianus had taken arms against him.[28] The
destruction of Demetrius, son to Philip the Second of Macedon,
turned upon the father, who died of repentance.[29] And many like
examples there are, but few or none where the fathers had good by
such distrust; except it were where the sons were up in open arms
against them, as was Selymus the First against Bajazet, and the
three sons[30] of Henry the Second, King of England.

For their prelates: when they are proud and great, there is also
danger from them. As it was in the times of Anselmus and Thomas
Becket, archbishops of Canterbury, who with their crosiers did
almost try it with the king's sword; and yet they had to deal with
stout and haughty kings, William Rufus, Henry the First, and
Henry the Second.[31] The danger is not from that state[32] but where it
hath a dependence of[33] foreign authority, or where the churchmen
come in and are elected, not by the collation of the king or particular
patrons, but by the people.

For their nobles: to keep them at a distance, it is not amiss; but to
depress them may make a king more absolute, but less safe, and less
able to perform anything that he desires. I have noted it in my
history of King Henry the Seventh of England,[34] who depressed his
nobility; whereupon it came to pass that his times were full of
difficulties and troubles, for the nobility, though they continued

26. See note 23.　　　27. Of great promise.
28. Constantine the Great, Roman emperor 306–37, executed his son Crispus in
326. At Constantine's death, the empire was divided between his sons: Constantine
II was killed while attempting to overthrow his brother Constans (whom Bacon calls
Constance); Constans himself was murdered in his bed by his own men; and
Constantius died in 361 on his way to oppose Julian, who had been proclaimed
emperor by his troops.
29. Demetrius, son of Philip V of Macedon, was falsely accused of treason by his
brother, the crown-prince Perseus. His father had him put to death in 179 B.C. Bacon
has confused Philip V with Philip II, father of Alexander the Great.
30. Henry, Geoffrey, King Richard I (and later, King John).
31. Anselm, d. 1109, was twice sent into exile for asserting the rights of the clergy
against the secular authority of William Rufus and Henry I. Thomas à Becket was
murdered in Canterbury Cathedral in 1170 after violent disputes with Henry II.
32. Social rank (i.e. the clergy).　　　33. It receives support from some.
34. See *Works*, VI.242.

loyal unto him, yet did they not co-operate with him in his business. So that in effect he was fain to do all things himself.

For their second-nobles:[35] there is not much danger from them, being a body dispersed. They may sometimes discourse high, but that doth little hurt; besides, they are a counterpoise to the higher nobility, that they grow not too potent; and lastly, being the most immediate in authority with the common people, they do best temper popular commotions.

For their merchants: they are *vena porta*,[36] and if they flourish not, a kingdom may have good limbs, but will have empty veins and nourish little.[37] Taxes and imposts upon them do seldom good to the king's revenue, for that that he wins in the hundred,[38] he loseth in the shire, the particular rates being increased, but the total bulk of trading rather decreased.

For their commons: there is little danger from them, except it be where they have great and potent heads, or where you meddle with the point of religion or their customs or means of life.

For their men of war: it is a dangerous state where they live and remain in a body, and are used to donatives; whereof we see examples in the janizaries,[39] and Praetorian bands[40] of Rome. But trainings of men, and arming them in several places,[41] and under several[42] commanders, and without donatives, are things of defence, and no danger.

Princes are like to heavenly bodies, which cause good or evil times, and which have much veneration, but no rest. All precepts concerning kings are in effect comprehended in those two remembrances: *Memento quod es homo*, and *Memento quod es Deus*, or *vice Dei*:[43] the one bridleth their power, and the other their will.

---

35. Gentry.   36. The gate vein (to the liver).
37. Receive little nourishment.   38. A subdivision of the shire.
39. Bodyguards to the Turkish sultans.
40. Bodyguards to the Roman emperors.
41. In different parts of the country.   42. Different.
43. Remember that you are a man, and remember that you are a god, or God's vicegerent (for sources, see Ernst H. Kantorowicz, *The King's Two Bodies*, Princeton, 1957, pp. 496–7).

20.

Of Counsel

The greatest trust between man and man is the trust of giving counsel. For in other confidences men commit the parts of life; their lands, their goods, their children, their credit, some particular affair: but to such as they make their counsellors they commit the whole; by how much the more they are obliged to all faith and integrity. The wisest princes need not think it any diminution to their greatness or derogation to their sufficiency to rely upon counsel. God himself is not without, but hath made it one of the great names of his blessed Son, *the Counsellor*.[1] Solomon hath pronounced that *in counsel is stability*.[2] Things will have their first or second agitation: if they be not tossed upon the arguments of counsel, they will be tossed upon the waves of fortune, and be full of inconstancy, doing and undoing, like the reeling of a drunken man. Solomon's son[3] found the force of counsel, as his father saw the necessity of it. For the beloved kingdom of God was first rent and broken by ill counsel; upon which counsel there are set for our instruction the two marks whereby bad counsel is for ever best discerned: that it was young counsel, for the persons, and violent counsel, for the matter.

The ancient times do set forth in figure both the incorporation and inseparable conjunction of counsel with kings, and the wise and politic use of counsel by kings: the one, in that they say Jupiter did marry Metis, which signifieth counsel, whereby they intend that sovereignty is married to counsel; the other in that which followeth, which was thus: they say, after Jupiter was married to Metis, she conceived by him and was with child, but Jupiter suffered her not to stay till she brought forth, but ate her up; whereby he became himself with child, and was delivered of Pallas armed out of his head. Which monstrous fable containeth a secret of empire: how

Texts: MS, 1612, 1625

1. Isaiah 9.6.   2. Derived from Proverbs 20.18.
3. Rehoboam, from whom the ten tribes of Israel revolted (see 1 Kings 12).

kings are to make use of their council of state. That first they ought
to refer matters unto them, which is the first begetting or impregna-
tion; but when they are elaborate, moulded, and shaped in the
womb of their council, and grow ripe and ready to be brought forth,
that then they suffer not their council to go through with the
resolution and direction, as if it depended on them, but take the
matter back into their own hands, and make it appear to the world
that the decrees and final directions (which, because they come forth
with prudence and power, are resembled to Pallas armed) proceeded
from themselves; and not only from their authority, but (the more
to add reputation to themselves) from their head and device.

Let us now speak of the inconveniences of counsel, and of the
remedies. The inconveniences that have been noted in calling and
using counsel are three. First, the revealing of affairs, whereby they
become less secret. Secondly, the weakening of the authority of
princes, as if they were less of themselves. Thirdly, the danger of
being unfaithfully counselled, and more for the good of them that
counsel than of him that is counselled. For which inconveniences,
the doctrine of Italy, and practice of France, in some kings' times,
hath introduced cabinet[4] councils, a remedy worse than the disease.

As to secrecy, princes are not bound to communicate all matters
with all counsellors, but may extract and select. Neither is it
necessary that he that consulteth what he should do, should declare
what he will do. But let princes beware that the unsecreting of their
affairs comes not from themselves. And as for cabinet councils, it
may be their motto, *Plenus rimarum sum*:[5] one futile[6] person, that
maketh it his glory to tell, will do more hurt than many that know it
their duty to conceal. It is true there be some affairs which require
extreme secrecy, which will hardly go beyond one or two persons
besides the king. Neither are those counsels unprosperous, for,
besides the secrecy, they commonly go on constantly in one spirit of
direction without distraction. But then it must be a prudent king,
such as is able to grind with a hand-mill,[7] and those inward[8]
counsellors had need also be wise men, and especially true and
trusty to the king's ends: as it was with King Henry the Seventh of

4. Secret, unofficial.
5. I am full of leaks (Terence, *The Eunuch*, I.2.25).   6. Blabbing.
7. Able to conduct his own affairs (i.e. without the elaborate machinery of
government).   8. Confidential.

England, who in his greatest business imparted himself to none, except it were to Morton[9] and Fox.[10]

For weakening of authority, the fable[11] showeth the remedy. Nay, the majesty of kings is rather exalted than diminished when they are in the chair of counsel. Neither was there ever prince bereaved of his dependences[12] by his council, except where there hath been either an over-greatness in one counsellor or an over-strict combination in divers; which are things soon found and holpen.[13]

For the last inconvenience, that men will counsel with an eye to themselves; certainly, *non inveniet fidem super terram*[14] is meant of the nature of times, and not of all particular persons. There be that are in nature faithful and sincere, and plain and direct, not crafty and involved: let princes, above all, draw to themselves such natures. Besides, counsellors are not commonly so united but that one counsellor keepeth sentinel over another: so that if any do counsel out of faction or private ends, it commonly comes to the king's ear. But the best remedy is if princes know their counsellors as well as their counsellors know them:

Principis est virtus maxima nosse suos.[15]

And on the other side, counsellors should not be too speculative into their sovereign's person. The true composition of a counsellor is rather to be skilful in their master's business than in his nature, for then he is like to advise him, and not to feed his humour. It is of singular use to princes if they take the opinions of their council both separately and together. For private opinion is more free, but opinion before others is more reverend.[16] In private, men are more bold in their own humours, and in consort, men are more obnoxious[17] to others' humours. Therefore it is good to take both: and of the inferior sort rather in private, to preserve freedom; of the greater rather in consort, to preserve respect. It is in vain for princes to take counsel concerning matters, if they take no counsel likewise

9. Archbishop of Canterbury, Lord Chancellor, and Cardinal, d. 1500.
10. Bishop of Winchester, Privy Councillor and Keeper of the Privy Seal, d. 1528.
11. i.e. the story of Jupiter and Metis given above.   12. Prerogatives.
13. Remedied.
14. He shall not find faith upon the earth (alluding to Luke 18.8).
15. It is a prince's greatest virtue to know his own men (Martial, *Epigrams*, VIII.15).   16. Bacon may mean 'reverent' by this.   17. Subservient.

concerning persons: for all matters are as dead images, and the life of the execution of affairs resteth in the good choice of persons. Neither is it enough to consult concerning persons, *secundum genera*[18] (as in an idea or mathematical description), what the kind and character of the person should be; for the greatest errors are committed, and the most judgement is shown, in the choice of individuals. It was truly said, *Optimi consiliarii mortui:*[19] books will speak plain when counsellors blanch.[20] Therefore it is good to be conversant in them, specially the books of such as themselves have been actors upon the stage.

The councils at this day in most places are but familiar meetings, where matters are rather talked on than debated. And they run too swift to the order or act of counsel. It were better that in causes of weight the matter were propounded one day and not spoken to till the next day; *in nocte consilium.*[21] So was it done in the commission of union between England and Scotland, which was a grave and orderly assembly.[22] I commend set days for petitions, for both it gives the suitors more certainty for their attendance, and it frees the meetings for matters of estate,[23] that they may *hoc agere.*[24] In choice of committees for ripening business for the council, it is better to choose indifferent[25] persons than to make an indifferency by putting in those that are strong on both sides. I commend also standing commissions, as for trade, for treasure, for war, for suits, for some provinces. For where there be divers particular councils, and but one council of estate (as it is in Spain), they are in effect no more than standing commissions, save that they have greater authority. Let such as are to inform councils out of their particular professions (as lawyers, seamen, mintmen, and the like) be first heard before committees, and then, as occasion serves, before the council. And let them not come in multitudes, or in a tribunitious manner;[26] for that is to clamour[27] councils, not to inform them. A long table, and a square table, or seats about the walls, seem things

18. According to classes.
19. The best counsellors are the dead (a saying about books attributed to Alonso of Aragon, d. 1458: see *Works*, VII.140).   20. Flatter or gloss over.
21. In the night there is counsel (i.e. the interval of a night brings counsel for the following day).
22. In 1603 James VI of Scotland became King of England: a year later Bacon assisted the commission set up to consider the union of the kingdoms.   23. State.
24. Concentrate on the business in hand.   25. Impartial.
26. Or be turbulent in behaviour (like tribunes).   27. Disturb.

of form, but are things of substance; for at a long table, a few at the upper end in effect sway all the business, but in the other form there is more use of the counsellors' opinions that sit lower. A king, when he presides in council, let him beware how he opens his own inclination too much in that which he propoundeth: for else counsellors will but take the wind of him,[28] and instead of giving free counsel, sing him a song of *placebo*.[29]

28. Make themselves conform to his wishes.   29. Will follow his humour.

21.

Of Delays

Fortune is like the market; where many times, if you can stay a little, the price will fall. And again, it is sometimes like Sibylla's offer,[1] which at first offereth the commodity at full, then consumeth part and part, and still holdeth up the price. For *Occasion*[2] (as it is in the common verse) *turneth a bald noddle, after she hath presented her locks in front, and no hold taken*; or at least turneth the handle of the bottle first to be received, and after the belly, which is hard to clasp. There is surely no greater wisdom than well to time the beginnings and onsets of things. Dangers are no more light, if they once seem light; and more dangers have deceived men than forced them. Nay, it were better to meet some dangers half-way, though they come nothing near, than to keep too long a watch upon their approaches; for if a man watch too long, it is odds he will fall asleep. On the other side, to be deceived with too long shadows (as some have been when the moon was low and shone on their enemies' back), and so to shoot off before the time, or to teach dangers to come on, by over-early buckling towards[3] them, is another extreme. The ripeness or unripeness of the occasion (as we said) must ever be well weighed: and generally it is good to commit the beginnings of all great actions to Argus with his hundred eyes, and the ends to Briareus with his hundred hands, first to watch, and then to speed. For the helmet of Pluto,[4] which maketh the politic man go invisible, is secrecy in the counsel and celerity in the execution. For when things are once come to the execution, there is no secrecy comparable to celerity – like the motion of a bullet in the air, which flieth so swift as it outruns the eye.

Text: 1625

1. One of the Sibyls, ancient prophetesses, offered to sell nine books to the Roman king, Tarquin. When he refused, she burnt three but asked the same price for the remaining six books. Again Tarquin refused, and she destroyed three more, still asking the original price for the last three. Finally he bought them, and the Sibylline Books became precious to the Romans for the prophecies they contained.

2. Opportunity.   3. Girding oneself for.

4. The god of the underworld. During the war between the gods and the Titans, the Cyclops gave Pluto a helmet which made the wearer invisible.

22.

Of Cunning

We take cunning for a sinister or crooked wisdom. And certainly there is great difference between a cunning man and a wise man, not only in point of honesty, but in point of ability. There be that can pack[1] the cards, and yet cannot play well; so there are some that are good in canvasses[2] and factions, that are otherwise weak men. Again, it is one thing to understand persons, and another thing to understand matters: for many are perfect in men's humours, that are not greatly capable of the real part of business, which is the constitution of one that hath studied men more than books. Such men are fitter for practice[3] than for counsel, and they are good but in their own alley:[4] turn them to new men, and they have lost their aim; so as the old rule to know a fool from a wise man, *Mitte ambos nudos ad ignotos et videbis,*[5] doth scarce hold for them. And because these cunning men are like haberdashers[6] of small wares, it is not amiss to set forth their shop.

It is a point of cunning to wait upon[7] him with whom you speak, with your eye, as the Jesuits give it in precept; for there be many wise men that have secret hearts and transparent countenances. Yet this would be done with a demure abasing of your eye sometimes, as the Jesuits also do use.

Another is that when you have anything to obtain of present dispatch,[8] you entertain and amuse the party with whom you deal with some other discourse, that he be not too much awake to make objections. I knew a counsellor and secretary that never came to Queen Elizabeth of England with bills to sign, but he would always first put her into some discourse of estate,[9] that she mought[10] the less mind the bills.

Texts: 1612, 1625

1. Stack, shuffle fraudulently.   2. Intrigues.   3. Plotting.
4. Bowling-alley.
5. Send both of them naked among strangers and *then* you will see (attributed to Aristippus in Diogenes Laertius, *Lives of Eminent Philosophers*, II.73).
6. Shopkeepers.   7. Watch carefully.   8. Great urgency.   9. State.
10. Might.

The like surprise may be made by moving[11] things when the party is in haste and cannot stay to consider advisedly of that is moved.

If a man would cross[12] a business that he doubts[13] some other would handsomely and effectually move, let him pretend to wish it well, and move it himself in such sort as may foil it.

The breaking off in the midst of that one was about to say, as if he took himself up, breeds a greater appetite in him with whom you confer, to know more.

And because it works better when anything seemeth to be gotten from you by question than if you offer it of yourself, you may lay a bait for a question by showing another visage and countenance than you are wont; to the end to give occasion for the party to ask what the matter is of the change. As Nehemias did: *And I had not before that time been sad before the king.*[14]

In things that are tender[15] and unpleasing, it is good to break the ice by some whose words are of less weight, and to reserve the more weighty voice to come in as by chance, so that he may be asked the question upon the other's speech. As Narcissus did, in relating to Claudius the marriage of Messalina and Silius.[16]

In things that a man would not be seen in himself, it is a point of cunning to borrow the name of the world; as to say, *The world says*, or, *There is a speech abroad.*

I knew one that, when he wrote a letter, he would put that which was most material in the postscript, as if it had been a by-matter.

I knew another that, when he came to have speech, he would pass over that that he intended most, and go forth, and come back again and speak of it as of a thing that he had almost forgot.

Some procure themselves to be surprised at such times as it is like the party that they work upon will suddenly come upon them, and to be found with a letter in their hand, or doing somewhat which they are not accustomed; to the end they may be apposed of[17] those things which of themselves they are desirous to utter.

11. Proposing.   12. Thwart.   13. Suspects.

14. Nehemiah 2.1. Nehemiah, cupbearer to King Artaxerxes, appeared sorrowful before his master when the walls of Jerusalem were torn down. On being asked why he was sad, he persuaded the king to allow the city walls to be rebuilt.   15. Delicate.

16. Narcissus persuaded two women to inform the emperor Claudius that his wife Messalina had secretly married her lover Silius. When Narcissus revealed the details of their affair, Silius was executed (see Tacitus, *Annals*, XI.29–30).

17. Questioned about.

It is a point of cunning to let fall those words in a man's own name, which he would have another man learn and use, and thereupon take advantage. I knew two that were competitors for the secretary's place in Queen Elizabeth's time, and yet kept good quarter[18] between themselves, and would confer one with another upon the business; and the one of them said that to be a secretary in the *declination of a monarchy* was a ticklish thing, and that he did not affect[19] it. The other straight caught up those words and discoursed with divers of his friends that he had no reason to desire to be secretary in the *declination of a monarchy*. The first man took hold of it and found means it was told the Queen; who, hearing of *a declination of a monarchy*, took it so ill as she would never after hear of the other's suit.

There is a cunning, which we in England call *The turning of the cat*[20] *in the pan*, which is, when that which a man says to another, he lays it as if another had said it to him. And to say truth, it is not easy, when such a matter passed between two, to make it appear from which of them it first moved and began.

It is a way that some men have, to glance and dart at others by justifying themselves by negatives, as to say, *This I do not*; as Tigellinus did towards Burrhus, *Se non diversas spes, sed incolumitatem imperatoris simpliciter spectare*.[21]

Some have in readiness so many tales and stories, as there is nothing they would insinuate but they can wrap it into a tale, which serveth both to keep themselves more in guard and to make others carry it with more pleasure.

It is a good point of cunning for a man to shape the answer he would have, in his own words and propositions, for it makes the other party stick the less.

It is strange how long some men will lie in wait to speak somewhat they desire to say, and how far about they will fetch,[22] and how many other matters they will beat over to come near it. It is a thing of great patience, but yet of much use.

A sudden, bold, and unexpected question doth many times surprise a man, and lay him open. Like to him, that having changed

18. On good terms.   19. Desire.   20. Cate, or cake.
21. He said he did not have irreconcilable aims (as Burrhus did): his one object was the emperor's safety (Tacitus, *Annals*, XIV.57). Tigellinus was a minister under the emperor Nero; Burrhus was the commander of Nero's Praetorian bodyguards.
22. Go.

his name, and walking in Paul's,[23] another suddenly came behind him and called him by his true name, whereat straightways he looked back.

But these small wares and petty points of cunning are infinite, and it were a good deed to make a list of them, for that nothing doth more hurt in a state than that cunning men pass for wise.

But certainly some there are that know the resorts and falls[24] of business, that cannot sink into the main[25] of it; like a house that hath convenient stairs and entries but never a fair room. Therefore you shall see them find out pretty looses in the conclusion,[26] but are no ways able to examine or debate matters. And yet commonly they take advantage of their inability, and would be thought wits of direction.[27] Some build rather upon the abusing of others, and (as we now say) *putting tricks upon them*, than upon soundness of their own proceedings. But Solomon saith: *Prudens advertit ad gressus suos; stultus divertit ad dolos.*[28]

23. St Paul's Cathedral (a fashionable meeting-place in Bacon's day).
24. The beginnings and the outcome.   25. Get to the heart.
26. Get in some good shots at the end.
27. Men who have a talent for directing affairs.
28. The wise man pays attention to the steps he is taking: the fool turns aside to the snares (derived from Proverbs 14.8 and 15).

23.

Of Wisdom for a Man's Self

An ant is a wise creature for itself, but it is a shrewd[1] thing in an orchard or garden. And certainly men that are great lovers of themselves waste the public. Divide with reason between self-love and society, and be so true to thyself as thou be not false to others, specially to thy king and country. It is a poor centre of a man's actions, *himself*. It is right earth, for that only stands fast upon his own centre, whereas all things that have affinity with the heavens move upon the centre of another, which they benefit.[2] The referring of all to a man's self is more tolerable in a sovereign prince, because themselves are not only themselves, but their good and evil is at the peril of the public fortune. But it is a desperate evil in a servant to a prince, or a citizen in a republic. For whatsoever affairs pass such a man's hands, he crooketh them to his own ends; which must needs be often eccentric to[3] the ends of his master or state. Therefore let princes or states choose such servants as have not this mark, except they mean their service should be made but the accessary.[4] That which maketh the effect more pernicious is that all proportion is lost. It were disproportion enough for the servant's good to be preferred before the master's, but yet it is a greater extreme when a little good of the servant shall carry things against a great good of the master's. And yet that is the case of bad officers, treasurers, ambassadors, generals, and other false and corrupt servants, which set a bias upon their bowl, of[5] their own petty ends and envies, to the overthrow of their master's great and important affairs. And for the most part, the good such servants receive is after the model of[6] their own fortune, but the hurt they sell for that good is after the model of

Texts: MS, 1612, 1625

1. Mischievous.
2. i.e. a man's self is exactly like the earth, for it alone, according to Ptolemaic astronomy, remains fixed while the planetary spheres move around it.
3. Different from.　　4. Of assistance only.
5. Who are diverted from their proper, faithful course in favour of.
6. On the scale of, proportionate to.

their master's fortune. And certainly it is the nature of extreme self-lovers, as they will set an house on fire, and it[7] were but to roast their eggs. And yet these men many times hold credit with their masters, because their study is but to please them and profit themselves; and for either respect they will abandon the good of their affairs.

Wisdom for a man's self is, in many branches thereof, a depraved thing. It is the wisdom of rats, that will be sure to leave a house somewhat before it fall. It is the wisdom of the fox, that thrusts out the badger, who digged and made room for him. It is the wisdom of crocodiles, that shed tears when they would devour. But that which is specially to be noted is, that those which (as Cicero says of Pompey) are *sui amantes sine rivali*,[8] are many times unfortunate. And whereas they have all their time sacrificed to themselves, they become in the end themselves sacrifices to the inconstancy of fortune, whose wings they thought by their self-wisdom to have pinioned.

7. Even if it.
8. Lovers of themselves without rivals (from *Letters to his Brother Quintus*, III.8).

24.

Of Innovations

As the births of living creatures at first are ill-shapen, so are all innovations, which are the births of time. Yet notwithstanding, as those that first bring honour into their family are commonly more worthy than most that succeed, so the first precedent (if it be good) is seldom attained[1] by imitation. For ill, to man's nature as it stands perverted, hath a natural motion, strongest in continuance; but good, as a forced motion, strongest at first. Surely ever medicine is an innovation, and he that will not apply new remedies must expect new evils. For time is the greatest innovator, and if time of course[2] alter things to the worse, and wisdom and counsel shall not alter them to the better, what shall be the end? It is true that what is settled by custom, though it be not good, yet at least it is fit. And those things which have long gone together are as it were confederate within themselves:[3] whereas new things piece not[4] so well, but though they help by their utility, yet they trouble by their inconformity.[5] Besides, they are like strangers, more admired and less favoured. All this is true, if time stood still, which contrariwise moveth so round[6] that a froward retention of custom is as turbulent a thing as an innovation; and they that reverence too much old times are but a scorn to the new. It were good therefore that men in their innovations would follow the example of time itself, which indeed innovateth greatly, but quietly and by degrees scarce to be perceived. For otherwise, whatsoever is new is unlooked for, and ever it mends some, and pairs[7] other: and he that is holpen[8] takes it for a fortune,[9] and thanks the time; and he that is hurt, for a wrong, and imputeth it to the author. It is good also not to try experiments in states, except the necessity be urgent or the utility evident; and well to beware that it be the reformation that draweth on the

Text: 1625

1. Equalled.   2. By its course.   3. i.e. well fitted together.
4. Do not fit in.   5. Dissimilarity.   6. Quickly.
7. Impairs.   8. Helped.   9. A stroke of luck.

change, and not the desire of change that pretendeth the reformation.[10] And lastly, that the novelty, though it be not rejected, yet be held for a suspect, and, as the Scripture saith, *that we make a stand upon the ancient way, and then look about us, and discover what is the straight and right way, and so to walk in it.*[11]

---

10. Uses the reform as an excuse.   11. From Jeremiah 6.16.

25.

Of Dispatch

Affected dispatch[1] is one of the most dangerous things to business that can be. It is like that which the physicians call predigestion, or hasty digestion, which is sure to fill the body full of crudities and secret seeds of diseases. Therefore measure not dispatch by the times of sitting, but by the advancement of the business. And as in races it is not the large stride or high lift that makes the speed, so in business the keeping close to the matter and not taking of it too much at once, procureth dispatch. It is the care of some, only to come off speedily for the time,[2] or to contrive some false periods of business,[3] because[4] they may seem men of dispatch. But it is one thing to abbreviate by contracting, another by cutting off: and business so handled at several sittings or meetings goeth commonly backward and forward in an unsteady manner. I knew a wise man that had it for a by-word, when he saw men hasten to a conclusion: *Stay a little, that we may make an end the sooner.*

On the other side, true dispatch is a rich thing. For time is the measure of business, as money is of wares; and business is bought at a dear hand[5] where there is small dispatch. The Spartans and Spaniards have been noted to be of small dispatch: *Mi venga la muerte de[6] Spagna: Let my death come from Spain*; for then it will be sure to be long in coming.

Give good hearing to those that give the first information in business, and rather direct them in the beginning than interrupt them in the continuance of their speeches: for he that is put out of his own order will go forward and backward, and be more tedious while he waits upon his memory than he could have been if he had

---

Texts: MS, 1612, 1625

1. An excessive desire for dispatch.
2. For the moment *or* in proportion to the time taken.
3. Apparent conclusions to the business.   4. So that.   5. Rate.
6. Most of this saying is in Italian, but Bacon gives the Spanish *muerte de* for what should be the Italian *morte di.*

gone on in his own course. But sometimes it is seen that the moderator[7] is more troublesome than the actor.[8]

Iterations are commonly loss of time; but there is no such gain of time as to iterate often the state of the question, for it chaseth away many a frivolous speech as it is coming forth. Long and curious[9] speeches are as fit for dispatch as a robe or mantle with a long train is for race. Prefaces and passages[10] and excusations[11] and other speeches of reference to the person[12] are great wastes of time; and though they seem to proceed of[13] modesty, they are bravery.[14] Yet beware of being too material[15] when there is any impediment or obstruction in men's wills; for preoccupation of mind ever requireth preface of speech, like a fomentation to make the unguent enter.

Above all things, order and distribution and singling out of parts is the life of dispatch, so as the distribution be not too subtle: for he that doth not divide will never enter well into business, and he that divideth too much will never come out of it clearly. To choose time is to save time, and an unseasonable motion is but beating the air. There be three parts of business: the preparation, the debate or examination, and the perfection. Whereof, if you look for dispatch, let the middle only be the work of many, and the first and last the work of few. The proceeding upon somewhat[16] conceived in writing doth for the most part facilitate dispatch; for though it should be wholly rejected, yet that negative is more pregnant of direction[17] than an indefinite, as ashes are more generative than dust.

---

7. Person presiding.   8. Speaker.   9. Elaborate.
10. Connecting parts of a speech used to pass from one topic to another.
11. Apologies.   12. i.e. to the speaker himself.   13. From.
14. Mere ostentation.   15. Coming to the point too soon.
16. Something.   17. Suggestive.

26.

Of Seeming Wise

It has been an opinion that the French are wiser than they seem, and the Spaniards seem wiser than they are. But howsoever it be between nations, certainly it is so between man and man. For, as the Apostle saith of godliness, *Having a show of godliness, but denying the power thereof,*[1] so certainly there are,[2] in point of wisdom and sufficiency,[3] that do nothing or little very solemnly: *magno conatu nugas.*[4] It is a ridiculous thing, and fit for a satire to persons of judgement, to see what shifts these formalists[5] have, and what prospectives[6] to make superficies to seem body that hath depth and bulk. Some are so close and reserved as they will not show their wares but by a dark light, and seem always to keep back somewhat; and when they know within themselves they speak of that they do not well know, would nevertheless seem to others to know of[7] that which they may not well speak. Some help themselves with countenance and gesture, and are wise by signs; as Cicero saith of Piso, that when he answered him he fetched one of his brows up to his forehead, and bent the other down to his chin: *Respondes, altero ad frontem sublato, altero ad mentum depresso supercilio, crudelitatem tibi non placere.*[8] Some think to bear it[9] by speaking a great word and being peremptory, and go on and take by admittance that which they cannot make good. Some, whatsoever is beyond their reach, will seem to despise or make light of it as impertinent or curious,[10] and so would have their ignorance seem judgement. Some are never without a difference,[11] and commonly by amusing

Texts: MS, 1612, 1625

1. St Paul, 2 Timothy 3.5.   2. There are those.   3. Ability.
4. (Performing) trifles with great effort (from Terence, *The Self-Tormentor*, IV.1.8).
5. People of only outward show.   6. Perspective glasses (optical device).
7. Nevertheless wish to make it appear to others that they know of.
8. You reply, with one eyebrow hoisted to your forehead, and the other drawn down to your chin, that you do not approve of cruelty (*The Speech against Piso*, 6).
9. To carry it off.   10. Irrelevant or over-subtle.
11. Subtle qualification or distinction.

men with a subtlety, blanch[12] the matter; of whom A. Gellius saith, *Hominem delirum, qui verborum minutiis rerum frangit pondera.*[13] Of which kind also, Plato in his *Protagoras* bringeth in Prodicus in scorn, and maketh him make a speech that consisteth of distinctions from the beginning to the end.[14] Generally such men, in all deliberations, find ease[15] to be of the negative side, and affect a credit to object and foretell difficulties.[16] For when propositions are denied, there is an end of them; but if they be allowed,[17] it requireth a new work: which false point of wisdom is the bane of business. To conclude, there is no decaying merchant or inward beggar[18] hath so many tricks to uphold the credit of their wealth, as these empty persons have to maintain the credit of their sufficiency. Seeming wise men may make shift to get opinion,[19] but let no man choose them for employment; for certainly you were better take for business a man somewhat absurd than over-formal.[20]

12. Gloss over.

13. A foolish man who breaks up the weighty reality of things with fine verbal quibbles (not Aulus Gellius but another Roman rhetorician, Quintilian. Bacon quotes freely from *The Education of an Orator*, X.1.130, where Quintilian is describing Seneca).

14. *Protagoras*, 337A–C. Protagoras and Prodicus taught philosophy and rhetoric in Athens in the fifth and fourth centuries B.C.   15. Find it easy.

16. And try to gain credit by objecting and foretelling difficulties.

17. Accepted.

18. A penniless man, though to the world he does not appear so.

19. To be thought well of.

20. A man who is somewhat ridiculous rather than one who is all show.

27.

Of Friendship

It had been hard for him that spake it to have put more truth and untruth together in a few words, than in that speech, *Whosoever is delighted in solitude is either a wild beast or a god.*[1] For it is most true that a natural and secret hatred and aversation[2] towards society, in any man, hath somewhat of the savage beast; but it is most untrue that it should have any character at all of the divine nature, except it proceed, not out of a pleasure in solitude, but out of a love and desire to sequester a man's self for a higher conversation:[3] such as is found to have been falsely and feignedly in some of the heathen, as Epimenides the Candian,[4] Numa the Roman,[5] Empedocles the Sicilian,[6] and Apollonius of Tyana;[7] and truly and really in divers of the ancient hermits and holy fathers of the church. But little do men perceive what solitude is, and how far it extendeth. For a crowd is not company, and faces are but a gallery of pictures, and talk but a tinkling cymbal, where there is no love.[8] The Latin adage meeteth with it a little:[9] *Magna civitas, magna solitudo,*[10] because in a great town friends are scattered, so that there is not that fellowship, for the most part, which is in less neighbourhoods. But we may go further, and affirm most truly that it is a mere[11] and miserable solitude to want true friends, without which the world is but a wilderness: and even in this sense also of solitude, whosoever in the frame of his nature and affections

Texts: MS, 1612, 1625

1. From Aristotle, *Politics*, I.2.   2. Aversion.   3. Way of life.
   4. Poet of Crete (Candia), sixth century B.C., said to have fallen asleep in a cave and slept there for fifty-seven years without waking.
   5. Second king of Rome, traditionally the founder of the Roman religious system. He claimed that the goddess Egeria had taught him legislation in a grove near Rome.
   6. Greek philosopher, fifth century B.C., reputed to have thrown himself into the flames of Mount Etna so that his disappearance without trace might be taken as a sign that he was a god.
   7. Pythagorean philosopher and magician of the first century A.D.
   8. Alluding to 1 Corinthians 13.1.   9. Expresses some of its meaning.
   10. A great city is a great solitude (from Erasmus, *Adages*).   11. An entire.

is unfit for friendship, he taketh it of the beast, and not from humanity.

A principal fruit of friendship is the ease and discharge of the fullness and swellings of the heart, which passions of all kinds do cause and induce. We know diseases of stoppings and suffocations are the most dangerous in the body, and it is not much otherwise in the mind: you may take sarza[12] to open the liver, steel[13] to open the spleen, flowers of sulphur[14] for the lungs, castoreum[15] for the brain; but no receipt[16] openeth the heart but a true friend, to whom you may impart griefs, joys, fears, hopes, suspicions, counsels, and whatsoever lieth upon the heart to oppress it, in a kind of civil shrift[17] or confession.

It is a strange thing to observe how high a rate great kings and monarchs do set upon this fruit of friendship whereof we speak – so great, as they purchase it many times at the hazard of their own safety and greatness. For princes, in regard of the distance of their fortune from that of their subjects and servants, cannot gather this fruit, except (to make themselves capable thereof) they raise some persons to be as it were companions and almost equals to themselves, which many times sorteth to[18] inconvenience. The modern languages give unto such persons the name of *favourites*, or *privadoes*, as if it were matter of grace, or conversation.[19] But the Roman name attaineth the true use and cause thereof, naming them *participes curarum*,[20] for it is that which tieth the knot. And we see plainly that this hath been done, not by weak and passionate princes only, but by the wisest and most politic that ever reigned; who have oftentimes joined to themselves some of their servants, whom both themselves have called *friends*, and allowed others likewise to call them in the same manner, using the word which is received between private men.

L. Sulla, when he commanded Rome, raised Pompey (after surnamed the Great) to that height, that Pompey vaunted himself for Sulla's overmatch. For when he had carried the consulship for a friend of his, against the pursuit of Sulla, and that Sulla did a little resent thereat, and began to speak great, Pompey turned upon him again, and in effect bade him be quiet; *for that more men adored the*

12. Sarsaparilla.   13. Iron (administered medicinally).
14. Purified sulphur.   15. Medicine obtained from the beaver.
16. Prescription.   17. Secular confession.   18. Results in.
19. Social intercourse.   20. Partners in (their) cares.

sun rising than the sun setting.[21] With Julius Caesar, Decimus Brutus had obtained that interest as he set him down in his testament for heir in remainder after his nephew. And this was the man that had power with him to draw him forth to his death. For when Caesar would have discharged the senate, in regard of some ill presages, and specially a dream of Calpurnia, this man lifted him gently by the arm out of his chair, telling him he hoped he would not dismiss the senate till his wife had dreamt a better dream.[22] And it seemeth his favour was so great, as Antonius, in a letter which is recited *verbatim* in one of Cicero's *Philippics*, calleth him[23] *venefica*, 'witch', as if he had enchanted Caesar. Augustus raised Agrippa (though of mean birth) to that height, as, when he consulted with Maecenas about the marriage of his daughter Julia, Maecenas took the liberty to tell him, *that he must either marry his daughter to Agrippa, or take away his life; there was no third way, he had made him so great.*[24] With Tiberius Caesar, Sejanus had ascended to that height as they two were termed and reckoned as a pair of friends. Tiberius in a letter to him saith, *Haec pro amicitia nostra non occultavi;*[25] and the whole senate dedicated an altar to Friendship, as to a goddess, in respect of the great dearness of friendship between them two.[26] The like or more was between Septimius Severus and Plautianus. For he forced his eldest son to marry the daughter of Plautianus, and would often maintain Plautianus in doing affronts to his son, and did write also in a letter to the senate by these words: *I love the man so well, as I wish he may over-live me.*[27] Now if these princes had been as a Trajan, or a Marcus Aurelius,[28] a man might have thought that this had proceeded of an abundant goodness of nature, but being men so wise, of such strength and severity of mind, and so extreme lovers of themselves as all these were, it proveth most plainly that they found their own felicity (though as

21. Plutarch, *Pompey*, XIV.3. Sulla, d. 78 B.C., was Roman dictator; Pompey, d. 48 B.C., a great Roman general.
22. See Plutarch, *Caesar*, LXIV.1–4 (and Shakespeare, *Julius Caesar*, II.2.99).
23. i.e. Decimus Brutus (*Philippics*, XIII.11).
24. Dio, *Roman History*, LIV.6. Agrippa and Maecenas were Roman statesmen.
25. Out of regard for our friendship, I have not concealed these things (Tacitus, *Annals*, IV.40). Tiberius was Roman emperor, 14–37; Sejanus was commander of the Praetorian Guard until his execution in 31.   26. See Tacitus, *Annals*, IV.74.
27. Dio, *Roman History*, LXXVI.15. Septimius Severus was Roman emperor, 193–211; Plautianus (spelt *Plantianus* in the 1625 edition) was commander of the Praetorian Guard until he was executed in 204.
28. Trajan, d. 117, and Marcus Aurelius, d. 180, were Roman emperors.

great as ever happened to mortal men) but as an half piece,[29] except they mought[30] have a friend to make it entire: and yet, which is more, they were princes that had wives, sons, nephews; and yet all these could not supply the comfort of friendship.

It is not to be forgotten what Commineus[31] observeth of his first master, Duke Charles the Hardy;[32] namely, that he would communicate his secrets with none, and least of all, those secrets which troubled him most. Whereupon he goeth on and saith that towards his latter time *that closeness did impair and a little perish his understanding.*[33] Surely Commineus mought have made the same judgement also, if it had pleased him, of his second master, Lewis the Eleventh,[34] whose closeness was indeed his tormentor. The parable of Pythagoras is dark, but true: *Cor ne edito*, 'Eat not the heart.'[35] Certainly, if a man would give it a hard phrase, those that want[36] friends to open themselves unto are cannibals of their own hearts. But one thing is most admirable (wherewith I will conclude this first fruit of friendship), which is, that this communicating of a man's self to his friend works two contrary effects, for it redoubleth joys, and cutteth griefs in halfs. For there is no man that imparteth his joys to his friend, but he joyeth the more; and no man that imparteth his griefs to his friend, but he grieveth the less. So that it is in truth of operation upon a man's mind, of like virtue as the alchemists use to attribute to their stone[37] for man's body, that it worketh all contrary effects, but still to the good and benefit of nature. But yet without praying in[38] aid of alchemists, there is a manifest image of this in the ordinary course of nature. For in bodies,[39] union strengtheneth and cherisheth any natural action, and on the other side weakeneth and dulleth any violent impression; and even so is it of minds.

The second fruit of friendship is healthful and sovereign for the understanding, as the first is for the affections. For friendship

29. Incomplete (i.e. lacking the other half).   30. Might.
31. Philippe de Comines, French historian, d. 1509.
32. Charles the Bold, Duke of Burgundy, d. 1477.
33. See *The Memoirs of Comines*, V.3.   34. King of France, d. 1483.
35. A saying of Pythagoras, Greek philosopher of the sixth century B.C., recorded in Plutarch, *The Education of Children*, 12 (*Moralia*, 17E).   36. Lack.
37. The philosopher's stone (a substance which, it was claimed, would change base metals into gold, and cure diseases).   38. Calling in the.
39. All material things.

maketh indeed a fair day in the affections, from storm and tempests; but it maketh daylight in the understanding, out of darkness and confusion of thoughts. Neither is this to be understood only of faithful counsel, which a man receiveth from his friend; but before you come to that, certain it is that whosoever hath his mind fraught with many thoughts, his wits and understanding do clarify and break up, in the communicating and discoursing with another: he tosseth his thoughts more easily; he marshalleth them more orderly; he seeth how they look when they are turned into words; finally, he waxeth wiser than himself; and that more by an hour's discourse than by a day's meditation. It was well said by Themistocles[40] to the king of Persia, *that speech was like cloth of Arras,*[41] *opened and put abroad; whereby the imagery doth appear in figure; whereas in thoughts they lie but as in packs.*[42] Neither is this second fruit of friendship, in opening the understanding, restrained only to such friends as are able to give a man counsel (they indeed are best); but even without that, a man learneth of himself and bringeth his own thoughts to light and whetteth his wits as against a stone, which itself cuts not. In a word, a man were better relate himself to a statua[43] or picture than to suffer his thoughts to pass in smother.[44]

Add now, to make this second fruit of friendship complete, that other point which lieth more open and falleth within vulgar observation, which is faithful counsel from a friend. Heraclitus[45] saith well in one of his enigmas, *Dry light is ever the best.* And certain it is that the light that a man receiveth by counsel from another is drier and purer than that which cometh from his own understanding and judgement, which is ever infused and drenched in his affections and customs. So as there is as much difference between the counsel that a friend giveth, and that a man giveth himself, as there is between the counsel of a friend and of a flatterer. For there is no such flatterer as is a man's self, and there is no such remedy against flattery of a man's self as the liberty of a friend. Counsel is of two sorts: the one concerning manners,[46] the other concerning business. For the first, the best preservative to keep the mind in health is the faithful

---

40. Athenian general and statesman, d. 462 B.C.
41. A tapestry.   42. Plutarch, *Themistocles*, XXIX.3.   43. Statue.
44. To be smothered.
45. Greek philosopher, d. 475 B.C. For the saying, see above, p. 31.
46. Morals.

admonition of a friend. The calling of a man's self to a strict account is a medicine sometime too piercing and corrosive. Reading good books of morality is a little flat and dead.[47] Observing our faults in others is sometimes unproper[48] for our case. But the best receipt (best, I say, to work, and best to take) is the admonition of a friend. It is a strange thing to behold what gross errors and extreme absurdities many (especially of the greater sort) do commit for want of a friend to tell them of them, to the great damage both of their fame and fortune. For, as St James saith,[49] they are as men *that look sometimes into a glass, and presently[50] forget their own shape and favour.*[51] As for business, a man may think, if he will, that two eyes see no more than one; or that a gamester seeth always more than a looker-on; or that a man in anger is as wise as he that hath said over the four and twenty letters[52]; or that a musket may be shot off as well upon the arm as upon a rest; and such other fond[53] and high imaginations, to think himself all in all. But when all is done, the help of good counsel is that which setteth business straight. And if any man think that he will take counsel, but it shall be by pieces, asking counsel in one business of one man, and in another business of another man, it is well (that is to say, better perhaps than if he asked none at all), but he runneth two dangers. One, that he shall not be faithfully counselled, for it is a rare thing, except it be from a perfect and entire friend, to have counsel given, but such as shall be bowed and crooked to some ends which he hath that giveth it. The other, that he shall have counsel given, hurtful and unsafe (though with good meaning), and mixed partly of mischief and partly of remedy: even as if you would call a physician that is thought good for the cure of the disease you complain of, but is unacquainted with your body, and therefore may put you in way for a present cure, but overthroweth your health in some other kind; and so cure the disease and kill the patient. But a friend that is wholly acquainted with a man's estate will beware, by furthering any present business, how he dasheth upon other inconvenience. And therefore rest not upon scattered counsels; they will rather distract and mislead than settle and direct.

47. Dull.   48. Inappropriate.
49. James 1.23–4.   50. Immediately.   51. Features.
52. i.e. the alphabet (since *i* and *j*, like *u* and *v*, were regarded as the same letter in Bacon's day). The time taken to recite the alphabet might be enough for an angry man to cool down.   53. Foolish.

After these two noble fruits of friendship (peace in the affections, and support of the judgement) followeth the last fruit, which is like the pomegranate, full of many kernels: I mean aid and bearing a part in all actions and occasions. Here the best way to represent to life[54] the manifold use of friendship is to cast and see[55] how many things there are which a man cannot do himself, and then it will appear that it was a sparing speech of the ancients,[56] to say, *that a friend is another himself*, for that a friend is far more than himself. Men have their time, and die many times in desire of[57] some things which they principally take to heart: the bestowing of a child, the finishing of a work, or the like. If a man have a true friend, he may rest almost secure that the care of those things will continue after him. So that a man hath as it were two lives in his desires.[58] A man hath a body, and that body is confined to a place; but where friendship is, all offices of life are as it were granted to him and his deputy, for he may exercise them by his friend. How many things are there which a man cannot, with any face or comeliness,[59] say or do himself! A man can scarce allege his own merits with modesty, much less extol them; a man cannot sometimes brook to supplicate or beg; and a number of the like.[60] But all these things are graceful in a friend's mouth, which are blushing in a man's own. So again, a man's person[61] hath many proper relations[62] which he cannot put off. A man cannot speak to his son but as a father; to his wife but as a husband; to his enemy but upon terms;[63] whereas a friend may speak as the case requires, and not as it sorteth with[64] the person. But to enumerate these things were endless. I have given the rule, where a man cannot fitly play his own part: if he have not a friend, he may quit the stage.

54. To the life.   55. Reckon up.
56. For example, Zeno Cittieus and Aristotle. See Cicero, *On Friendship*, XXI. 80.
57. Still desiring.   58. As far as his desires are concerned.   59. Propriety.
60. See Cicero, *On Friendship*, XVI. 57.   61. Role.
62. Relationships peculiar to it.   63. On terms of formality.   64. Suits.

Certainly, who hath a state to repair, may not despise small things;
and commonly it is less dishonourable to abridge petty charges than
to stoop to petty gettings. A man may not rashly to begin charges
which once begun will continue; but in matters that return not he
may be more magnificent.

28.

Of Expense

Riches are for spending; and spending for honour and good actions.
Therefore extraordinary expense must be limited by the worth of
the occasion, for voluntary undoing may be as well for a man's
country as for the kingdom of heaven. But ordinary expense ought
to be limited by a man's estate, and governed with such regard, as
it be within his compass,[1] and not subject to deceit and abuse of
servants, and ordered to the best show, that the bills may be less
than the estimation abroad. Certainly if a man will keep but of even
hand,[2] his ordinary expenses ought to be but to the half of his
receipts; and if he think to wax rich, but to the third part. It is no
baseness for the greatest to descend and look into their own estate.
Some forbear it, not upon negligence alone, but doubting to[3] bring
themselves into melancholy, in respect[4] they shall find it broken.
But wounds cannot be cured without searching. He that cannot look
into his own estate at all, had need both choose well those whom he
employeth, and change them often; for new are more timorous and
less subtle. He that can look into his estate but seldom, it behoveth
him to turn all to certainties.[5] A man had need, if he be plentiful in
some kind of expense, to be as saving again in some other. As, if he
be plentiful in diet, to be saving in apparel; if he be plentiful in the
hall, to be saving in the stable; and the like. For he that is plentiful in
expenses of all kinds will hardly be preserved from decay. In
clearing of a man's estate, he may as well hurt himself in being too
sudden, as in letting it run on too long. For hasty selling is
commonly as disadvantageable as interest. Besides, he that clears at
once will relapse, for, finding himself out of straits, he will revert to
his customs: but he that cleareth by degrees induceth a habit of
frugality, and gaineth as well upon his mind as upon his estate.

Texts: 1597, MS, 1612, 1625

1. Within his means.   2. Wishes to avoid fluctuations in his wealth.
3. Fearful that they may.   4. In case.
5. He needs to make all his finances (income and expenses) exact and fixed.

Certainly, who hath a state[6] to repair may not despise small things,
and commonly it is less dishonourable to abridge petty charges than
to stoop to petty gettings. A man ought warily to begin charges
which once begun will continue; but in matters that return not he
may be more magnificent.

6. An estate.

29.

Of the True Greatness
of Kingdoms and Estates

The speech of Themistocles the Athenian,[1] which was haughty and arrogant in taking so much to himself, had been a grave and wise observation and censure,[2] applied at large to others. Desired at a feast to touch a lute, he said, *He could not fiddle, but yet he could make a small town a great city.*[3] These words (holpen[4] a little with a metaphor) may express two differing abilities in those that deal in business of estate. For if a true survey be taken of counsellors and statesmen, there may be found (though rarely) those which can make a small state great, and yet cannot fiddle: as, on the other side, there will be found a great many that can fiddle very cunningly, but yet are so far from being able to make a small state great, as their gift lieth the other way – to bring a great and flourishing estate to ruin and decay. And certainly those degenerate arts and shifts, whereby many counsellors and governors gain both favour with their masters and estimation with the vulgar,[5] deserve no better name than fiddling; being things rather pleasing for the time, and graceful to themselves only, than tending to the weal and advancement of the state which they serve. There are also (no doubt) counsellors and governors, which may be held sufficient (*negotiis pares*),[6] able to manage affairs, and to keep them from precipices and manifest inconveniences; which nevertheless are far from the ability to raise and amplify an estate in power, means, and fortune. But be the workmen what they may be, let us speak of the work; that is, the true greatness of kingdoms and estates, and the means thereof. An argument fit for great and mighty princes to have in their hand, to the end that neither by over-measuring their forces they leese[7]

Texts: 1612, 1625

1. Athenian general and statesman, d. 460 B.C.   2. Judgement.
3. Plutarch, *Themistocles*, II.3, and *Cimon*, IX.1.   4. Helped.
5. Common people.   6. (Men who are) equal to conducting business.
7. Lose.

themselves in vain enterprises, nor, on the other side, by under-valuing them they descend to fearful and pusillanimous counsels.

The greatness of an estate in bulk and territory doth fall under measure, and the greatness of finances and revenue doth fall under computation. The population may appear by musters, and the number and greatness of cities and towns, by cards[8] and maps. But yet there is not anything amongst civil affairs more subject to error than the right valuation and true judgement concerning the power and forces of an estate. The kingdom of heaven is compared, not to any great kernel or nut, but to a grain of mustard-seed,[9] which is one of the least grains, but hath in it a property and spirit hastily to get up and spread. So are there states great in territory, and yet not apt to enlarge or command; and some that have but a small dimension of stem, and yet apt to be the foundations of great monarchies.

Walled towns, stored arsenals and armouries, goodly races of horse, chariots of war, elephants, ordnance, artillery, and the like: all this is but a sheep in a lion's skin, except the breed and disposition of the people be stout and warlike. Nay, number itself in armies importeth not much[10] where the people is of weak courage; for (as Virgil saith) *It never troubles a wolf how many the sheep be.*[11] The army of the Persians, in the plains of Arbela, was such a vast sea of people as it did somewhat astonish the commanders in Alexander's army; who came to him therefore and wished him to set upon them by night, but he answered, *He would not pilfer the victory.*[12] And the defeat was easy. When Tigranes the Armenian,[13] being en-camped upon a hill with 400,000 men, discovered the army of the Romans, being not above 14,000, marching towards him, he made himself merry with it and said, *Yonder men are too many for an ambassage*[14] *and too few for a fight.*[15] But before the sun set he found them enough to give him the chase, with infinite slaughter. Many are the examples of the great odds between number and courage: so that a man may truly make a judgement that the principal point of greatness in any state is to have a race of military men. Neither is money the sinews of war (as it is trivially said), where the sinews of men's arms, in base and effeminate people, are

---

8. Charts.   9. See Matthew 13.31.   10. Is not of much importance.
11. See *Eclogues*, VII.52.   12. Plutarch, *Alexander*, XXXI.7.
13. King of Armenia, first century B.C.; defeated by a Roman army under the consul Lucullus, he finally submitted to Pompey.   14. Embassy.
15. Plutarch, *Lucullus*, XXVII.4.

failing. For Solon said well to Croesus (when in ostentation he showed him his gold), *Sir, if any other come that hath better iron than you, he will be master of all this gold.*[16] Therefore let any prince or state think soberly of his forces, except his militia of natives be of good and valiant soldiers. And let princes, on the other side, that have subjects of martial disposition, know their own strength, unless they be otherwise wanting unto themselves. As for mercenary forces (which is the help in this case), all examples show that whatsoever estate[17] or prince doth rest upon them, *He may spread his feathers for a time, but he will mew them*[18] *soon after.*

The blessing of Judah and Issachar will never meet, *that the same people or nation should be both the lion's whelp* and *the ass between burthens:*[19] neither will it be that a people overlaid with taxes should ever become valiant and martial. It is true that taxes levied by consent of the estate do abate men's courage less, as it hath been seen notably in the excises of the Low Countries, and in some degree in the subsidies of England. For you must note that we speak now of the heart and not of the purse. So that although the same tribute and tax, laid by consent or by imposing, be all one to the purse, yet it works diversely upon the courage. So that you may conclude, *that no people overcharged with tribute is fit for empire.*

Let states that aim at greatness take heed how their nobility and gentlemen[20] do multiply too fast. For that maketh the common subject grow to be a peasant and base swain, driven out of heart, and in effect but the gentleman's labourer. Even as you may see in coppice woods: if you leave your staddles[21] too thick, you shall never have clean underwood, but shrubs and bushes. So in countries, if the gentlemen be too many, the commons will be base, and you will bring it to that, that not the hundred poll[22] will be fit for an helmet; especially as to the infantry, which is the nerve of an army: and so there will be great population and little strength. This which I speak of hath been nowhere better seen than by comparing of

16. Bacon derives this passage (and much of the essay) from Machiavelli, *Discourses*: here from II.10, a section headed 'Money is not the Sinews of War, as it is commonly supposed to be'. Solon was an Athenian statesman, legislator and poet, who was later revered as one of the Seven Sages of Greece. Croesus, proverbial for his wealth, was king of Lydia, sixth century B.C.

17. State (the meaning throughout the essay).   18. Shed them (the feathers).

19. From Genesis 49.9 and 14. Judah and Issachar were sons of Jacob.

20. i.e. the gentry.   21. Young trees.

22. Not one man (or head) in a hundred.

England and France; whereof England, though far less in territory and population, hath been nevertheless an over-match, in regard[23] the middle people of England make good soldiers, which the peasants of France do not. And herein the device of King Henry the Seventh (whereof I have spoken largely in the history of his life[24]) was profound and admirable, in making farms and houses of husbandry of a standard; that is, maintained with such a proportion of land unto them, as may breed a subject to live in convenient plenty and no servile condition, and to keep the plough in the hands of the owners, and not mere hirelings. And thus indeed you shall attain to Virgil's character, which he gives to ancient Italy:

Terra potens armis atque ubere glebae.[25]

Neither is that state[26] (which, for anything I know, is almost peculiar to England, and hardly to be found anywhere else, except it be perhaps in Poland) to be passed over; I mean the state of free servants and attendants upon noblemen and gentlemen, which are no ways inferior unto the yeomanry for arms. And therefore, out of all question, the splendour and magnificence and great retinues and hospitality of noblemen and gentlemen, received into custom, doth much conduce unto martial greatness. Whereas, contrariwise, the close and reserved living of noblemen and gentlemen causeth a penury of military forces.

By all means it is to be procured that the trunk of Nebuchadnezzar's tree of monarchy be great enough to bear the branches and the boughs; that is, that the natural subjects of the crown or state bear a sufficient proportion to the stranger subjects that they govern.[27] Therefore all states that are liberal of naturalization towards strangers are fit for empire. For to think[28] that an handful of people can, with the greatest courage and policy in the world, embrace too large extent of dominion – it may hold for a time, but it will fail suddenly. The Spartans were a nice[29] people in point of naturalization: whereby, while they kept their compass,[30] they stood firm, but when they did spread, and their boughs were

23. Because.   24. See *Works*, VI.93–5.
25. A land powerful in arms and in the richness of the soil (*Aeneid*, I.531).
26. Part of society.
27. See Daniel 4.10–12 (for Nebuchadnezzar's dream), and Machiavelli, *Discourses*, II.3.   28. As for thinking.   29. Niggardly.
30. i.e. kept within their own frontiers.

becomen too great for their stem, they became a windfall upon the
sudden. Never any state was in this point so open to receive
strangers into their body as were the Romans. Therefore it sorted
with them[31] accordingly, for they grew to the greatest monarchy.
Their manner was to grant naturalization (which they called *jus
civitatis*[32]) and to grant it in the highest degree, that is, not only *jus
commercii, jus connubii, jus haereditatis*, but also *jus suffragii* and
jus honorum.[33] And this, not to singular[34] persons alone, but
likewise to whole families, yea, to cities, and sometimes to nations.
Add to this their custom of plantation of colonies, whereby the
Roman plant was removed into the soil of other nations. And
putting both constitutions together, you will say that it was not the
Romans that spread upon the world, but it was the world that spread
upon the Romans: and that was the sure way of greatness. I have
marvelled sometimes at Spain, how they clasp and contain[35] so large
dominions with so few natural Spaniards: but sure the whole
compass of Spain is a very great body of a tree, far above Rome and
Sparta at the first. And besides, though they have not had that usage
to naturalize liberally, yet they have that which is next to it; that is,
to employ almost indifferently all nations in their militia of ordinary soldiers, yea, and sometimes in their highest commands. Nay, it
seemeth at this instant they are sensible of this want of natives, as
by the Pragmatical Sanction, now published, appeareth.[36]

It is certain that sedentary and within-door arts and delicate
manufactures (that require rather the finger than the arm) have in
their nature a contrariety to a military disposition. And generally all
warlike people are a little idle, and love danger better than travail:
neither must they be too much broken of it, if they shall be
preserved in vigour. Therefore it was great advantage in the ancient
states of Sparta, Athens, Rome, and others, that they had the use of
slaves, which commonly did rid those manufactures.[37] But that is
abolished, in greatest part, by the Christian law. That which cometh
nearest to it is to leave those arts chiefly to strangers (which for that
purpose are the more easily to be received), and to contain the

31. Things turned out for them.   32. Right of citizenship.
33. Not only the rights of trading, marriage and inheritance, but also the right to
vote and the right to hold public office.   34. Single.   35. Restrain.
36. In 1622, King Philip IV issued a decree which gave privileges to natives of Spain
who were married, and further immunities to those who had six children or more.
37. Got those tasks done.

principal bulk of the vulgar natives[38] within those three kinds: tillers of the ground, free servants, and handicraftsmen of strong and manly arts (as smiths, masons, carpenters, etc.) not reckoning professed soldiers.

But above all, for empire and greatness it importeth most[39] that a nation do profess arms as their principal honour, study, and occupation. For the things which we formerly have spoken of are but habilitations towards[40] arms, and what is habilitation without intention and act? Romulus, after his death (as they report or feign), sent a present[41] to the Romans, that above all they should intend[42] arms, and then they should prove the greatest empire of the world. The fabric of the state of Sparta was wholly (though not wisely) framed and composed to that scope[43] and end. The Persians and Macedonians had it for a flash.[44] The Gauls, Germans, Goths, Saxons, Normans, and others, had it for a time. The Turks have it at this day, though in great declination. Of Christian Europe, they that have it are in effect only the Spaniards. But it is so plain *that every man profiteth in that he most intendeth*, that it needeth not to be stood upon.[45] It is enough to point at it: that no nation which doth not directly profess arms may look to have greatness fall into their mouths. And, on the other side, it is a most certain oracle of time, that those states that continue long in that profession (as the Romans and Turks principally have done) do wonders. And those that have professed arms but for an age have, notwithstanding, commonly attained that greatness in that age which maintained them long after, when their profession and exercise of arms hath grown to decay.

Incident to this point is for a state to have those laws or customs which may reach forth unto them just occasions (as may be pretended)[46] of war. For there is that justice imprinted in the nature of men that they enter not upon wars (whereof so many calamities do ensue) but upon some, at the least specious grounds and quarrels. The Turk hath at hand, for cause of war, the propagation of his law or sect, a quarrel[47] that he may always command. The Romans,

38. Native common people.   39. It matters most.
40. Means of attaining ability in.
41. i.e. a message. According to Livy, *History*, I.16, Romulus, the legendary founder of Rome, conveyed his advice to the Romans after his death.
42. Pay constant attention to.   43. Object.   44. Brief moment.
45. Insisted upon.   46. Such as may be used as an excuse.   47. Cause.

though they esteemed the extending the limits of their empire to be great honour to their generals when it was done, yet they never rested upon that alone to begin a war. First, therefore, let nations that pretend to greatness have this: that they be sensible of[48] wrongs, either upon borderers, merchants, or politic ministers,[49] and that they sit not too long upon a provocation. Secondly, let them be prest[50] and ready to give aids and succours to their confederates. As it ever was with the Romans, insomuch as if the confederate had leagues defensive with divers other states, and, upon invasion offered, did implore their aids severally, yet the Romans would ever be the foremost and leave it to none other to have the honour. As for the wars which were anciently made on the behalf of a kind of party, or tacit conformity of estate,[51] I do not see how they may be well justified: as when the Romans made a war for the liberty of Graecia;[52] or when the Lacedaemonians and Athenians made wars[53] to set up or pull down democracies and oligarchies; or when wars were made by foreigners, under the pretence of justice or protection, to deliver the subjects of others from tyranny and oppression; and the like. Let it suffice, that no estate expect to be great that is not awake upon any just occasion of arming.

No body can be healthful without exercise, neither natural body nor politic:[54] and certainly to a kingdom or estate, a just and honourable war is the true exercise. A civil war, indeed, is like the heat of a fever; but a foreign war is like the heat of exercise, and serveth to keep the body in health; for in a slothful peace, both courages will effeminate and manners corrupt. But howsoever it be for happiness, without all question for greatness it maketh to be still for the most part in arms,[55] and the strength of a veteran army (though it be a chargeable[56] business), always on foot, is that which commonly giveth the law,[57] or at least the reputation, amongst all neighbour states. As may well be seen in Spain, which hath had, in

---

48. Sensitive to.   49. Ministers of state.   50. Prompt.

51. On behalf of factions within states, or for governments which were tacitly under foreign influence.

52. When the second Macedonian War ended in victory for Rome in 197 B.C. the Romans declared Greece free from dominion by Philip V of Macedon.

53. i.e. the Peloponnesian War fought in the fifth century B.C. between Athens and Sparta (or Lacedaemon).   54. Body of the state.

55. It is an advantage to be almost always in arms.   56. Expensive.

57. Gives supremacy.

one part or other, a veteran army almost continually now by the space of six-score years.

To be master of the sea is an abridgement[58] of a monarchy. Cicero, writing to Atticus of Pompey his preparation against Caesar, saith: *Consilium Pompeii plane Themistocleum est; putat enim, qui mari potitur, eum rerum potiri.*[59] And without doubt Pompey had tired out Caesar, if upon vain confidence he had not left that way. We see the great effects of battles by sea. The battle of Actium[60] decided the empire of the world. The battle of Lepanto[61] arrested the greatness of the Turk. There be many examples where sea-fights have been final to the war; but this is when princes or states have set up their rest upon[62] the battles. But thus much is certain, that he that commands the sea is at great liberty, and may take as much and as little of the war as he will. Whereas those that be strongest by land are many times nevertheless in great straits. Surely, at this day, with us of Europe, the vantage of strength at sea (which is one of the principal dowries of this kingdom of Great Britain) is great: both because most of the kingdoms of Europe are not merely[63] inland, but girt with the sea most part of their compass; and because the wealth of both Indies seems in great part but an accessary to the command of the seas.

The wars of latter ages seem to be made in the dark, in respect of the glory and honour which reflected upon men from the wars in ancient time. There be now, for martial encouragement, some degrees and orders of chivalry, which nevertheless are conferred promiscuously upon soldiers and no soldiers; and some remembrance perhaps upon the scutcheon; and some hospitals for maimed soldiers; and such like things. But in ancient times, the trophies erected upon the place of the victory; the funeral laudatives[64] and monuments for those that died in the wars; the crowns and garlands

58. Epitome.

59. Pompey's plan is truly Themistoclean, for he thinks that whoever has command of the sea has mastery over everything (from *Letters to Atticus*, X.8). Pompey's struggle with Julius Caesar ended with his defeat in the land battle of Pharsalus. Pompey escaped to Egypt but was murdered there in 48 B.C.

60. Fought in 31 B.C., when Augustus defeated Mark Antony and Cleopatra. Afterwards he became the first Roman emperor.

61. Fought in 1571, when the galleys of Spain defeated those of the Ottoman empire.   62. Staked everything upon.   63. Entirely.   64. Encomiums.

personal;[65] the style of *emperor*,[66] which the great kings of the world after borrowed; the triumphs[67] of the generals upon their return; the great donatives and largesses upon the disbanding of the armies, were things able to inflame all men's courages. But above all, that of the triumph amongst the Romans was not pageants or gaudery,[68] but one of the wisest and noblest institutions that ever was. For it contained three things: honour to the general, riches to the treasury out of the spoils, and donatives to the army. But that honour perhaps were not fit for monarchies, except it be in the person of the monarch himself, or his sons; as it came to pass in the times of the Roman emperors, who did impropriate[69] the actual triumphs to themselves and their sons, for such wars as they did achieve in person, and left only, for wars achieved by subjects, some triumphal garments and ensigns to the general.

To conclude: no man can by *care taking* (as the Scripture saith)[70] *add a cubit to his stature*, in this little model of a man's body:[71] but in the great frame of kingdoms and commonwealths, it is in the power of princes or estates to add amplitude and greatness to their kingdoms. For by introducing such ordinances, constitutions, and customs as we have now touched, they may sow greatness to their posterity and succession. But these things are commonly not observed, but left to take their chance.

---

65. Awarded to individuals.
66. It was customary for Roman soldiers after a victory to salute their general with the title of 'imperator' or *emperor*.   67. Triumphal processions.
68. Worthless finery.   69. Appropriated.
70. Matthew 6.27 and Luke 12.25.
71. In this thing on so small a scale, a man's body.

30.

Of Regiment[1] of Health

There is a wisdom in this beyond the rules of physic: a man's own observation, what he finds good of,[2] and what he finds hurt of, is the best physic to preserve health. But it is a safer conclusion to say, *This agreeth not well with me, therefore I will not continue it*, than this, *I find no offence of[3] this, therefore I may use it*. For strength of nature in youth passeth over many excesses which are owing a man till his age.[4] Discern of the coming on of years, and think not to do the same things still; for age will not be defied. Beware of sudden change in any great point of diet, and if necessity enforce it, fit the rest to it. For it is a secret, both in nature and state, that it is safer to change many things than one. Examine thy customs of diet, sleep, exercise, apparel and the like, and try in anything thou shalt judge hurtful, to discontinue it by little and little; but so as if thou dost find any inconvenience by the change, thou come back to it again: for it is hard to distinguish that which is generally held good and wholesome from that which is good particularly[5] and fit for thine own body. To be free-minded and cheerfully disposed at hours of meat and of sleep and of exercise, is one of the best precepts of long lasting.[6] As for the passions and studies of the mind, avoid envy, anxious fears, anger fretting inwards, subtle and knotty inquisitions, joys and exhilarations in excess, sadness not communicated. Entertain hopes, mirth rather than joy, variety of delights rather than surfeit of them, wonder and admiration (and therefore novelties), studies that fill the mind with splendid and illustrious objects (as histories, fables, and contemplations of nature). If you fly physic in health altogether, it will be too strange for your body when you shall need it. If you make it too familiar, it will work no extraordinary effect when sickness cometh. I commend rather some diet for

Texts: 1597, MS, 1612, 1625

1. Regimen, or governance.   2. From.
3. Harm from.   4. Which a man will have to pay for in old age.
5. Good for you individually.   6. For prolonging life.

certain seasons than frequent use of physic, except it be grown into a custom: for those diets alter the body more, and trouble it less. Despise no new accident[7] in your body, but ask opinion of it.[8] In sickness, respect health principally; and in health, action. For those that put their bodies to endure in health may, in most sicknesses which are not very sharp, be cured only with diet and tendering.[9] Celsus[10] could never have spoken it as a physician, had he not been a wise man withal, when he giveth it for one of the great precepts of health and lasting, that a man do vary and interchange contraries, but with an inclination to the more benign extreme: use fasting and full eating, but rather full eating; watching and sleep, but rather sleep; sitting and exercise, but rather exercise; and the like. So shall nature be cherished and yet taught masteries.[11] Physicians are some of them so pleasing[12] and conformable to the humour of the patient, as they press not the true cure of the disease; and some other are so regular in proceeding according to art for the disease, as they respect not sufficiently the condition of the patient. Take one of a middle temper;[13] or, if it may not be found in one man, combine two of either sort; and forget not to call as well the best acquainted with your body, as the best reputed of for his faculty.[14]

---

7. Unexpected alteration.   8. Medical advice about it.
9. Careful nursing.
10. Roman writer of the first century A.D. who compiled an encyclopedia, nearly all of which, except for the medical books, is lost. Bacon refers to (and misrepresents) these 'precepts of health' elsewhere (see *Works*, V.262).
11. Control over disease.   12. Anxious to please.
13. Choose a doctor whose nature is midway between these types.   14. Ability.

31.

Of Suspicion

Suspicions amongst thoughts are like bats amongst birds: they ever fly by twilight. Certainly they are to be repressed, or at the least well guarded,[1] for they cloud the mind, they leese[2] friends, and they check[3] with business, whereby business cannot go on currently[4] and constantly. They dispose kings to tyranny, husbands to jealousy, wise men to irresolution and melancholy. They are defects, not in the heart but in the brain, for they take place in the stoutest natures, as in the example of Henry the Seventh of England. There was not a more suspicious man, nor a more stout. And in such a composition[5] they do small hurt, for commonly they are not admitted but with examination whether they be likely or no: but in fearful natures they gain ground too fast. There is nothing makes a man suspect much, more than to know little; and therefore men should remedy suspicion by procuring to know more, and not to keep their suspicions in smother.[6] What would men have? Do they think those they employ and deal with are saints? Do they not think they will have their own ends, and be truer to themselves than to them? Therefore there is no better way to moderate suspicions than to account upon such suspicions as true and yet to bridle them as false. For so far a man ought to make use of suspicions, as to provide as, if that should be true that he suspects, yet it may do him no hurt. Suspicions that the mind of itself gathers are but buzzes, but suspicions that are artificially nourished and put into men's heads by the tales and whisperings of others, have stings. Certainly the best mean[7] to clear the way in this same wood of suspicions is frankly to communicate them with the party that he suspects: for thereby he shall be sure to know more of the truth of them than he did before, and withal shall make that party more circumspect not to

Text: 1625

1. Controlled.   2. Lose.   3. Interfere.   4. Smoothly.
5. Temperament.   6. Stifled (but waiting to break out).
7. Means.

give further cause of suspicion. But this would not be[8] done to men of base natures, for they, if they find themselves once suspected, will never be true. The Italian says, *Sospetto licentia fede*,[9] as if suspicion did give a passport to faith; but it ought rather to kindle it to discharge itself.[10]

8. Ought not to be.
9. Suspicion permits fidelity to depart (i.e. frees a man from his obligations).
10. Clear itself of the charge (of allowing faith to leave).

32

Of Discourse

Some in their discourse desire rather commendation of wit,[1] in being able to hold all arguments, than of judgement, in discerning what is true; as if it were a praise to know what might be said, and not what should be thought. Some have certain commonplaces and themes wherein they are good, and want variety; which kind of poverty is for the most part tedious, and, when it is once perceived, ridiculous. The honourablest part of talk is to give the occasion,[2] and again to moderate[3] and pass to somewhat else, for then a man leads the dance. It is good, in discourse and speech of conversation, to vary and intermingle speech of the present occasion with arguments,[4] tales with reasons, asking of questions with telling of opinions, and jest with earnest: for it is a dull thing to tire, and, as we say now, to jade anything too far.[5] As for jest, there be certain things which ought to be privileged from it; namely, religion, matters of state, great persons, any man's present business of importance, and any case that deserveth pity. Yet there be some that think their wits have been asleep, except they dart out somewhat that is piquant and to the quick. That is a vein which would be[6] bridled:

> Parce, puer, stimulis, et fortius utere loris.[7]

And generally, men ought to find the difference between saltness[8] and bitterness. Certainly he that hath a satirical vein, as he maketh others afraid of his wit, so he had need be afraid of others' memory. He that questioneth much shall learn much and content[9] much, but especially if he apply his questions to the skill of the persons whom

Texts: 1597, MS, 1612, 1625

1. For cleverness.   2. Suggest the topic of conversation.
3. Take charge of the discussion.
4. Of what is of current and temporary interest with subjects of lasting significance.   5. Work a subject to death.
6. An inclination which needs to be.
7. Spare the whip, boy, and pull harder on the reins (Ovid, *Metamorphoses*, II.127).   8. Pungent wit.   9. Please.

he asketh; for he shall give them occasion to please themselves in speaking, and himself shall continually gather knowledge. But let his questions not be troublesome, for that is fit for a poser.[10] And let him be sure to leave other men their turns to speak. Nay, if there be any that would reign and take up all the time, let him find means to take them off and to bring others on, as musicians use to do with those that dance too long galliards. If you dissemble sometimes your knowledge of that you are thought to know, you shall be thought another time to know that you know not. Speech of a man's self ought to be seldom and well chosen. I knew one was wont to say in scorn, *He must needs be a wise man, he speaks so much of himself.* And there is but one case wherein a man may commend himself with good grace, and that is in commending virtue in another, especially if it be such a virtue whereunto himself pretendeth. Speech of touch towards others[11] should be sparingly used, for discourse ought to be as a field, without coming home to any man. I knew two noblemen, of the west part of England, whereof the one was given to scoff, but kept ever royal cheer in his house; the other would ask of those that had been at the other's table, *Tell truly, was there never a flout or dry blow[12] given?* To which the guest would answer, *Such and such a thing passed.* The lord would say, *I thought he would mar a good dinner.* Discretion of speech is more than eloquence, and to speak agreeably[13] to him with whom we deal is more than to speak in good words or in good order. A good continued speech, without a good speech of interlocution, shows slowness; and a good reply or second speech, without a good settled speech, showeth shallowness and weakness. As we see in beasts, that those that are weakest in the course are yet nimblest in the turn, as it is betwixt the greyhound and the hare. To use too many circumstances[14] ere one come to the matter is wearisome; to use none at all is blunt.

---

10. Interrogator, university examiner.
11. Remarks which refer to individuals.   12. A jibe or sarcastic comment.
13. Suitably.   14. Introductory remarks.

33.

Of Plantations[1]

Plantations are amongst ancient, primitive, and heroical works. When the world was young it begat more children, but now it is old, it begets fewer;[2] for I may justly account new plantations to be the children of former kingdoms. I like a plantation in a pure soil, that is, where people are not displanted to the end to plant in others. For else it is rather an extirpation than a plantation. Planting of countries is like planting of woods, for you must make account to leese[3] almost twenty years' profit, and expect your recompense in the end. For the principal thing that hath been the destruction of most plantations hath been the base and hasty drawing of profit in the first years. It is true, speedy profit is not to be neglected, as far as may stand with the good of the plantation, but no further. It is a shameful and unblessed thing to take the scum of people and wicked condemned men, to be the people with whom you plant: and not only so, but it spoileth the plantation; for they will ever live like rogues, and not fall to work, but be lazy, and do mischief, and spend victuals, and be quickly weary, and then certify over[4] to their country to the discredit of the plantation. The people wherewith you plant ought to be gardeners, ploughmen, labourers, smiths, carpenters, joiners, fishermen, fowlers, with some few apothecaries, surgeons, cooks, and bakers. In a country of plantation, first look about what kind of victual the country yields of itself to hand, as chestnuts, walnuts, pineapples, olives, dates, plums, cherries, wild honey, and the like, and make use of them. Then consider what victual or esculent things there are, which grow speedily, and within the year; as parsnips, carrots, turnips, onions, radish, artichokes of Jerusalem, maize, and the like. For wheat, barley, and oats, they ask too much labour; but with peas and beans you may begin, both

Text: 1625

1. Colonies.
2. In Bacon's day it was believed that nature was decaying, and that the universe and mankind were declining into impotence.
3. Lose.   4. Report back.

because they ask less labour, and because they serve for meat as well as for bread. And of rice likewise cometh a great increase, and it is a kind of meat. Above all, there ought to be brought store of biscuit, oatmeal, flour, meal, and the like, in the beginning, till bread may be had. For beasts or birds, take chiefly such as are least subject to diseases, and multiply fastest, as swine, goats, cocks, hens, turkeys, geese, house-doves, and the like. The victual in plantations ought to be expended almost as in a besieged town, that is, with certain allowance. And let the main part of the ground employed to gardens or corn be to[5] a common stock, and to be laid in, and stored up, and then delivered out in proportion; besides some spots of ground that any particular person will manure for his own private.[6] Consider likewise what commodities the soil where the plantation is doth naturally yield, that they may some way help to defray the charge of the plantation: so it be not, as was said, to the untimely prejudice of the main business, as it hath fared with tobacco in Virginia. Wood commonly aboundeth but too much, and therefore timber is fit to be one.[7] If there be iron ore, and streams whereupon to set the mills, iron is a brave[8] commodity where wood aboundeth. Making of bay salt,[9] if the climate be proper for it, would be put in experience.[10] Growing silk likewise, if any be, is a likely commodity. Pitch and tar, where store of firs and pines are, will not fail. So drugs and sweet woods, where they are, cannot but yield great profit. Soap-ashes likewise, and other things that may be thought of. But moil[11] not too much under ground, for the hope of mines is very uncertain, and useth to make the planters lazy in other things. For government, let it be in the hands of one, assisted with some council; and let them have a commission to exercise martial laws, with some limitation. And above all, let men make that profit of being in the wilderness, as they have God always and his service before their eyes. Let not the government of the plantation depend upon too many counsellors and undertakers[12] in the country that planteth, but upon a temperate number: and let those be rather noblemen and gentlemen than merchants, for they look ever to the present gain. Let there be freedoms from custom till the plantation be of strength, and not only freedom from custom,[13] but freedom to carry their

5. For.   6. Cultivate for his personal benefit.   7. One of the commodities.
8. Excellent.   9. Salt crystals made by evaporating sea-water.
10. Ought to be tried.   11. Toil.   12. Contractors.
13. Import and export duties.

commodities where they may make their best of them, except there be some special cause of caution. Cram not in people by sending too fast, company after company, but rather hearken how they waste, and send supplies proportionably; but so as the number may live well in the plantation, and not by surcharge be in penury. It hath been a great endangering to the health of some plantations, that they have built along the sea and rivers, in marish and unwholesome grounds. Therefore, though you begin there, to avoid carriage and other like discommodities, yet build still rather upwards from the streams than along. It concerneth likewise the health of the plantation that they have good store of salt with them, that they may use it in their victuals when it shall be necessary. If you plant where savages are, do not only entertain them with trifles and gingles,[14] but use them justly and graciously, with sufficient guard nevertheless: and do not win their favour by helping them to invade their enemies, but for their defence it is not amiss. And send oft of them over to the country that plants, that they may see a better condition than their own, and commend it when they return. When the plantation grows to strength, then it is time to plant with women as well as with men, that the plantation may spread into generations, and not be ever pieced[15] from without. It is the sinfullest thing in the world to forsake or destitute[16] a plantation once in forwardness: for, besides the dishonour, it is the guiltiness of blood of many commiserable persons.[17]

14. Rattles.   15. Patched up.   16. Desert.
17. People who deserve compassion.

34.

Of Riches

I cannot call riches better than the baggage of virtue. The Roman word is better, *impedimenta*.[1] For as the baggage is to an army, so is riches to virtue. It cannot be spared nor left behind, but it hindereth the march; yea, and the care of it sometimes loseth or disturbeth the victory. Of great riches there is no real use, except it be in the distribution; the rest is but conceit.[2] So saith Solomon, *Where much is, there are many to consume it; and what hath the owner but the sight of it with his eyes?*[3] The personal fruition in any man cannot reach to feel great riches: there is a custody of them, or a power of dole and donative of them, or a fame of them; but no solid use to the owner. Do you not see what feigned prices are set upon little stones and rarities, and what works of ostentation are undertaken, because[4] there might seem to be some use of great riches? But then you will say, they may be of use to buy men out of dangers or troubles. As Solomon saith, *Riches are as a stronghold in the imagination of the rich man.*[5] But this is excellently expressed, that it is in imagination, and not always in fact. For certainly great riches have sold more men than they have bought out. Seek not proud riches,[6] but such as thou mayest get justly, use soberly, distribute cheerfully, and leave contentedly. Yet have no abstract[7] nor friarly contempt of them. But distinguish, as Cicero saith well of Rabirius Postumus: *In studio rei amplificandae apparebat non avaritiae praedam sed instrumentum bonitati quaeri.*[8] Hearken also to Solomon, and beware of hasty gathering of riches: *Qui festinat ad divitias, non erit insons.*[9] The poets feign that when Plutus (which is

Texts: MS, 1612, 1625

1. Impediments, things which hinder.   2. Imagination.
3. Ecclesiastes 5.11.   4. So that.   5. Proverbs 18.11.
6. Wealth for ostentation.   7. Other-worldly.
8. In his keenness to increase his wealth it was apparent that he was not seeking a prey for avarice to feed upon, but an instrument for good to work with (*The Speech on behalf of Rabirius Postumus*, II). Cicero is not speaking of Rabirius Postumus, but his father, Gaius Curtius.
9. He who makes haste to be rich shall not be innocent (Proverbs 28.20).

riches) is sent from Jupiter, he limps and goes slowly, but when he is sent from Pluto, he runs and is swift of foot: meaning, that riches gotten by good means and just labour pace slowly, but when they come by the death of others (as by the course of inheritance, testaments, and the like), they come tumbling upon a man. But it mought[10] be applied likewise to Pluto, taking him for the devil. For when riches come from the devil (as by fraud and oppression and unjust means), they come upon speed. The ways to enrich are many, and most of them foul. Parsimony is one of the best, and yet is not innocent, for it withholdeth men from works of liberality and charity. The improvement of the ground is the most natural obtaining of riches, for it is our great mother's blessing, the earth's; but it is slow. And yet where men of great wealth do stoop to husbandry, it multiplieth riches exceedingly. I knew a nobleman in England, that had the greatest audits of any man in my time: a great grazier, a great sheep-master, a great timber-man, a great collier, a great corn-master, a great lead-man, and so of iron, and a number of the like points of husbandry: so as the earth seemed a sea to him, in respect of the perpetual importation. It was truly observed by one, that himself came very hardly[11] to a little riches, and very easily to great riches. For when a man's stock is come to that, that he can expect[12] the prime of markets, and overcome those bargains which for their greatness are few men's money,[13] and be partner in the industries of younger men, he cannot but increase mainly.[14] The gains of ordinary trades and vocations are honest, and furthered by two things chiefly: by diligence, and by a good name for good and fair dealing. But the gains of bargains are of a more doubtful nature, when men shall wait upon others' necessity, broke by[15] servants and instruments to draw them on, put off others cunningly that would be better chapmen,[16] and the like practices, which are crafty and naught.[17] As for the chopping of[18] bargains, when a man buys not to hold, but to sell over again, that commonly grindeth double, both upon the seller and upon the buyer.[19] Sharings[20] do greatly enrich, if the hands be well chosen that are trusted. Usury is the certainest means of gain, though one of the worst, as that whereby a man doth

10. Might.   11. With great difficulty.   12. Wait for.
13. Is able to take advantage of those bargains which are so costly that few men have enough money for them.   14. Greatly.   15. Do business through.
16. Purchasers.   17. Bad.   18. Dealing in.
19. On both the original seller and then the final buyer.   20. Partnerships.

eat his bread *in sudore vultus alieni*,²¹ and besides, doth plough
upon Sundays. But yet certain though it be, it hath flaws, for that
the scriveners and brokers do value unsound men to serve their own
turn.²² The fortune in being the first in an invention or in a privilege
doth cause sometimes a wonderful overgrowth in riches, as it was
with the first sugar man in the Canaries. Therefore if a man can play
the true logician, to have as well judgement as invention,²³ he may
do great matters, especially if the times be fit. He that resteth upon
gains certain shall hardly grow to great riches, and he that puts all
upon adventures²⁴ doth oftentimes break and come to poverty: it is
good therefore to guard adventures with certainties that may
uphold losses. Monopolies and coemption of wares²⁵ for re-sale,
where they are not restrained, are great means to enrich, especially
if the party have intelligence what things are like to come into
request, and so store himself beforehand. Riches gotten by service,
though it be of the best rise,²⁶ yet when they are gotten by flattery,
feeding humours,²⁷ and other servile conditions, they may be placed
amongst the worst. As for fishing for testaments and executorships
(as Tacitus saith of Seneca, *testamenta et orbos tanquam indagine
capi*²⁸), it is yet worse, by how much men submit themselves to
meaner persons than in service. Believe not much them that seem to
despise riches, for they despise them that despair of them; and none
worse when they come to them. Be not penny-wise; riches have
wings, and sometimes they fly away of themselves, sometimes they
must be set flying to bring in more. Men leave their riches either to
their kindred, or to the public, and moderate portions prosper best in
both. A great state left to an heir is as a lure to all the birds of prey
round about to seize on him, if he be not the better stablished in
years and judgement. Likewise glorious gifts and foundations are
like *sacrifices without salt*, and but the painted sepulchres of alms,

21. In the sweat of another man's brow (see Genesis 3.19).
22. Because money-lenders and brokers, for their own ends, deliberately over-
value men who are financially unsound, so representing them as good risks.
23. Bacon says that there are four Arts to Logic: Invention, Judgement, Custody
(or Memory) and Elocution (or Tradition) (*Works*, IV.407). Other Renaissance
definitions confined the Arts to Invention and Judgement.
24. Speculations, risky enterprises.
25. Buying up commodities to control (or corner) the market.
26. Though service is one of the most honourable ways of obtaining wealth.
27. Catering to a superior's whims.
28. He seized wills and wardships as with a net (*Annals*, XIII.42). It is not Tacitus,
but Seneca's enemy, Suillus, who brings this accusation.

which soon will putrefy and corrupt inwardly. Therefore measure not thine advancements[29] by quantity, but frame them by measure:[30] and defer not charities till death, for certainly if a man weigh it rightly, he that doth so is rather liberal of another man's than of his own.

29. Gifts.   30. Appropriately

35.

Of Prophecies

I mean not to speak of divine prophecies, nor of heathen oracles, nor of natural predictions,[1] but only of prophecies that have been of certain memory, and from hidden causes. Saith the Pythonissa to Saul: *Tomorrow thou and thy son shall be with me.*[2] Homer hath these verses:

> *At domus Aeneae cunctis dominabitur oris,*
> *Et nati natorum, et qui nascentur ab illis,*[3]

a prophecy, as it seems, of the Roman empire. Seneca the tragedian hath these verses:

> *Venient annis*
> *Saecula seris, quibus Oceanus*
> *Vincula rerum laxet, et ingens*
> *Pateat tellus, Tiphysque novos*
> *Detegat orbes, nec sit terris*
> *Ultima Thule,*[4]

a prophecy of the discovery of America. The daughter of Polycrates dreamed that Jupiter bathed her father, and Apollo anointed him: and it came to pass that he was crucified in an open place, where the sun made his body run with sweat, and the rain washed it.[5] Philip of Macedon dreamed he sealed up his wife's belly, whereby he did

Text: 1625

1. Predictions from known data.
2. 1 Samuel 28.19. In the Vulgate, the *Pythonissa* was the witch whom Saul consulted.
3. But the family of Aeneas shall rule over all the lands – even his children's children, and those that shall be born of them (Virgil, *Aeneid*, III.97–8, adapted from Homer, *Iliad*, XX.307–8).
4. In far-off years, there shall come a time when the Ocean shall loosen nature's bands, and a vast continent shall lie revealed, and Typhis shall disclose new worlds, and Thule shall no longer be the end of the earth (from *Medea*, 375–9).
5. The story of the dream, and the execution of Polycrates is told by Herodotus, *History*, III.124–5.

expound it, that his wife should be barren: but Aristander the soothsayer told him his wife was with child, because men do not use to seal vessels that are empty.[6] A phantasm that appeared to M. Brutus in his tent said to him: *Philippis iterum me videbis.*[7] Tiberius said to Galba: *Tu quoque, Galba, degustabis imperium.*[8] In Vespasian's time, there went a prophecy in the East, that those that should come forth of Judea should reign over the world: which though it may be was meant of our Saviour, yet Tacitus expounds it of Vespasian.[9] Domitian dreamed, the night before he was slain, that a golden head was growing out of the nape of his neck;[10] and indeed the succession that followed him, for many years, made golden times. Henry the Sixth of England said of Henry the Seventh, when he was a lad, and gave him water, *This is the lad that shall enjoy the crown for which we strive.*[11] When I was in France, I heard from one Dr Pena, that the Queen Mother, who was given to curious arts, caused the King her husband's nativity to be calculated, under a false name; and the astrologer gave a judgement, that he should be killed in a duel, at which the Queen laughed, thinking her husband to be above challenges and duels: but he was slain upon a course at tilt, the splinters of the staff of Montgomery going in at his beaver.[12] The trivial[13] prophecy which I heard when I was a child, and Queen Elizabeth was in the flower of her years, was:

> When Hempe is spun,
> England's done.

Whereby it was generally conceived that after the princes had reigned which had the principal[14] letters of that word *hempe* (which were Henry, Edward, Mary, Philip, and Elizabeth), England should come to utter confusion: which, thanks be to God, is verified only in the change of the name, for that the King's style is now no more of

6. Philip of Macedon's dream is in Plutarch, *Alexander*, II.2–4.
7. You shall see me again at Philippi (Plutarch, *Brutus*, XXXVI.4).
8. You too, Galba, shall have your taste of empire (Tacitus, *Annals*, VI.20).
9. Tacitus, *Histories*, V.13.
10. Suetonius, *Domitian*, XXIII (concluding words).
11. Bacon tells the story in more detail in his *History of Henry VII* (*Works*, VI.245). The episode is recounted in Hall and Holinshed, whence it passed to Shakespeare, *3 Henry VI*, IV.6.68–70.
12. Henry II of France was accidentally killed at a tournament in 1559.
13. Common.   14. Initial.

England, but of Britain.[15] There was also another prophecy, before the year of 88,[16] which I do not well understand:

> There shall be seen upon a day,
> Between the Baugh and the May,[17]
> The Black Fleet of Norway.
> When that that is come and gone,
> England build houses of lime and stone,
> For after wars shall you have none.

It was generally conceived to be meant of the Spanish fleet that came in 88, for that the king of Spain's surname, as they say, is *Norway*. The prediction of Regiomontanus,

Octogesimus octavus mirabilis annus,[18]

was thought likewise accomplished in the sending of that great fleet, being the greatest in strength, though not in number, of all that ever swam upon the sea. As for Cleon's dream, I think it was a jest. It was, that he was devoured of a long dragon; and it was expounded of a maker of sausages, that troubled him exceedingly.[19] There are numbers of the like kind, especially if you include dreams and predictions of astrology. But I have set down these few only of certain credit, for example. My judgement is, that they ought all to be despised, and ought to serve but for winter talk by the fire side. Though when I say despised, I mean it as for belief, for otherwise, the spreading or publishing of them is in no sort to be despised. For they have done much mischief, and I see many severe laws made to suppress them. That that hath given them grace, and some credit, consisteth in three things. First, that men mark when they hit, and never mark when they miss, as they do generally also of dreams. The second is, that probable conjectures or obscure traditions many times turn themselves into prophecies; while the nature of man, which coveteth divination, thinks it no peril to foretell that which

15. In 1603, when James VI of Scotland succeeded to the English throne, he styled himself King of Great Britain.

16. 1588, when the Spanish Armada attacked England and was defeated.

17. Between the Bass Rock and the Isle of May, in the Firth of Forth. Some ships from the Armada were driven there by storms.

18. Eighty-eight, a year of wonders (a line from a prophecy written by Regiomontanus, or John Muller of Königsberg, *c.* 1470).

19. The reference is to Aristophanes, *The Knights*, 197ff. Bacon has added the devouring dragon, and confused other details.

indeed they do but collect.[20] As that of Seneca's verse. For so much was then subject to demonstration, that the globe of the earth had great parts beyond the Atlantic, which mought[21] be probably conceived not to be all sea: and adding thereto the tradition in Plato's *Timaeus* and his *Atlanticus*,[22] it mought encourage one to turn it to a prediction. The third and last (which is the great one) is, that almost all of them, being infinite in number, have been impostures, and by idle and crafty brains, merely[23] contrived and feigned after the event past.

20. Infer.   21. Might.
22. The tradition was that there had once been a huge island to the west of Europe, beyond which lay another continent. The island, called Atlantis, was said to have been swallowed up by an earthquake, leaving behind a great ocean, the Atlantic, separating Europe from the unknown continent. There is an account of the inhabitants and laws of the lost Atlantis in the *Critias*, or *Atlanticus* as it was subtitled in early editions of Plato.   23. Entirely.

36.

Of Ambition

Ambition is like choler, which is an humour that maketh men active, earnest, full of alacrity, and stirring, if it be not stopped. But if it be stopped, and cannot have his way, it becometh adust, and thereby malign and venomous.[1] So ambitious men, if they find the way open for their rising, and still get forward, they are rather busy than dangerous; but if they be checked in their desires, they become secretly discontent and look upon men and matters with an evil eye, and are best pleased when things go backward, which is the worst property[2] in a servant of a prince or state. Therefore it is good for princes, if they use ambitious men, to handle it so as they be still progressive and not retrograde;[3] which because it cannot be without inconvenience, it is good not to use such natures at all. For if they rise not with their service, they will take order[4] to make their service fall with them. But since we have said it were good not to use men of ambitious natures, except it be upon necessity, it is fit we speak in what cases they are of necessity. Good commanders in the wars must be taken, be they never so ambitious; for the use of their service dispenseth with[5] the rest, and to take a soldier without ambition is to pull off his spurs. There is also great use of ambitious men in being screens to princes in matters of danger and envy, for no man will take that part, except he be like a seeled dove,[6] that mounts and mounts because he cannot see about him. There is use also of ambitious men in pulling down the greatness of any subject that overtops: as Tiberius used Macro in the pulling down of

Texts: MS, 1612, 1625

1. In Renaissance medical theory, *choler* (or bile) was one of the four humours, or fluids in the body, which were thought to determine human temperament. The other three were blood, phlegm and melancholy (or black bile). Choler was supposed to make a man irascible; choler *adust* was the condition where too much black bile made him melancholic.   2. Worst possible characteristic.

3. So that they continue to progress in their advancement, and never fall back.   4. Arrange things.   5. Makes up for.

6. A dove with its eyelids sewn up.

Sejanus.[7] Since therefore they must be used in such cases, there resteth to speak how they are to be bridled that they may be less dangerous. There is less danger of them if they be of mean birth, than if they be noble; and if they be rather harsh of nature, than gracious and popular; and if they be rather new raised, than grown cunning and fortified in their greatness. It is counted by some a weakness in princes to have favourites, but it is of all others the best remedy against ambitious great ones. For when the way of pleasuring and displeasuring lieth by the favourite, it is impossible any other should be over-great. Another means to curb them is to balance them by others as proud as they. But then there must be some middle counsellors to keep things steady, for without that ballast the ship will roll too much. At the least, a prince may animate and inure[8] some meaner persons to be as it were scourges to ambitious men. As for the having of them obnoxious[9] to ruin, if they be of fearful natures, it may do well, but if they be stout[10] and daring, it may precipitate their designs and prove dangerous. As for the pulling of them down, if the affairs require it, and that it may not be done with safety suddenly, the only way is the interchange continually of favours and disgraces, whereby they may not know what to expect, and be as it were in a wood. Of ambitions, it is less harmful, the ambition to prevail in great things, than that other, to appear in everything, for that breeds confusion, and mars business. But yet it is less danger to have an ambitious man stirring in business, than great in dependences.[11] He that seeketh to be eminent amongst able men hath a great task, but that is ever good for the public. But he that plots to be the only figure amongst ciphers is the decay of an whole age. Honour hath three things in it: the vantage ground to do good, the approach to kings and principal persons, and the raising of a man's own fortunes. He that hath the best of these intentions, when he aspireth, is an honest man; and that prince that can discern of these intentions in another that aspireth, is a wise prince. Generally let princes and states choose such ministers as are more sensible of duty than of rising; and such as love business rather upon conscience than upon bravery;[12] and let them discern a busy nature from a willing mind.

---

7. See Dio, *Roman History*, LVIII.9.   8. Accustom.   9. Exposed.
10. Bold.   11. Followers.
12. Out of a sense of duty rather than a desire to show off.

37.

Of Masques[1] and Triumphs[2]

These things are but toys, to come amongst such serious observations. But yet, since princes will have such things, it is better they should be graced with elegancy than daubed with cost. Dancing to song is a thing of great state and pleasure. I understand it, that the song be in quire, placed aloft,[3] and accompanied with some broken music,[4] and the ditty fitted to the device.[5] Acting in song, especially in dialogues, hath an extreme good grace: I say acting, not dancing (for that is a mean and vulgar thing);[6] and the voices of the dialogue would[7] be strong and manly (a bass and a tenor, no treble); and the ditty high and tragical,[8] not nice or dainty. Several quires, placed one over against another, and taking the voice by catches, anthemwise, give great pleasure. Turning dances into figure[9] is a childish curiosity. And generally let it be noted, that those things which I here set down are such as do naturally take the sense,[10] and not respect[11] petty wonderments. It is true, the alterations of scenes, so it be quietly and without noise, are things of great beauty and pleasure, for they feed and relieve the eye before it be full of the same object. Let the scenes abound with light, specially coloured and varied, and let the masquers or any other that are to come down from the scene, have some motions upon the scene itself before their coming down; for it draws the eye strangely, and makes it with great pleasure to desire to see that it cannot perfectly discern. Let the

Text: 1625

1. Court entertainments which combined music, song, dance and poetry, and in which members of the court, and often the royal family, participated. The most famous masque, though not one written for court, is Milton's *Comus*.

2. Pageants, magnificent shows.   3. In the gallery.

4. Music divided into parts arranged for different instruments.

5. The words made appropriate to the action and dances.

6. i.e. the dancers are not to accompany themselves in song.   7. Should.

8. Lofty and grave.

9. Having the dancers arrange themselves to represent the age of someone present (on birthdays, etc.), or spell out the letters of their name.

10. Appeal to the senses.   11. Do not concern.

songs be loud and cheerful, and not chirpings or pulings. Let the music likewise be sharp and loud and well placed. The colours that show best by candle-light are white, carnation, and a kind of sea-water-green; and oes[12] or spangs,[13] as they are of no great cost, so they are of most glory. As for rich embroidery, it is lost and not discerned. Let the suits of the masquers be graceful and such as become the person when the vizors are off, not after examples of known attires, Turks, soldiers, mariners, and the like. Let anti-masques[14] not be long; they have been commonly of fools, satyrs, baboons, wild-men, antics,[15] beasts, sprites, witches, Ethiopes, pygmies, turquets,[16] nymphs, rustics, Cupids, statuas moving,[17] and the like. As for angels, it is not comical enough to put them in antimasques; and anything that is hideous, as devils, giants, is on the other side[18] as unfit. But chiefly, let the music of them be recreative and with some strange changes. Some sweet odours suddenly coming forth without any drops falling are, in such a company as there is steam and heat, things of great pleasure and refreshment. Double masques, one of men, another of ladies, addeth state and variety. But all is nothing, except the room be kept clear and neat.

For justs, and tourneys,[19] and barriers,[20] the glories of them are chiefly in the chariots wherein the challengers make their entry, especially if they be drawn with strange beasts, as lions, bears, camels, and the like; or in the devices of their entrance; or in the bravery[21] of their liveries; or in the goodly furniture[22] of their horses and armour. But enough of these toys.

12. Sparkling decorations (in the shape of a letter O).   13. Spangles.
14. Often a comic or antic performance which preceded the main masque, or served as a foil to it.
15. Buffoons (but spelt *Antiques* in the original, so perhaps an antimasque made up of old hags, or something of the like).   16. Perhaps Turkish dwarfs.
17. Moving statues.   18. In the main masque (which is to be serious).
19. As for jousts, and tournaments.
20. Combat with swords or lances across a barrier or wooden railing.
21. Splendour.   22. Equipment.

38.

Of Nature in Men

Nature is often hidden, sometimes overcome, seldom extinguished. Force maketh nature more violent in the return; doctrine and discourse maketh nature less importune;[1] but custom only doth alter and subdue nature. He that seeketh victory over his nature, let him not set himself too great nor too small tasks: for the first will make him dejected by often failings, and the second will make him a small proceeder, though by often prevailings. And at the first let him practise with helps, as swimmers do with bladders or rushes; but after a time let him practise with disadvantages, as dancers do with thick shoes. For it breeds great perfection, if the practice be harder than the use. Where nature is mighty, and therefore the victory hard, the degrees had need be: first, to stay and arrest nature in time, like to him that would say over the four and twenty letters[2] when he was angry; then, to go less in quantity, as if one should, in forbearing wine, come from drinking healths to a draught at a meal; and lastly, to discontinue altogether. But if a man have the fortitude and resolution to enfranchise himself at once, that is the best:

> *Optimus ille animi vindex laedentia pectus*
> *Vincula qui rupit, dedoluitque semel.*[3]

Neither is the ancient rule amiss, to bend nature as a wand to a contrary extreme, whereby to set it right, understanding it, where the contrary extreme is no vice. Let not a man force a habit upon himself with a perpetual continuance, but with some intermission. For both the pause reinforceth the new onset, and if a man that is not perfect be ever in practice, he shall as well practise his errors as his abilities, and induce one habit of both; and there is no means to help this but by seasonable intermissions. But let not a man trust his

Texts: MS, 1612, 1625

1. Importunate.   2. The letters of the alphabet. See Essay 27, note 52.
3. He is the best liberator of his mind who breaks the chains that afflict his heart, and is at once free from grieving (Ovid, *Remedies for Love*, 293–4).

victory over his nature too far, for nature will lay buried a great time, and yet revive upon the occasion or temptation. Like as it was with Aesop's damsel, turned from a cat to a woman, who sat very demurely at the board's end till a mouse ran before her.[4] Therefore let a man either avoid the occasion altogether, or put himself often to it, that he may be little moved with it. A man's nature is best perceived in privateness, for there is no affectation; in passion, for that putteth a man out of his precepts; and in a new case or experiment, for there custom leaveth him. They are happy men whose natures sort with[5] their vocations; otherwise they may say, *Multum incola fuit anima mea*,[6] when they converse in[7] those things they do not affect.[8] In studies, whatsoever a man commandeth upon himself, let him set hours for it; but whatsoever is agreeable to his nature, let him take no care for any set times, for his thoughts will fly to it of themselves, so as[9] the spaces of other business or studies will suffice. A man's nature runs either to herbs or weeds; therefore let him seasonably water the one, and destroy the other.

4. For the source, see above, pp. 47–8.   5. Suit.
6. My soul has long been a sojourner (Psalms 120.6, Vulgate text). The 1611 Authorized Version translates it 'My soul hath long dwelt with him that hateth peace'.   7. Are occupied with.   8. Desire.   9. So that.

39

Of Custom and Education

Men's thoughts are much according to their inclination; their discourse and speeches according to their learning and infused opinions; but their deeds are after as they have been accustomed.[1] And therefore, as Machiavel well noteth[2] (though in an evil-favoured[3] instance), there is no trusting to the force of nature nor to the bravery[4] of words, except it be corroborate[5] by custom. His instance is, that for the achieving of a desperate conspiracy, a man should not rest upon[6] the fierceness of any man's nature, or his resolute undertakings, but take such an one as hath had his hands formerly in blood. But Machiavel knew not of a Friar Clement,[7] nor a Ravillac,[8] nor a Jaureguy, nor a Baltazar Gerard[9]; yet his rule holdeth still, that nature, nor the engagement of words are not so forcible as custom. Only superstition is now so well advanced, that men of the first blood[10] are as firm as butchers by occupation, and votary[11] resolution is made equipollent to custom, even in matter of blood. In other things the predominancy of custom is everywhere visible; insomuch as a man would wonder to hear men profess, protest, engage, give great words, and then do just as they have done before; as if they were dead images and engines moved only by the wheels of custom. We see also the reign or tyranny of custom, what it is. The Indians (I mean the sect of their wise men[12]) lay themselves quietly upon a stack of wood, and so sacrifice themselves by fire. Nay, the wives strive to be burned with the corpses of their

Texts: MS, 1612, 1625

1. Their actions conform to what they have been used to.
2. *Discourses*, III.6 (where Machiavelli is writing about the difficulties of assassinating a prince).   3. Ugly.   4. Showiness.   5. Confirmed.
6. Rely on.   7. Assassinated Henry III of France in 1589.
8. Assassinated Henry IV of France in 1610.
9. Jaureguy tried to murder William of Orange in 1582: Gerard shot and killed the prince in 1584.   10. Men who are committing murder for the first time.
11. Based on a vow.
12. The Gymnosophists, an ancient Hindu sect. Cicero describes the manner of their death, and the behaviour of their wives in *Tusculan Disputations*, V.27.

husbands. The lads of Sparta of ancient time were wont to be scourged upon the altar of Diana, without so much as queching.[13] I remember, in the beginning of Queen Elizabeth's time of England, an Irish rebel,[14] condemned, put up a petition to the deputy that he might be hanged in a withe, and not in an halter, because it had been so used with former rebels. There be monks in Russia, for penance, that will sit a whole night in a vessel of water, till they be engaged[15] with hard ice. Many examples may be put of the force of custom, both upon mind and body. Therefore, since custom is the principal magistrate of man's life, let men by all means endeavour to obtain good customs. Certainly custom is most perfect when it beginneth in young years: this we call education, which is in effect but an early custom. So we see, in languages the tongue is more pliant to all expressions and sounds, the joints are more supple to all feats of activity and motions, in youth than afterwards. For it is true that late learners cannot so well take the ply,[16] except it be in some minds that have not suffered themselves to fix, but have kept themselves open and prepared to receive continual amendment, which is exceeding rare. But if the force of custom simple and separate be great, the force of custom copulate[17] and conjoined and collegiate[18] is far greater. For there example teacheth, company comforteth,[19] emulation quickeneth, glory raiseth, so as in such places the force of custom is in his exaltation.[20] Certainly the great multiplication of virtues upon human nature resteth upon societies well ordained and disciplined. For commonwealths and good governments do nourish virtue grown, but do not much mend the seeds. But the misery is that the most effectual means are now applied to the ends least to be desired.

13. Flinching *or* crying out.
14. Probably Brian O'Rourke, who was hanged, not at the beginning of Elizabeth's reign, but in 1597.   15. Bound fast.   16. Are not as pliant.
17. Linked together.   18. Incorporated into one body (as in a college).
19. Strengthens.   20. At its zenith, exercising its greatest influence.

40.

Of Fortune

It cannot be denied but outward accidents conduce much to fortune: favour, opportunity, death of others, occasion fitting virtue.[1] But chiefly the mould of a man's fortune is in his own hands. *Faber quisque fortunae suae,*[2] saith the poet. And the most frequent of external causes is that the folly of one man is the fortune of another. For no man prospers so suddenly as by others' errors. *Serpens nisi serpentem comederit non fit draco.*[3] Overt and apparent[4] virtues bring forth praise, but there be secret and hidden virtues that bring forth fortune: certain deliveries of[5] a man's self, which have no name. The Spanish name, *desemboltura,*[6] partly expresseth them, when there be not stonds[7] nor restiveness in a man's nature, but that the wheels of his mind keep way with the wheels of his fortune. For so Livy (after he had described Cato Major in these words, *In illo viro tantum robur corporis et animi fuit, ut quocunque loco natus esset, fortunam sibi facturus videretur*[8]) falleth upon that, that he had *versatile ingenium.*[9] Therefore if a man look sharply and attentively, he shall see Fortune: for though she be blind, yet she is not invisible. The way of fortune is like the milken way in the sky, which is a meeting or knot of a number of small stars, not seen asunder but giving light together. So are there a number of little and scarce discerned virtues, or rather faculties and customs, that make men fortunate. The Italians note some of them, such as a man would little think. When they speak of one that cannot do amiss, they will throw in, into his other conditions, that he hath *poco di matto.*[10]

Texts: MS, 1612, 1625

1. Opportunity meeting with talent.
2. Every man is the architect of his own fortune (from Plautus, *Three Bob Day*, II.2.87. See *Works*, III.454).
3. A serpent must have eaten another serpent before it can become a dragon.
4. Manifest.   5. Ways of disclosing.   6. Assured facility in speaking.
7. Hindrances.
8. In this man there was such strength of body and mind that wherever he had been born it seems certain he would have made fortune his own (from Livy, *History*, XXXIX.40).   9. A versatile nature.   10. A little of the fool (*or* madman).

And certainly there be not two more fortunate properties than to
have a little of the fool and not too much of the honest. Therefore
extreme lovers of their country or masters were never fortunate,
neither can they be. For when a man placeth his thoughts without
himself, he goeth not his own way. An hasty fortune maketh an
enterpriser and remover[11] (the French hath it better, *entreprenant*,
or *remuant*), but the exercised fortune[12] maketh the able man.
Fortune is to be honoured and respected, and it be but for[13] her
daughters, Confidence and Reputation. For those two felicity
breedeth: the first within a man's self, the latter in others towards
him. All wise men, to decline[14] the envy of their own virtues, use to
ascribe them to Providence and Fortune, for so they may the better
assume them; and besides, it is greatness in a man to be the care of
the higher powers. So Caesar said to the pilot in the tempest,
Caesarem portas, et fortunam eius.[15] So Sulla chose the name of
Felix and not of *Magnus.*[16] And it hath been noted that those that
ascribe openly too much to their own wisdom and policy, end
infortunate. It is written that Timotheus the Athenian, after he had,
in the account he gave to the state of his government, often
interlaced this speech, *And in this Fortune had no part*, never
prospered in anything he undertook afterwards.[17] Certainly there
be whose fortunes are like Homer's verses, that have a slide[18] and
easiness more than the verses of other poets; as Plutarch saith of
Timoleon's fortune,[19] in respect of that of Agesilaus or
Epaminondas.[20] And that this should be, no doubt it is much in a
man's self.

---

11. An adventurer, and someone forever on the move, hustling.
12. Fortune put to the test.   13. If only because of.   14. Avert.
15. You carry Caesar and his fortune (Plutarch, *Caesar*, XXXVIII.3).
16. Chose to be called *the Fortunate*, and not *the Great* (see Plutarch, *Sulla*,
XXXIV.2).   17. Plutarch, *Sulla*, VI.3–4.   18. Smoothness.
19. Plutarch, *Timoleon*, XXXVI.1–3.   20. Greek generals, fourth century B.C.

41.

Of Usury

Many have made witty invectives against usury.[1] They say that it is pity the devil should have God's part, which is the tithe;[2] that the usurer is the greatest Sabbath-breaker, because his plough goeth every Sunday; that the usurer is the drone that Virgil speaketh of:

Ignavum fucos pecus a praesepibus arcent;[3]

that the usurer breaketh the first law that was made for mankind after the fall,[4] which was, *in sudore vultus tui comedes panem tuum*, not, *in sudore vultus alieni;*[5] that usurers should have orange-tawny bonnets,[6] because they do judaize;[7] that it is against nature for money to beget money; and the like. I say this only, that usury is a *concessum propter duritiem cordis;*[8] for since there must be borrowing and lending, and men are so hard of heart as[9] they will not lend freely, usury must be permitted. Some others have made suspicious and cunning propositions of banks, discovery of men's estates, and other inventions.[10] But few have spoken of usury usefully. It is good to set before us the incommodities and

Text: 1625

1. Earning interest (rather than the present meaning, to lend at an exorbitant or unlawful rate).
2. Ten per cent (the lawful rate of interest in Bacon's day).
3. They drive the lazy swarm of drones from their hives (*Georgics*, IV.168).
4. The fall of man in the Garden of Eden.
5. In the sweat of your face you shall eat your bread; not, in the sweat of another's face (derived from Genesis 3.19).
6. In some parts of medieval Europe the Jews were compelled by law to wear yellow caps or bonnets.
7. Behave like a Jew, i.e. lend out money for interest (the Jews were the chief money-lenders at this time).
8. A thing allowed on account of the hardness of men's hearts (Matthew 19.8).
9. That.
10. Some others have made perspicacious remarks, based on their suspicions, about banks, the disclosure of men's estates and incomes, and other revelations (of how their money was obtained and used).

commodites[11] of usury, that the good may be either weighed out or culled out; and warily to provide that while we make forth to that which is better we meet not with that which is worse.

The discommodities of usury are, first, that it makes fewer merchants. For were it not for this lazy trade of usury, money would not lie still, but would in great part be employed upon merchandising, which is the *vena porta*[12] of wealth in a state. The second, that it makes poor merchants: for as a farmer cannot husband his ground so well if he sit[13] at a great rent, so the merchant cannot drive his trade so well if he sit at great usury. The third is incident to the other two, and that is, the decay of customs of kings or states, which ebb or flow with merchandising. The fourth, that it bringeth the treasure of a realm or state into a few hands. For the usurer being at certainties, and others at uncertainties, at the end of the game most of the money will be in the box;[14] and ever a state flourisheth when wealth is more equally spread. The fifth, that it beats down the price of land. For the employment of money is chiefly either merchandising or purchasing, and usury waylays both. The sixth, that it doth dull and damp all industries, improvements, and new inventions, wherein money would be stirring if it were not for this slug.[15] The last, that it is the canker and ruin of many men's estates, which in process of time breeds a public poverty.

On the other side, the commodities of usury are, first, that howsoever usury in some respect hindereth merchandising, yet in some other it advanceth it, for it is certain that the greatest part of trade is driven by young merchants upon borrowing at interest; so as[16] if the usurer either call in or keep back his money, there will ensue presently a great stand of trade. The second is, that were it not for this easy borrowing upon interest, men's necessities would draw upon them a most sudden undoing, in that they would be forced to sell their means (be it lands or goods) far under foot;[17] and so, whereas usury doth but gnaw upon them, bad markets would swallow them quite up. As for mortgaging or pawning, it will little mend the matter, for either men will not take pawns without use,[18]

11. Disadvantages and advantages.   12. Gate vein (to the liver).
13. Holds possession of it *or* pays for it.   14. In the usurer's hands.
15. Hindrance.   16. So that.   17. Far below their real value.
18. Will not accept pledges of security, when lending out money, unless there is interest to be earned.

or if they do, they will look precisely for the forfeiture. I remember a cruel monied man in the country, that would say, *The devil take this usury, it keeps us from forfeitures of mortgages and bonds*. The third and last is, that it is a vanity to conceive that there would be ordinary borrowing without profit, and it is impossible to conceive the number of inconveniences that will ensue if borrowing be cramped. Therefore to speak of the abolishing of usury is idle: all states have ever had it, in one kind or rate or other. So as that opinion must be sent to Utopia.[19]

To speak now of the reformation and reglement[20] of usury: how the discommodities of it may be best avoided and the commodities retained. It appears by the balance of commodities and discommodities of usury, two things are to be reconciled. The one, that the tooth of usury be grinded, that it bite not too much; the other, that there be left open a means to invite monied men to lend to the merchants, for the continuing and quickening of trade. This cannot be done except you introduce two several sorts[21] of usury, a less and a greater. For if you reduce usury to one low rate, it will ease the common borrower, but the merchant will be to seek for money.[22] And it is to be noted, that the trade of merchandise, being the most lucrative, may bear usury at a good rate; other contracts not so.

To serve both intentions, the way would be briefly thus: that there be two rates of usury, the one free and general for all, the other under licence only to certain persons and in certain places of merchandising. First, therefore, let usury in general be reduced to five in the hundred,[23] and let that rate be proclaimed to be free and current, and let the state shut itself out to take[24] any penalty for the same. This will preserve borrowing from any general stop or dryness. This will ease infinite borrowers in the country. This will, in good part, raise the price of land, because land purchased at sixteen years' purchase will yield six in the hundred, and somewhat more, whereas this rate of interest yields but five. This, by like reason, will encourage and edge[25] industrious and profitable improvements, because many will rather venture in that kind than take five in the hundred, especially having been used to greater profit. Secondly, let there be certain persons licensed to lend to

19. The imaginary country described by Sir Thomas More, where, because there was no private property, there could be no usury. 20. Regulation.
21. Two different kinds. 22. At a loss for money. 23. Five per cent.
24. Restrain itself from taking. 25. Stimulate.

known merchants upon usury at a higher rate, and let it be with the cautions following. Let the rate be, even with the merchant himself, somewhat more easy than that he used formerly to pay; for by that means all borrowers shall have some ease by this reformation, be he merchant or whosoever. Let it be no bank or common stock, but every man be master of his own money – not that I altogether mislike banks, but they will hardly be brooked, in regard of certain suspicions.[26] Let the state be answered[27] some small matter for the licence, and the rest left to the lender; for if the abatement be but small, it will no whit discourage the lender. For he, for example, that took before ten or nine in the hundred, will sooner descend to eight in the hundred than give over his trade of usury and go from certain gains to gains of hazard. Let these licensed lenders be in number indefinite, but restrained to certain principal cities and towns of merchandising, for then they will be hardly able to colour other men's monies[28] in the country; so as[29] the licence of nine will not suck away the current rate of five, for no man will lend his monies far off, nor put them into unknown hands.

If it be objected that this doth in a sort authorize usury, which before was in some places but permissive, the answer is that it is better to mitigate usury by declaration than to suffer it to rage by connivance.

26. On account of certain practices which arouse suspicion.   27. Paid.
28. Lend out other men's money under the pretence that it is their own.
29. With the result that.

42.

Of Youth and Age

A man that is young in years may be old in hours, if he have lost no time. But that happeneth rarely. Generally, youth is like the first cogitations, not so wise as the second. For there is a youth in thoughts as well as in ages. And yet the invention of young men is more lively than that of old, and imaginations stream into their minds better, and as it were more divinely. Natures that have much heat, and great and violent desires and perturbations, are not ripe for action till they have passed the meridian of their years: as it was with Julius Caesar, and Septimius Severus. Of the latter of whom it is said, *Juventutem egit erroribus, imo furoribus, plenam*:[1] and yet he was the ablest emperor, almost, of all the list. But reposed[2] natures may do well in youth. As it is seen in Augustus Caesar, Cosmus, Duke of Florence,[3] Gaston de Foix,[4] and others. On the other side, heat and vivacity in age is an excellent composition[5] for business. Young men are fitter to invent than to judge, fitter for execution than for counsel, and fitter for new projects than for settled business. For the experience of age, in things that fall within the compass of it, directeth them, but in new things abuseth[6] them. The errors of young men are the ruin of business; but the errors of aged men amount but to this, that more might have been done, or sooner. Young men, in the conduct and manage[7] of actions, embrace more than they can hold; stir more than they can quiet; fly to the end, without consideration of the means and degrees; pursue some few principles which they have chanced upon absurdly; care not to innovate,[8] which draws unknown inconveniences; use extreme remedies at first; and, that which doubleth all errors, will not acknowledge or retract them; like an unready horse that will neither

Texts: MS, 1612, 1625

1. He passed a youth full of folly, or rather of madness (from Spartianus, *Life of Severus*, II).   2. Calm, settled.   3. Cosimo de' Medici, d. 1574.
4. Duke of Nemours, nephew of Louis XII of France; he died at the battle of Ravenna in 1512.   5. Temperament.   6. Misdirects.   7. Management.
8. Are not careful about changing things.

stop nor turn. Men of age object too much, consult too long, adventure too little, repent too soon, and seldom drive business home to the full period,[9] but content themselves with a mediocrity of success. Certainly it is good to compound employments of both; for that will be good for the present, because the virtues of either age may correct the defects of both; and good for succession, that young men may be learners while men in age are actors; and, lastly, good for extern[10] accidents, because authority followeth old men, and favour and popularity youth. But for the moral part, perhaps youth will have the pre-eminence, as age hath for the politic. A certain rabbin, upon the text, *Your young men shall see visions, and your old men shall dream dreams*,[11] inferreth that young men are admitted nearer to God than old, because vision is a clearer revelation than a dream. And certainly, the more a man drinketh of the world, the more it intoxicateth; and age doth profit rather in the powers of understanding than in the virtues of the will and affections. There be some have an over-early ripeness in their years, which fadeth betimes. These are, first, such as have brittle wits, the edge whereof is soon turned; such as was Hermogenes the rhetorician,[12] whose books are exceeding subtle, who afterwards waxed stupid. A second sort is of those that have some natural dispositions which have better grace in youth than in age, such as is a fluent and luxuriant speech, which becomes youth well, but not age: so Tully[13] saith of Hortensius,[14] *Idem manebat, neque idem docebat*.[15] The third is of such as take too high a strain at the first, and are magnanimous more than tract[16] of years can uphold. As was Scipio Africanus,[17] of whom Livy saith in effect, *Ultima primis cedebant*.[18]

9. Completion.   10. External.

11. Joel 2.28. The *rabbin*, or rabbi, is Abravanel.

12. Greek rhetorician of the second century A.D. He is said to have lost his memory at the age of twenty-five.   13. Cicero.

14. Roman orator, at one time a rival of Cicero.

15. He remained the same when the same (style) no longer became him (Cicero, *Brutus*, XCV).   16. Length.

17. Roman general, d. 183 B.C. According to Livy, *History*, XXXVIII.53, Scipio was more suited to war than the peaceful times of his later years.

18. His last actions were not equal to his first (from Ovid, *Heroides*, IX.23).

43.

Of Beauty

Virtue[1] is like a rich stone, best plain set: and surely virtue is best in a body that is comely, though not of delicate features, and that hath rather dignity of presence than beauty of aspect. Neither is it almost[2] seen, that very beautiful persons are otherwise of great virtue, as if nature were rather busy not to err, than in labour to produce excellency. And therefore they prove accomplished,[3] but not of great spirit, and study rather behaviour than virtue. But this holds not always; for Augustus Caesar, Titus Vespasianus, Philip le Bel of France,[4] Edward the Fourth of England, Alcibiades of Athens,[5] Ismael the Sophy of Persia,[6] were all high and great spirits, and yet the most beautiful men of their times. In beauty, that of favour is more than that of colour, and that of decent and gracious motion more than that of favour.[7] That is the best part of beauty[8] which a picture cannot express; no, nor the first sight of the life.[9] There is no excellent beauty that hath not some strangeness in the proportion. A man cannot tell whether Apelles[10] or Albert Dürer were the more trifler; whereof the one would make a personage by geometrical proportions,[11] the other, by taking the best parts out of

Texts: MS, 1612, 1625

    1. Excellence of any kind (not merely moral virtue). Elsewhere Bacon notes that 'virtue is nothing but inward beauty' and 'beauty nothing but outward virtue' (Works, IV.473).   2. Generally.

    3. They prove to be accomplished in outward attainments.

    4. Philip the Fair, King of France, d. 1314.

    5. Athenian general and statesman, d. 404 B.C.

    6. The first Shah of Persia (Iran), d. 1524.

    7. In beauty, features and countenance matter more than colouring, and a seemly and graceful demeanour is more important than the features.

    8. i.e. the seemly and graceful behaviour.

    9. The reality, the person who is depicted.

    10. Greek painter, fourth century B.C. It was not Apelles but Zeuxis, an earlier artist, who, when he wished to paint an ideal face, chose five beautiful girls as his models (see Cicero, On Invention, II.1).

    11. In his treatise Four Books on Human Proportion, Dürer expounded the theory that geometrical laws could be used to depict the human body.

divers faces to make one excellent. Such personages, I think, would please nobody but the painter that made them. Not but I think a painter may make a better face than ever was, but he must do it by a kind of felicity (as a musician that maketh an excellent air in music), and not by rule. A man shall see faces that, if you examine them part by part, you shall find never a good, and yet all together do well. If it be true that the principal part of beauty is in decent motion, certainly it is no marvel though persons in years seem many times[12] more amiable: *pulchrorum autumnus pulcher;*[13] for no youth can be comely but by pardon, and considering the youth as to make up the comeliness.[14] Beauty is as summer fruits, which are easy to corrupt, and cannot last; and for the most part it makes a dissolute youth, and an age a little out of countenance: but yet certainly again, if it light well,[15] it maketh virtues shine, and vices blush.

12. Often seem.

13. The autumn of the beautiful is beautiful (a saying of Euripides, preserved in Plutarch, *Alcibiades*, I.3, and recorded by Bacon in his *Apophthegms*, 145: see *Works*, VII.145).

14. For no youth can be regarded as comely unless it is forgiven what it lacks in grace, and the youthfulness itself be allowed to make up for what is lacking.

15. If it alights on a worthy person.

44.

Of Deformity

Deformed persons are commonly even with nature: for as nature hath done ill by them, so do they by nature, being for the most part (as the Scripture saith) *void of natural affection;*[1] and so they have their revenge of nature. Certainly there is a consent between the body and the mind, and *where nature erreth in the one, she ventureth in the other: Ubi peccat in uno, periclitatur in altero.*[2] But because there is in man an election[3] touching the frame of his mind, and a necessity in the frame of his body, the stars of natural inclination are sometimes obscured by the sun of discipline and virtue. Therefore it is good to consider of deformity, not as a sign, which is more deceivable,[4] but as a cause, which seldom faileth of the effect. Whosoever hath anything fixed in his person that doth induce contempt, hath also a perpetual spur in himself to rescue and deliver himself from scorn. Therefore all deformed persons are extreme bold – first, as in their own defence, as being exposed to scorn, but in process of time, by a general habit. Also, it stirreth in them industry, and especially of this kind, to watch and observe the weakness of others, that they may have somewhat to repay. Again, in their superiors, it quencheth jealousy towards them, as persons that they think they may at pleasure despise; and it layeth their competitors and emulators asleep, as never believing they should be in possibility of advancement, till they see them in possession. So that upon the matter,[5] in a great wit[6] deformity is an advantage to rising. Kings in ancient times (and at this present in some countries) were wont to put great trust in eunuchs, because they that are envious towards all are more obnoxious and officious[7] towards one. But yet their trust towards them hath rather been as to good spials[8]

Texts: MS, 1612, 1625

1. The phrase, but not the discussion of deformity, is in Romans 1.31.
2. While she errs in the one, she runs a risk in the other.   3. Choice.
4. Deceptive.   5. On the whole.   6. Intellect.
7. Submissive and dutiful.   8. Spies.

and good whisperers than good magistrates and officers. And much like is the reason[9] of deformed persons. Still the ground is,[10] they will, if they be of spirit, seek to free themselves from scorn, which must be either by virtue or malice. And therefore let it not be marvelled if sometimes they prove excellent persons; as was Agesilaus,[11] Zanger the son of Solyman,[12] Aesop,[13] Gasca, President of Peru;[14] and Socrates[15] may go likewise amongst them, with others.

9. Condition.

10. In both cases, with eunuchs and deformed persons, the principle is the same.

11. King of Sparta, fourth century B.C., who inflicted defeats on the Persians. He was deformed and lame.

12. Zanger, son of Solyman the Magnificent, Sultan of Turkey, was said to have committed suicide, in about 1553, on learning that his brother Mustapha had been executed by Solyman. He was known as the Crooked.

13. In an unreliable medieval biography, Aesop is alleged to have been ugly and deformed.

14. Pedro de la Gasca, who put down the rebellion of Pizarro in Peru in 1547. He is said to have been awkward and disproportioned, with limbs too long for his body.

15. Socrates was ugly, but not deformed.

45.
Of Building

Houses are built to live in, and not to look on; therefore let use be preferred before uniformity, except where both may be had. Leave the goodly fabrics of houses, for beauty only, to the enchanted palaces of the poets; who build them with small cost. He that builds a fair house upon an ill seat,[1] committeth himself to prison. Neither do I reckon it an ill seat only where the air is unwholesome, but likewise where the air is unequal. As you shall see many fine seats set upon a knap[2] of ground, environed with higher hills round about it, whereby the heat of the sun is pent in and the wind gathereth as in troughs; so as you shall have, and that suddenly, as great diversity of heat and cold as if you dwelt in several places. Neither is it ill air only that maketh an ill seat, but ill ways, ill markets, and (if you will consult with Momus) ill neighbours.[3] I speak not of many more: want of water; want of wood, shade, and shelter; want of fruitfulness, and mixture of grounds of several natures; want of prospect; want of level grounds; want of places at some near distance for sports of hunting, hawking, and races; too near the sea, too remote; having the commodity[4] of navigable rivers, or the discommodity[5] of their overflowing; too far off from great cities, which may hinder business, or too near them, which lurcheth[6] all provisions, and maketh everything dear; where a man hath a great living laid together, and where he is scanted.[7] All which, as it is impossible perhaps to find together, so it is good to know them and think of them, that a man may take as many as he can, and, if he have several dwellings, that he sort[8] them so, that what he wanteth in the one he may find in the other. Lucullus[9] answered Pompey

Text: 1625

1. Site.   2. Knoll.

3. Momus, the god of carping, criticized Athena's house because it had no wheels to move it away from bad neighbours (*Fables of Aesop*, Penguin translation, No. 155, p. 159).   4. Advantage.   5. Disadvantage.   6. Swallows up.

7. Short of space *or* supplies.   8. Arrange.

9. Roman general, first century B.C. The exchange with Pompey is recorded by Plutarch, *Lucullus*, XXXIX.4.

well, who, when he saw his stately galleries and rooms so large and
lightsome in one of his houses, said, *Surely an excellent place for
summer, but how do you in winter?* Lucullus answered, *Why, do
you not think me as wise as some fowl are, that ever change their
abode towards the winter?*

To pass from the seat to the house itself; we will do as Cicero doth
in the orator's art, who writes books *De Oratore*,[10] and a book he
entitles *Orator*, whereof the former delivers the precepts of the art,
and the latter the perfection.[11] We will therefore describe a princely
palace, making a brief model thereof. For it is strange to see, now in
Europe, such huge buildings as the Vatican and Escurial[12] and some
others be, and yet scarce a very fair room in them.

First, therefore, I say you cannot have a perfect palace except you
have two several[13] sides: a side for the banquet, as is spoken of in the
book of Hester,[14] and a side for the household; the one for feasts and
triumphs,[15] and the other for dwelling. I understand both these
sides to be not only returns,[16] but parts of the front, and to be
uniform without, though severally partitioned within; and to be on
both sides of a great and stately tower in the midst of the front, that,
as it were, joineth them together on either hand. I would have on the
side of the banquet, in front, one only goodly room above stairs, of
some forty foot high, and under it a room for a dressing or preparing
place at times of triumphs. On the other side, which is the household side, I wish it divided at the first into a hall and a chapel (with a
partition between), both of good state and bigness; and those not to
go all the length, but to have at the further end a winter and a
summer parlour, both fair. And under these rooms, a fair and large
cellar, sunk under ground, and likewise some privy kitchens, with
butteries and pantries, and the like. As for the tower, I would have it
two stories, of eighteen foot high apiece, above the two wings; and a
goodly leads upon the top,[17] railed with statuas[18] interposed; and
the same tower to be divided into rooms, as shall be thought fit. The
stairs likewise to the upper rooms, let them be upon a fair open
newel,[19] and finely railed in with images of wood cast into a brass

---

10. On the orator.   11. Practice.
12. The great palace of the Spanish kings, near Madrid. Begun by Philip II in 1563.
13. Separate.   14. Esther 1.5.   15. Shows, magnificent spectacles.
16. Wings of the house.   17. A fine leaded roof.   18. Statues.
19. A *newel* is the central column of a winding staircase; an *open newel* is where
there is no column and the stairs are pinned to the wall.

colour; and a very fair landing place at the top. But this to be, if you do not point[20] any of the lower rooms for a dining place of servants. For otherwise you shall have the servants' dinner after your own: for the steam of it will come up as in a tunnel. And so much for the front. Only, I understand the height of the first stairs to be sixteen foot, which is the height of the lower room.

Beyond this front is there to be a fair court, but three sides of it of a far lower building than the front. And in all the four corners of that court, fair staircases, cast into turrets on the outside, and not within the row of buildings themselves. But those towers are not to be of the height of the front, but rather proportionable to the lower building. Let the court not be paved, for that striketh up a great heat in summer and much cold in winter. But only some side alleys, with a cross, and the quarters to graze, being kept shorn, but not too near shorn.[21] The row of return, on the banquet side, let it be all stately galleries, in which galleries let there be three or five fine cupolas in the length of it, placed at equal distance, and fine coloured windows of several works. On the household side, chambers of presence[22] and ordinary entertainments, with some bedchambers; and let all three sides be a double house,[23] without thorough-lights on the sides,[24] that you may have rooms from the sun, both for forenoon and afternoon. Cast it also that you may have rooms both for summer and winter, shady for summer, and warm for winter. You shall have sometimes fair houses so full of glass that one cannot tell where to become[25] to be out of the sun or cold. For inbowed windows, I hold them of good use (in cities, indeed, upright[26] do better, in respect of the uniformity towards the street), for they be pretty retiring places for conference; and besides, they keep both the wind and sun off, for that which would strike almost thorough the room doth scarce pass the window. But let them be but few, four in the court, on the sides only.

Beyond this court, let there be an inward[27] court of the same square and height, which is to be environed with the garden on all sides; and in the inside, cloistered on all sides, upon decent and

20. Appoint.
21. Paths along each side of the court, with two paths crossing at right angles at the centre and dividing the court into four quarters, each of which is turfed, with its grass kept short.   22. Rooms for receiving guests.   23. Have rooms back and front.
24. Without windows which, by their position or size, allow light to reach right into the room.   25. Place oneself.
26. Windows flush with the front of the house, not projecting.   27. Inner.

beautiful arches, as high as the first storey. On the under storey, towards the garden, let it be turned to a grotta, or place of shade or estivation;[28] and only have opening and windows towards the garden; and be level upon the floor, no whit sunk under ground, to avoid all dampishness. And let there be a fountain, or some fair work of statuas, in the midst of this court; and to be paved as the other court was. These buildings to be for privy lodgings on both sides, and the end for privy galleries. Whereof you must foresee that one of them be for an infirmary, if the prince or any special person should be sick, with chambers, bedchamber, antecamera, and recamera[29] joining to it. This upon the second storey. Upon the ground storey, a fair gallery, open, upon pillars; and upon the third storey likewise, an open gallery upon pillars, to take the prospect and freshness of the garden. At both corners of the further side, by way of return, let there be two delicate or rich cabinets,[30] daintily paved, richly hanged, glazed with crystalline glass, and a rich cupola in the midst; and all other elegancy that may be thought upon. In the upper gallery too, I wish that there may be, if the place will yield it, some fountains running in divers places from the wall, with some fine avoidances.[31] And thus much for the model of the palace, save that you must have, before you come to the front, three courts. A green court plain, with a wall about it; a second court of the same, but more garnished, with little turrets, or rather embellishments, upon the wall; and a third court, to make a square with the front, but not to be built, nor yet enclosed with a naked wall, but enclosed with terraces, leaded aloft, and fairly garnished, on the three sides; and cloistered on the inside, with pillars and not with arches below. As for offices, let them stand at distance, with some low galleries, to pass from them to the palace itself.

28. A cool place away from the heat of the summer.
29. Ante-room and a room for withdrawing to.   30. Private rooms.
31. Outlets.

46.
Of Gardens

God Almighty first planted a garden. And indeed it is the purest of human pleasures. It is the greatest refreshment to the spirits of man, without which buildings and palaces are but gross handy-works: and a man shall ever see that when ages grow to civility[1] and elegancy, men come to build stately sooner than to garden finely, as if gardening were the greater perfection. I do hold it, in the royal ordering of gardens, there ought to be gardens for all the months in the year, in which severally things of beauty may be then in season. For December and January and the latter part of November, you must take such things as are green all winter: holly, ivy, bays, juniper, cypress-trees, yew, pineapple-trees;[2] fir-trees; rosemary, lavender; periwinkle, the white, the purple, and the blue; german-der, flags; orange-trees, lemon-trees; and myrtles, if they be stoved;[3] and sweet marjoram, warm set.[4] There followeth, for the latter part of January and February, the mezereon-tree, which then blossoms; crocus vernus,[5] both the yellow and the grey; primroses, anemones, the early tulippa, hyacinthus orientalis, chamaïris,[6] fritillaria. For March, there come violets, specially the single blue, which are the earliest; the yellow daffodil, the daisy, the almond-tree in blossom, the peach-tree in blossom, the cornelian-tree in blossom, sweet-briar. In April follow the double white violet, the wall-flower, the stock-gillyflower, the cowslip, flower-de-luces, and lilies of all natures; rosemary flowers, the tulippa, the double peony, the pale daffodil, the French honeysuckle; the cherry-tree in blos-som, the damson and plum-trees in blossom, the white-thorn in leaf, the lilac-tree. In May and June come pinks of all sorts, specially the blush pink; roses of all kinds, except the musk, which comes later; honeysuckles, strawberries, bugloss, columbine; the French

Text: 1625

1. Civilization.   2. Pine trees.   3. Kept in hot-houses.
4. Planted in a warm, sunny place.   5. Spring crocus.   6. Dwarf iris.

marigold, flos Africanus;[7] cherry-tree in fruit, ribes,[8] figs in fruit,
rasps,[9] vine-flowers, lavender in flowers; the sweet satyrian, with
the white flower; herba muscaria,[10] lilium convallium,[11] the apple-
tree in blossom. In July come gillyflowers of all varieties, musk-
roses, the lime-tree in blossom, early pears and plums in fruit,
jennetings, codlins.[12] In August come plums of all sorts in fruit,
pears, apricots, barberries, filberts, musk-melons, monk-hoods of
all colours. In September come grapes, apples, poppies of all colours,
peaches, melocotones,[13] nectarines, cornelians, wardens,[14] quinces.
In October and the beginning of November come services, medlars,
bullaces, roses cut or removed[15] to come late, hollyhocks, and such
like. These particulars are for the climate of London; but my
meaning is perceived, that you may have *ver perpetuum*,[16] as the
place affords.

And because the breath of flowers is far sweeter in the air (where
it comes and goes like the warbling of music) than in the hand,
therefore nothing is more fit for that delight than to know what be
the flowers and plants that do best perfume the air. Roses, damask
and red, are fast flowers of their smells,[17] so that you may walk by a
whole row of them, and find nothing of their sweetness, yea, though
it be in a morning's dew. Bays likewise yield no smell as they grow,
rosemary little, nor sweet marjoram. That which above all others
yields the sweetest smell in the air is the violet, specially the white
double violet, which comes twice a year, about the middle of April,
and about Bartholomew-tide.[18] Next to that is the musk-rose. Then
the strawberry-leaves dying, with[19] a most excellent cordial smell.
Then the flower of the vines; it is a little dust, like the dust of a bent,
which grows upon the cluster in the first coming forth. Then
sweet-briar. Then wall-flowers, which are very delightful to be set
under a parlour or lower chamber window. Then pinks and gillyflowers, specially the matted pink and clove gillyflower. Then the
flowers of the lime-tree. Then the honeysuckles, so they be somewhat afar off. Of bean-flowers I speak not, because they are field

---

7. A kind of marigold (here perhaps identical with the *French marigold*).
8. Currants.   9. Raspberries.   10. Grape-hyacinth.
11. Lily of the valley.   12. Kinds of early apple and cooking-apple.
13. Large peaches.   14. Kind of pears.   15. Transplanted.
16. A perpetual spring.
17. Flowers which retain their smells.   18. St Bartholomew's day, 24 August.
19. The 1625 edition reads *which* instead of *with*.

flowers. But those which perfume the air most delightfully, not passed by as the rest, but being trodden upon and crushed, are three: that is, burnet, wild thyme, and water-mints. Therefore you are to set whole alleys[20] of them, to have the pleasure when you walk or tread.

For gardens (speaking of those which are indeed prince-like, as we have done of buildings), the contents ought not well to be under thirty acres of ground, and to be divided into three parts: a green in the entrance; a heath or desert[21] in the going forth; and the main garden in the midst; besides alleys on both sides. And I like well that four acres of ground be assigned to the green, six to the heath, four and four to either side, and twelve to the main garden. The green hath two pleasures: the one, because nothing is more pleasant to the eye than green grass kept finely shorn; the other, because it will give you a fair alley in the midst by which you may go in front upon a stately hedge, which is to enclose the garden. But because the alley will be long, and, in great heat of the year or day, you ought not to buy the shade in the garden by going in the sun thorough the green, therefore you are, of either side the green, to plant a covert alley upon carpenter's work, about twelve foot in height, by which you may go in shade into the garden. As for the making of knots[22] or figures with divers coloured earths, that they may lie under the windows of the house on that side which the garden stands, they be but toys: you may see as good sights many times in tarts. The garden is best to be square, encompassed on all the four sides with a stately arched hedge, the arches to be upon pillars of carpenter's work, of some ten foot high and six foot broad, and the spaces between of the same dimension with the breadth of the arch. Over the arches let there be an entire[23] hedge of some four foot high, framed also upon carpenter's work; and upon the upper hedge, over every arch, a little turret, with a belly, enough to receive a cage of birds; and over every space between the arches some other little figure, with broad plates of round coloured glass, gilt, for the sun to play upon. But this hedge I intend to be raised upon a bank, not steep, but gently slope,[24] of some six foot, set all with flowers. Also I understand that this square of the garden should not be the whole breadth of the ground, but to leave on either side ground enough for

20. Paths.   21. Ground left in a wild, uncultivated state.
22. Plots of earth.   23. Continuous.   24. Sloping.

diversity of side alleys, unto which the two covert alleys of the green may deliver you. But there must be no alleys with hedges at either end of this great enclosure: not at the hither end, for letting[25] your prospect upon this fair hedge from the green; nor at the further end, for letting your prospect from the hedge, through the arches, upon the heath.

For the ordering of the ground within the great hedge, I leave it to variety of device, advising nevertheless that whatsoever form you cast it into, first, it be not too busy or full of work. Wherein I, for my part, do not like images cut out in juniper or other garden stuff: they be for children. Little low hedges, round, like welts,[26] with some pretty pyramides, I like well; and in some places, fair columns upon frames of carpenter's work. I would also have the alleys spacious and fair. You may have closer alleys upon the side grounds, but none in the main garden. I wish also, in the very middle, a fair mount, with three ascents and alleys, enough for four to walk abreast; which I would have to be perfect circles, without any bulwarks or embossments;[27] and the whole mount to be thirty foot high; and some fine banqueting-house, with some chimneys[28] neatly cast, and without too much glass.

For fountains, they are a great beauty and refreshment; but pools mar all, and make the garden unwholesome and full of flies and frogs. Fountains I intend to be of two natures: the one, that sprinkleth or spouteth water, the other, a fair receipt[29] of water, of some thirty or forty foot square, but without fish or slime or mud. For the first, the ornaments of images gilt or of marble, which are in use, do well: but the main matter is so to convey the water as it never stay, either in the bowls or in the cistern; that the water be never by rest discoloured, green or red or the like, or gather any mossiness or putrefaction. Besides that, it is to be cleansed every day by the hand. Also some steps up to it, and some fine pavement about it, doth well. As for the other kind of fountain, which we may call a bathing-pool, it may admit much curiosity[30] and beauty, wherewith we will not trouble ourselves: as that the bottom be finely paved, and with images, the sides likewise; and withal embellished with

25. Because it will obstruct.   26. Borders (like the edging on a garment).

27. i.e. each of the three pathways is to form a perfect circle at a different stage around the mount, with nothing jutting out to break up the line of the path. Access to each circle is by an *ascent* (steps, presumably).   28. Fireplaces.

29. Receptacle.   30. Elaborate workmanship.

coloured glass, and such things of lustre; encompassed also with fine rails of low statuas.[31] But the main point is the same which we mentioned in the former kind of fountain, which is that the water be in perpetual motion, fed by a water higher than the pool and delivered into it by fair spouts, and then discharged away under ground by some equality of bores,[32] that it stay little. And for fine devices, of arching water without spilling, and making it rise in several forms (of feathers, drinking-glasses, canopies, and the like), they be pretty things to look on, but nothing to health and sweetness.

For the heath, which was the third part of our plot, I wish it to be framed, as much as may be, to a natural wildness. Trees I would have none in it, but some thickets, made only of sweet-briar and honeysuckle, and some wild vine amongst; and the ground set with violets, strawberries, and primroses. For these are sweet, and prosper in the shade. And these to be in the heath, here and there, not in any order. I like also little heaps, in the nature of mole-hills (such as are in wild heaths), to be set, some with wild thyme; some with pinks; some with germander, that gives a good flower to the eye; some with periwinkle; some with violets; some with straw-berries; some with cowslips; some with daisies; some with red roses; some with lilium convallium; some with sweet-williams red; some with bear's-foot; and the like low flowers, being withal sweet and sightly. Part of which heaps to be with standards of little bushes pricked[33] upon their top, and part without. The standards to be roses, juniper, holly, barberries (but here and there, because of the smell of their blossom), red currants, gooseberries, rosemary, bays, sweet-briar, and such like. But these standards to be kept with cutting, that they grow not out of course.[34]

For the side grounds, you are to fill them with variety of alleys, private, to give a full shade, some of them, wheresoever the sun be. You are to frame some of them likewise for shelter, that when the wind blows sharp you may walk as in a gallery. And those alleys must be likewise hedged at both ends, to keep out the wind; and these closer alleys must be ever finely gravelled, and no grass, because of going wet.[35] In many of these alleys likewise, you are to

31. Statues.
32. i.e. through outlet pipes of the same bore as the spouts (so that the water may drain off as fast as it goes in).   33. Planted.
34. Irregularly.   35. For the times when you have to walk in the wet.

set fruit-trees of all sorts, as well upon the walls as in ranges. And this would be generally observed, that the borders wherein you plant your fruit-trees be fair and large, and low, and not steep, and set with fine flowers, but thin and sparingly, lest they deceive the trees.[36] At the end of both the side grounds, I would have a mount of some pretty height, leaving the wall of the enclosures breast high, to look abroad into the fields.

For the main garden, I do not deny but there should be some fair alleys ranged on both sides with fruit-trees, and some pretty tufts of fruit-trees, and arbours with seats, set in some decent order; but these to be by no means set too thick, but to leave the main garden so as it be not close, but the air open and free. For as for shade, I would have you rest upon the alleys of the side grounds, there to walk, if you be disposed, in the heat of the year or day; but to make account that the main garden is for the more temperate parts of the year, and, in the heat of summer, for the morning and the evening, or overcast days.

For aviaries, I like them not, except they be of that largeness as they may be turfed, and have living plants and bushes set in them; that the birds may have more scope and natural nestling, and that no foulness appear in the floor of the aviary. So I have made a platform[37] of a princely garden, partly by precept, partly by drawing, not a model, but some general lines of it; and in this I have spared for no cost. But it is nothing for great princes, that for the most part taking advice with workmen, with no less cost set their things together; and sometimes add statuas and such things for state and magnificence, but nothing to the true pleasure of a garden.

36. Rob the trees of nourishment.   37. Plan.

47.

Of Negotiating

It is generally better to deal by speech than by letter, and by the mediation of a third than by a man's self. Letters are good when a man would draw an answer by letter back again, or when it may serve for a man's justification afterwards to produce his own letter, or where it may be danger to be interrupted or heard by pieces. To deal in person is good when a man's face breedeth regard, as commonly with inferiors, or in tender[1] cases, where a man's eye upon the countenance of him with whom he speaketh may give him a direction how far to go; and generally, where a man will reserve to himself liberty either to disavow or to expound. In choice of instruments, it is better to choose men of a plainer sort, that are like to do that that is committed to them, and to report back again faithfully the success,[2] than those that are cunning[3] to contrive out of other men's business somewhat to grace themselves, and will help the matter in report for satisfaction sake.[4] Use also such persons as affect[5] the business wherein they are employed, for that quickeneth much; and such as are fit for the matter, as bold men for expostulation, fair-spoken men for persuasion, crafty men for inquiry and observation, froward and absurd[6] men for business that doth not well bear out itself. Use also such as have been lucky and prevailed before in things wherein you have employed them; for that breeds confidence, and they will strive to maintain their prescription.[7] It is better to sound a person with whom one deals afar off, than to fall upon the point at first, except you mean to surprise him by some short question. It is better dealing with men in appetite,[8] than with those that are where they would be. If a man deal with another upon conditions, the start or first performance is

Texts: 1597, MS, 1612, 1625

1. Delicate.   2. Outcome.   3. Who know how.
4. Report the outcome as better than it really is (in order to please their employer).   5. Like.   6. Unyielding.
7. Their claim to be considered lucky.   8. Keen for advancement.

all;[9] which a man cannot reasonably demand, except either the nature of the thing be such which must go before; or else a man can persuade the other party that he shall still need him in some other thing; or else that he be counted the honester man. All practice is to discover, or to work.[10] Men discover themselves in trust, in passion, at unawares, and of necessity, when they would have somewhat done and cannot find an apt pretext. If you would work any man, you must either know his nature and fashions,[11] and so lead him; or his ends, and so persuade him; or his weakness and disadvantages, and so awe him; or those that have interest in him, and so govern him. In dealing with cunning persons, we must ever consider their ends, to interpret their speeches; and it is good to say little to them, and that which they least look for. In all negotiations of difficulty, a man may not look to sow and reap at once, but must prepare business, and so ripen it by degrees.

9. All-important.
10. The purpose of all smart dealing is to find out things about men, or to manipulate them. 11. Habits.

48.

Of Followers and Friends

Costly followers are not to be liked, lest while a man maketh his train[1] longer, he make his wings shorter. I reckon to be costly, not them alone which charge the purse, but which are wearisome and importune[2] in suits. Ordinary followers ought to challenge no higher conditions than countenance, recommendation, and protection from wrongs. Factious followers are worse to be liked, which follow not upon affection to him with whom they range themselves, but upon discontentment conceived against some other; whereupon commonly ensueth that ill intelligence[3] that we many times see between great personages. Likewise glorious[4] followers, who make themselves as trumpets of the commendation of those they follow, are full of inconvenience, for they taint business through want of secrecy, and they export honour from a man and make him a return in envy. There is a kind of followers likewise which are dangerous, being indeed espials,[5] which inquire the secrets of the house, and bear tales of them to others. Yet such men, many times, are in great favour, for they are officious,[6] and commonly exchange tales. The following by certain estates[7] of men, answerable to[8] that which a great person himself professeth (as of soldiers to him that hath been employed in the wars, and the like), hath ever been a thing civil,[9] and well taken even in monarchies; so it be without too much pomp or popularity. But the most honourable kind of following is to be followed as one that apprehendeth[10] to advance virtue and desert in all sorts of persons. And yet, where there is no eminent odds in sufficiency,[11] it is better to take with the more passable[12] than with the more able. And besides, to speak truth, in base times active men

Texts: 1597, MS, 1612, 1625

1. Body of followers; but also the word for a peacock's tail.
2. Importunate.   3. Misunderstanding.   4. Boastful.   5. Spies.
6. Exact in the performance of their duties.   7. Orders, classes.
8. Corresponding to.   9. Seemly.   10. As someone who intends.
11. No marked difference in ability.   12. Mediocre.

are of more use than virtuous.[13] It is true that in government it is
good to use men of one rank equally, for to countenance some
extraordinarily is to make them insolent, and the rest discontent,
because they may claim a due.[14] But contrariwise, in favour, to use
men with much difference and election[15] is good, for it maketh
the persons preferred more thankful, and the rest more officious,
because all is of favour. It is good discretion not to make too much of
any man at the first, because one cannot hold out that proportion.
To be governed (as we call it) by one, is not safe, for it shows softness
and gives a freedom to scandal and disreputation;[16] for those that
would not censure or speak ill of a man immediately, will talk more
boldly of those that are so great with them, and thereby wound their
honour. Yet to be distracted with many is worse, for it makes men to
be of the last impression,[17] and full of change. To take advice of
some few friends is ever honourable, for *lookers-on many times see
more than gamesters; and the vale best discovereth the hill.* There
is little friendship in the world, and least of all between equals,
which was wont to be magnified.[18] That that is, is between superior
and inferior, whose fortunes may comprehend[19] the one the other.

13. Exceptionally talented ones.
14. Because men of equal rank are entitled, as a right, to be treated impartially.
15. Discrimination.　　16. Disrepute.
17. Under the influence of whatever they have most recently been impressed by, or
have experienced.　　18. Over-praised or exaggerated.　　19. Include.

49.

Of Suitors

Many ill matters and projects are undertaken, and private suits do putrefy the public good. Many good matters are undertaken with bad minds; I mean not only corrupt minds, but crafty minds that intend not performance. Some embrace suits which never mean to deal effectually in them, but if they see there may be life in the matter by some other mean,[1] they will be content to win a thank,[2] or take a second[3] reward, or at least to make use in the meantime of the suitor's hopes. Some take hold of suits only for an occasion to cross some other; or to make an information[4] whereof they could not otherwise have apt pretext, without care what become of the suit when that turn is served; or generally to make other men's business a kind of entertainment[5] to bring in their own. Nay, some undertake suits with a full purpose to let them fall, to the end to gratify the adverse party or competitor. Surely there is in some sort a right in every suit;[6] either a right of equity, if it be a suit of controversy, or a right of desert, if it be a suit of petition. If affection lead a man to favour the wrong side in justice, let him rather use his countenance to compound the matter than to carry it. If affection lead a man to favour the less worthy in desert, let him do it without depraving or disabling[7] the better deserver. In suits which a man doth not well understand, it is good to refer them to some friend of trust and judgement, that may report whether he may deal in them with honour; but let him choose well his referendaries,[8] for else he may be led by the nose. Suitors are so distasted[9] with delays and abuses, that plain dealing, in denying to deal in suits at first, and reporting the success[10] barely, and in challenging no more thanks than one hath deserved, is grown not only honourable, but also gracious. In

---

Texts: 1597, MS, 1612, 1625

1. Means.   2. Thanks.   3. Secondary, incidental.
4. Gain information about something, *or* make something known.
5. Prelude.   6. A lawsuit.   7. Without slandering or disparaging.
8. Those to whom he refers the matter.   9. Offended.   10. Result.

suits of favour, the first coming ought to take little place.[11] So far forth consideration may be had of his trust,[12] that if intelligence of the matter could not otherwise have been had but by him, advantage be not taken of the note[13] but the party left to his other means,[14] and in some sort recompensed for his discovery.[15] To be ignorant of the value of a suit is simplicity; as well as to be ignorant of the right thereof is want of conscience. Secrecy in suits is a great mean[16] of obtaining, for voicing them to be in forwardness[17] may discourage some kind of suitors, but doth quicken and awake others. But timing of the suit is the principal. Timing, I say, not only in respect of the person that should grant it, but in respect of those which are like to cross it. Let a man, in the choice of his mean,[18] rather choose the fittest mean than the greatest mean, and rather them that deal in certain things than those that are general.[19] The reparation of a denial[20] is sometimes equal to the first grant, if a man show himself neither dejected nor discontented. *Iniquum petas, ut aequum feras*[21] is a good rule where a man hath strength of favour, but otherwise a man were better rise in his suit,[22] for he that would have ventured at first to have lost the suitor,[23] will not in the conclusion lose both the suitor and his own former favour. Nothing is thought so easy a request to a great person as his letter, and yet if it be not in a good cause it is so much out of his reputation. There are no worse instruments than these general contrivers[24] of suits; for they are but a kind of poison and infection to public proceedings.

11. Priority in presenting a petition ought to be of small significance.

12. i.e. the petitioner's trust.   13. Information.

14. Means of obtaining the suit.   15. Disclosure.   16. Means.

17. Because giving out that suits are going ahead successfully.

18. The person to whom he entrusts the care of his suit.

19. Those who concern themselves with a few definite things, rather than everything in sight.

20. The gaining of one's suit, in a renewed petition, after it has first been denied.

21. Ask for more than what is just, so that you may get your due (Quintilian, *The Education of an Orator*, IV.5.16).

22. To increase slowly the demands he is making.

23. Run the risk, at the beginning, of losing the suitor.   24. Fixers, schemers.

50.
Of Studies

Studies serve for delight, for ornament, and for ability.[1] Their chief use for delight, is in privateness and retiring;[2] for ornament, is in discourse; and for ability, is in the judgement and disposition of business. For expert men[3] can execute, and perhaps judge of particulars, one by one; but the general counsels, and the plots and marshalling of affairs come best from those that are learned. To spend too much time in studies is sloth; to use them too much for ornament is affectation; to make judgement wholly by their rules is the humour of a scholar. They perfect nature, and are perfected by experience, for natural abilities are like natural plants that need proyning[4] by study; and studies themselves do give forth directions too much at large, except they be bounded in by experience. Crafty[5] men contemn studies, simple men admire them, and wise men use them; for they teach not their own use; but that is a wisdom without them and above them, won by observation. Read not to contradict and confute; nor to believe and take for granted; nor to find talk and discourse; but to weigh and consider. Some books are to be tasted, others to be swallowed, and some few to be chewed and digested: that is, some books are to be read only in parts; others to be read, but not curiously;[6] and some few to be read wholly and with diligence and attention. Some books also may be read by deputy, and extracts made of them by others, but that would be only in the less important arguments, and the meaner sort of books; else distilled books are like common distilled waters, flashy[7] things. Reading maketh a full man; conference a ready man; and writing an exact man. And therefore, if a man write little, he had need have a great memory; if he confer little, he had need have a present wit;[8] and if he read little, he had need have much cunning, to seem to know that he doth not.

Texts: 1597, MS, 1612, 1625

1. To make men able.   2. Seclusion.
3. Men who have learned only from experience, not study.   4. Cultivating.
5. Practical (but also, cunning).   6. With great care.   7. Insipid.
8. Ready mind.

Histories make men wise, poets witty,[9] the mathematics subtle, natural philosophy deep, moral grave, logic and rhetoric able to contend. *Abeunt studia in mores.*[10] Nay, there is no stond[11] or impediment in the wit[12] but may be wrought out by fit studies, like as diseases of the body may have appropriate exercises. Bowling is good for the stone and reins;[13] shooting[14] for the lungs and breast; gentle walking for the stomach; riding for the head; and the like. So if a man's wit be wandering, let him study the mathematics; for in demonstrations, if his wit be called away never so little, he must begin again. If his wit be not apt to distinguish or find differences, let him study the Schoolmen,[15] for they are *cymini sectores.*[16] If he be not apt to beat over matters,[17] and to call up one thing to prove and illustrate another, let him study the lawyers' cases. So every defect of the mind may have a special receipt.[18]

9. Ingenious.
10. Studies go to make up a man's character (Ovid, *Heroides*, XV.83).
11. Obstacle.   12. Mind.
13. Playing bowls is good for the bladder and kidneys.   14. Archery.
15. Medieval theologians and academics. See Essay 17, note 7.
16. Hair-splitters.   17. Cover the ground thoroughly.
18. Prescription (for remedy).

51.

Of Faction

Many have an opinion not wise, that for a prince to govern his estate[1] or for a great person to govern his proceedings according to the respect of factions, is a principal part of policy: whereas contrariwise, the chiefest wisdom is either in ordering those things which are general, and wherein men of several[2] factions do nevertheless agree, or in dealing with correspondence to particular persons,[3] one by one. But I say not that the consideration of factions is to be neglected. Mean[4] men, in their rising, must adhere;[5] but great men, that have strength in themselves, were better to maintain themselves indifferent and neutral. Yet even in beginners, to adhere so moderately, as he be[6] a man of the one faction which is most passable with[7] the other, commonly giveth best way. The lower and weaker faction is the firmer in conjunction; and it is often seen that a few that are stiff do tire out a greater number that are more moderate. When one of the factions is extinguished, the remaining subdivideth: as the faction between Lucullus and the rest of the nobles of the senate (which they called *Optimates*[8]) held out a while against the faction of Pompey and Caesar, but when the senate's authority was pulled down, Caesar and Pompey soon after brake. The faction or party of Antonius and Octavianus Caesar against Brutus and Cassius held out likewise for a time, but when Brutus and Cassius were overthrown, then soon after Antonius and Octavianus brake and subdivided. These examples are of wars, but the same holdeth in private factions. And therefore those that are seconds[9] in factions do many times, when the faction subdivideth, prove principals; but many times also they prove ciphers and cashiered, for many a man's strength is in opposition, and when that

Texts: 1597, MS, 1612, 1625

1. State. 2. Different.
3. Dealing in such a way as to suit the natures of individuals.
4. Ordinary. 5. Belong to a faction, or party. 6. So that he may be.
7. Acceptable to. 8. Aristocrats. 9. Subordinates.

faileth, he groweth out of use. It is commonly seen that men once placed take in with the contrary faction to that by which they enter, thinking belike[10] that they have the first sure, and now are ready for a new purchase.[11] The traitor in faction lightly goeth away with it,[12] for when matters have stuck long in balancing, the winning of some one man casteth them,[13] and he getteth all the thanks. The even carriage between two factions proceedeth not always of moderation, but of a trueness to a man's self,[14] with end to make use of both. Certainly in Italy they hold it a little suspect in popes, when they have often in their mouth *Padre commune*,[15] and take it to be a sign of one that meaneth to refer all to the greatness of his own house. Kings had need beware how they side themselves[16] and make themselves as of a faction or party, for leagues within the state are ever pernicious to monarchies; for they raise an obligation paramount to obligation of sovereignty, and make the king *tanquam unus ex nobis*,[17] as was to be seen in the League of France.[18] When factions are carried too high and too violently, it is a sign of weakness in princes, and much to the prejudice both of their authority and business. The motions of factions under kings ought to be like the motions (as the astronomers speak) of the inferior orbs, which may have their proper motions, but yet still are quietly carried by the higher motion of *primum mobile*.[19]

---

10. In all likelihood.   11. Acquisition.
12. Usually comes out of it a winner.   13. Turns the scale.
14. But from putting one's own interest first.   15. Father of all alike.
16. How they take sides.
17. As though he were one of us (from Genesis 3.22).
18. See Essay 15, note 11.   19. See Essay 15, note 12.

52.

Of Ceremonies and Respects[1]

He that is only real[2] had need have exceeding great parts of virtue; as the stone had need to be rich that is set without foil. But if a man mark it well, it is in praise and commendation of men as it is in gettings and gains; for the proverb is true, *that light gains make heavy purses*, for light gains come thick, whereas great come but now and then. So it is true that small matters win great commendation, because they are continually in use and in note, whereas the occasion of any great virtue cometh but on festivals. Therefore it doth much add to a man's reputation, and is (as Queen Isabella[3] said) *like perpetual letters commendatory*, to have good forms.[4] To attain them it almost sufficeth not to despise them, for so shall a man observe them in others; and let him trust himself with the rest. For if he labour too much to express them, he shall lose their grace, which is to be natural and unaffected. Some men's behaviour is like a verse, wherein every syllable is measured: how can a man comprehend great matters, that breaketh[5] his mind too much to small observations? Not to use ceremonies at all is to teach others not to use them again,[6] and so diminisheth respect to himself (especially they be not to be omitted to strangers and formal[7] natures); but the dwelling upon them and exalting them above the moon is not only tedious but doth diminish the faith and credit of him that speaks. And certainly there is a kind of conveying of effectual and imprinting[8] passages amongst compliments, which is of singular use, if a man can hit upon it. Amongst a man's peers, a man shall be sure of familiarity, and therefore it is good a little to keep state. Amongst a man's inferiors, one shall be sure of reverence, and therefore it is good a little to be familiar. He that is too much in anything, so that he giveth another occasion of satiety,

Texts: 1597, MS, 1612, 1625

1. Occasions for showing respect.   2. Sincere and straightforward.
3. Queen Isabella of Castile: her saying is recorded by Tunginius, *Apophtheg-mata*, 1609.   4. Manners.   5. Subdues.   6. In return.
7. Fastidious.   8. Impressive *or* memorable.

maketh himself cheap. To apply one's self to others is good, so it be
with demonstration that a man doth it upon regard and not upon
facility.[9] It is a good precept generally in seconding another, yet to
add somethat of one's own: as,[10] if you will grant his opinion, let it
be with some distinction; if you will follow his motion, let it be with
condition; if you will allow[11] his counsel, let it be with alleging
further reason. Men had need beware how they be too perfect in
compliments, for be they never so sufficient otherwise, their enviers
will be sure to give them that attribute, to the disadvantage of their
greater virtues. It is loss also in business to be too full of respects[12] or
to be too curious[13] in observing times and opportunities. Solomon
saith, *He that considereth the wind shall not sow, and he that
looketh to the clouds shall not reap.*[14] A wise man will make more
opportunities than he finds. Men's behaviour should be like their
apparel, not too strait or point device,[15] but free for exercise or
motion.

---

9. Provided that it is seen to be done out of personal regard, and not out of an
overwillingness to please.   10. For example.   11. Approve.
12. Formalities.   13. Too careful.   14. Ecclesiastes 11.4.   15. Precise.

53.

Of Praise

Praise is the reflection of virtue: but it is as the glass or body which giveth the reflection. If it be from the common people, it is commonly false and naught,[1] and rather followeth vain persons than virtuous. For the common people understand not many excellent virtues. The lowest virtues draw praise from them; the middle virtues work in them astonishment or admiration; but of the highest virtues they have no sense or perceiving at all. But shows, and *species virtutibus similes*,[2] serve best with them. Certainly fame is like a river that beareth up things light and swollen and drowns things weighty and solid. But if persons of quality and judgement concur, then it is (as the Scripture saith), *Nomen bonum instar unguenti fragrantis*:[3] it filleth all round about, and will not easily away. For the odours of ointments are more durable than those of flowers. There be so many false points of praise, that a man may justly hold it a suspect. Some praises proceed merely of flattery; and if he be an ordinary flatterer, he will have[4] certain common attributes[5] which may serve every man; if he be a cunning flatterer, he will follow the arch-flatterer, which is a man's self, and wherein a man thinketh best of himself, therein the flatterer will uphold him most; but if he be an impudent flatterer, look wherein a man is conscious to himself that he is most defective and is most out of countenance in himself,[6] that will the flatterer entitle him to perforce, *spreta conscientia*.[7] Some praises come of good wishes and respects, which is a form due in civility to kings and great persons, *laudando praecipere*,[8] when by telling men what they are, they represent to them what they should be. Some men are praised

Texts: MS, 1612, 1625

1. Worthless.　2. Appearances resembling virtues.
3. A good name is like a fragrant ointment (see Ecclesiastes 7.1).
4. Have to hand.　5. Epithets.　6. Ashamed of himself.
7. That quality the flatterer will inevitably attribute to him, scorning his victim's consciousness of imperfection (literally, 'disdaining conscience').
8. To teach by praising (derived from Pliny, *Letters*, III.18.1–3).

maliciously to their hurt, thereby to stir envy and jealousy towards them: *pessimum genus inimicorum laudantium;*[9] insomuch as it was a proverb amongst the Grecians, that *he that was praised to his hurt should have a push*[10] *rise upon his nose,*[11] as we say, *that a blister will rise upon one's tongue that tells a lie.* Certainly moderate praise, used with opportunity, and not vulgar, is that which doth the good. Solomon saith, *He that praiseth his friend aloud, rising early, it shall be to him no better than a curse.*[12] Too much magnifying of man or matter doth irritate[13] contradiction, and procure envy and scorn. To praise a man's self cannot be decent,[14] except it be in rare cases; but to praise a man's office or profession, he may do it with good grace and with a kind of magnanimity. The cardinals of Rome, which are theologues[15] and friars and Schoolmen,[16] have a phrase of notable contempt and scorn towards civil business: for they call all temporal business, of wars, embassages,[17] judicature, and other employments, *sbirrerie,*[18] which is *under-sheriffries,* as if they were but matters for under-sheriffs and catchpoles;[19] though many times those *under-sheriffries* do more good than their high speculations. St Paul, when he boasts of himself, he doth oft interlace, *I speak like a fool;*[20] but speaking of his calling, he saith, *Magnificabo apostolatum meum.*[21]

9. The worst class of enemies are men who praise you (Tacitus, *Agricola*, 41).

10. Pustule.   11. Compare Theocritus, *Idylls*, XII. 24 and IX. 30.

12. Proverbs 27.14.   13. Provoke.   14. Seemly.   15. Theologians.

16. See Essay 17, note 7.   17. Embassies.

18. In Italian, *sbirro* means a constable or a bailiff.   19. Bailiff's officers.

20. 2 Corinthians 11.23.   21. I will magnify my ministry (Romans 11.13).

54.

Of Vainglory

It was prettily devised of Aesop,[1] *The fly sat upon the axle-tree of the chariot wheel, and said, 'What a dust do I raise!'* So are there some vain persons that, whatsoever goeth alone or moveth upon greater means,[2] if they have never so little hand in it, they think it is they that carry it. They that are glorious[3] must needs be factious, for all bravery[4] stands upon comparisons. They must needs be violent to make good their own vaunts. Neither can they be secret, and therefore not effectual, but according to the French proverb, *Beaucoup de bruit, peu de fruit: much bruit,[5] little fruit.* Yet certainly there is use of this quality in civil affairs. Where there is an opinion and fame to be created, either of virtue or greatness, these men are good trumpeters. Again, as Titus Livius noteth in the case of Antiochus and the Aetolians,[6] *There are sometimes great effects of cross[7] lies,* as, if a man that negotiates between two princes to draw them to join in a war against the third, doth extol the forces of either of them above measure, the one to the other: and sometimes he that deals between man and man raiseth his own credit with both by pretending greater interest than he hath in either. And in these and the like kinds, it often falls out that somewhat is produced of nothing, for lies are sufficient to breed opinion, and opinion brings on substance. In militar[8] commanders and soldiers, vainglory is an essential point, for as iron sharpens iron, so by glory[9] one courage sharpeneth another. In cases of great enterprise, upon charge and adventure,[10] a composition of glorious[11] natures doth put life into business, and those that are of solid and sober natures have more of

Texts: 1612, 1625

1. Not Aesop, but Lorenzo Bevilaqua: see *Notes and Queries*, 202 (1957): 378.
2. Through other means than the vainglorious person.   3. Ostentatious.
4. Boasting.   5. Noise.
6. Antiochus, King of Syria, allied with the Aetolians against Rome, but was defeated. See Livy, *History*, XXXV.12 and 17–18.
7. Reciprocal.   8. Military.   9. Boasting.
10. Involving expense and risk.   11. Vainglorious.

the ballast than of the sail. In fame of learning, the flight will be slow
without some feathers of ostentation. *Qui de contemnenda gloria
libros scribunt, nomen suum inscribunt.*[12] Socrates, Aristotle,
Galen, were men full of ostentation. Certainly vainglory helpeth to
perpetuate a man's memory, and virtue was never so beholding[13] to
human nature, as it received his due at the second hand.[14] Neither
had the fame of Cicero, Seneca, Plinius Secundus,[15] borne her age[16]
so well, if it had not been joined with some vanity in themselves:
like unto varnish, that makes ceilings[17] not only shine but last. But
all this while, when I speak of vainglory, I mean not of that property
that Tacitus doth attribute to Mucianus, *Omnium quae dixerat
feceratque arte quadam ostentator,*[18] for that proceeds not of
vanity, but of natural magnanimity and discretion, and in some
persons is not only comely, but gracious. For excusations,
cessions,[19] modesty itself well governed, are but arts of ostentation.
And amongst those arts there is none better than that which Plinius
Secundus speaketh of, which is to be liberal of praise and commendation to others, in that wherein a man's self hath any perfection. For saith Pliny very wittily[20]: *In commending another you do
yourself right, for he that you commend is either superior to you in
that you commend, or inferior. If he be inferior, if he be to be
commended, you much more; if he be superior, if he be not to be
commended, you much less.*[21] Glorious men are the scorn of wise
men, the admiration of fools, the idols of parasites, and the slaves of
their own vaunts.

12. Men who write books on the worthlessness of glory take care to put their
names on the title-page (from Cicero, *Tusculan Disputations*, I.15).
13. Beholden.
14. That it received its due, not through its own efforts (i.e. at first hand), but
direct from human nature (i.e. at *second hand*).   15. Pliny the Younger.
16. Lasted.   17. Wooden panelling on floors, walls and ceilings.
18. He had a certain skill of displaying to advantage all that he had said or done
(from *Histories*, II.80). Mucianus, Roman consul three times, helped Vespasian to
become emperor.
19. For excuses, concessions.
20. Ingeniously.   21. From *Letters*, VI.17.4.

55.

Of Honour and Reputation

The winning of honour is but the revealing of a man's virtue and worth without disadvantage. For some in their actions do woo and affect[1] honour and reputation, which sort of men are commonly much talked of but inwardly little admired. And some, contrariwise, darken their virtue in the show of it, so as[2] they be undervalued in opinion. If a man perform that which hath not been attempted before, or attempted and given over, or hath been achieved, but not with so good circumstance, he shall purchase more honour than by effecting a matter of greater difficulty or virtue, wherein he is but a follower. If a man so temper his actions, as[3] in some one of them he doth content every faction or combination of people, the music will be the fuller. A man is an ill husband[4] of his honour that entereth into any action, the failing wherein may disgrace him more than the carrying of it through can honour him. Honour that is gained and broken upon another[5] hath the quickest[6] reflection, like diamonds cut with facets. And therefore let a man contend to excel any competitors of his in honour, in outshooting them, if he can, in their own bow. Discreet followers and servants help much to reputation: *Omnis fama a domesticis emanat.*[7] Envy, which is the canker of honour, is best extinguished by declaring[8] a man's self in his ends rather to seek merit than fame, and by attributing a man's successes rather to divine Providence and felicity, than to his own virtue or policy. The true marshalling of the degrees of sovereign honour are these. In the first place are *conditores imperiorum*, founders of states and commonwealths, such as were Romulus, Cyrus, Caesar, Ottoman, Ismael.[9] In the second place are *legislatores*, lawgivers,

Texts: 1597, MS, 1625

  1. Hunt after.   2. So that.   3. That.   4. Manager.
  5. Obtained at another's expense.   6. Most vivid.
  7. All of one's reputation comes from servants in the house (Cicero, *Handbook of Electioneering*, V).   8. Making clear.
  9. Founders respectively of Rome (according to legend); the Persian empire (sixth century B.C.); the Roman empire; the Turkish empire (Ottoman I, d.1326); and the Safavid dynasty, rulers of Persia (Iran) from the sixteenth century.

which are also called *second founders*, or *perpetui principes*,[10] because they govern by their ordinances after they are gone; such were Lycurgus, Solon, Justinian, Edgar, Alphonsus of Castile, the Wise, that made the *Siete Partidas*.[11] In the third place are *liberatores*, or *salvatores*,[12] such as compound the long miseries of civil wars, or deliver their countries from servitude of strangers or tyrants; as Augustus Caesar, Vespasianus,[13] Aurelianus,[14] Theodoricus,[15] King Henry the Seventh of England,[16] King Henry the Fourth of France.[17] In the fourth place are *propagatores* or *propugnatores imperii*,[18] such as in honourable wars enlarge their territories or make noble defence against invaders. And in the last place are *patres patriae*,[19] which reign justly, and make the times good wherein they live. Both which last kinds need no examples, they are in such number. Degrees of honour in subjects are, first, *participes curarum*,[20] those upon whom princes do discharge the greatest weight of their affairs, their *right hands*, as we call them. The next are *duces belli*,[21] great leaders, such as are princes' lieutenants and do them notable services in the wars. The third are *gratiosi*, favourites, such as exceed not this scantling,[22] to be solace to the sovereign and harmless to the people. And the fourth, *negotiis pares*,[23] such as have great places under princes, and execute their places with sufficiency. There is an honour, likewise,

10. Rulers in perpetuity.

11. Legislators respectively of Sparta, ninth century B.C.; Athens, sixth century B.C.; the Byzantine empire, sixth century; England, tenth century; and Castile, thirteenth century (Alfonso was the author of a legal code known as *Las siete partidas*, 'The Seven Parts'). 12. Liberators or saviours.

13. Roman emperor, 69–79; delivered the empire from civil wars after the death of Nero.

14. Roman emperor, 270–75; fought brilliant campaigns and restored unity to the empire.

15. Theodoric the Great, king of the Ostrogoths; liberated Italy in 493, and ruled it in peace until his death in 526.

16. Ruled 1485–1509; ended the Wars of the Roses and founded the House of Tudor. 17. Ruled 1589–1610; ended the wars of religion in France.

18. Extenders or defenders of empire. 19. Fathers of their country.

20. Partners in cares. 21. Military commanders.

22. Limit. 23. Those who are capable of conducting state affairs.

which may be ranked amongst the greatest, which happeneth rarely; that is, of such as sacrifice themselves to death or danger for the good of their country, as was M. Regulus,[24] and the two Decii.[25]

24. Roman general captured by the Carthaginians in the first Punic War. Sent to Rome on parole to ask for an exchange of prisoners, he persuaded the senate to refuse. He insisted on returning to Carthage, where he was executed (about 250 B.C.).

25. According to Livy, both Decius Mus and his son of the same name sacrificed their lives for Roman victories (in 340 and 295 B.C. respectively).

56

Of Judicature

Judges ought to remember that their office is *jus dicere*, and not *jus dare*: to interpret law, and not to make law or give law. Else will it be like the authority claimed by the Church of Rome, which under pretext of exposition of Scripture doth not stick[1] to add and alter, and to pronounce that which they do not find, and by show[2] of antiquity to introduce novelty. Judges ought to be more learned than witty,[3] more reverend than plausible,[4] and more advised[5] than confident. Above all things, integrity is their portion and proper virtue. *Cursed* (saith the law[6]) *is he that removeth the landmark.*[7] The mislayer of a mere-stone[8] is to blame. But it is the unjust judge that is the capital[9] remover of landmarks, when he defineth amiss of lands and property. One foul sentence doth more hurt than many foul examples. For these do but corrupt the stream, the other corrupteth the fountain. So saith Solomon: *Fons turbatus, et vena corrupta, est justus cadens in causa sua coram adversario.*[10] The office of judges may have reference unto the parties that sue, unto the advocates that plead, unto the clerks and ministers of justice underneath them, and to the sovereign or state above them.

First, for the causes or parties that sue. *There be* (saith the Scripture) *that turn judgement into wormwood;*[11] and surely there be also that turn it into vinegar, for injustice maketh it bitter, and delays make it sour. The principal duty of a judge is to suppress force and fraud, whereof force is the more pernicious when it is open, and fraud when it is close and disguised. Add thereto contentious suits, which ought to be spewed out, as the surfeit of courts. A judge ought to prepare his way to a just sentence, as God useth to prepare his way by *raising valleys* and *taking down hills*:[12] so when there appeareth

Texts: 1612, 1625

1. Hesitate.   2. Under the guise.   3. Ingenious.
4. More to be revered than applauded.   5. Deliberate.   6. Mosaic law.
7. Deuteronomy 27.17.   8. Boundary stone.   9. Chief.
10. A righteous man who gives way before the wicked is like a troubled fountain and a polluted spring (Proverbs 25.26).   11. Amos 5.7.   12. See Isaiah 40.4.

on either side an high hand, violent prosecution, cunning advantages taken, combination, power, great counsel, then is the virtue of a judge seen, to make inequality equal, that he may plant his judgement as upon an even ground. *Qui fortiter emungit, elicit sanguinem;*[13] and where the wine-press is hard wrought, it yields a harsh wine that tastes of the grape-stone. Judges must beware of hard constructions and strained inferences, for there is no worse torture than the torture of laws. Specially in case of laws penal, they ought to have care that that which was meant for terror be not turned into rigour; and that they bring not upon the people that shower whereof the Scripture speaketh, *Pluet super eos laqueos;*[14] for penal laws pressed are a *shower of snares* upon the people. Therefore let penal laws, if they have been sleepers of long,[15] or if they be grown unfit for the present time, be by wise judges confined in the execution: *Judicis officium est, ut res, ita tempora rerum,* etc.[16] In causes of life and death, judges ought (as far as the law permitteth) in justice to remember mercy, and to cast a severe eye upon the example, but a merciful eye upon the person.

Secondly, for the advocates and counsel that plead. Patience and gravity of hearing is an essential part of justice, and an over-speaking judge is no *well-tuned cymbal.*[17] It is no grace to a judge first to find that which he might have heard in due time from the bar; or to show quickness of conceit[18] in cutting off evidence or counsel too short; or to prevent[19] information by questions, though pertinent. The parts of a judge in hearing are four: to direct the evidence; to moderate length, repetition, or impertinency[20] of speech; to recapitulate, select, and collate the material points of that which hath been said; and to give the rule or sentence. Whatsoever is above these is too much, and proceedeth either of glory[21] and willingness to speak, or of impatience to hear, or of shortness of memory, or of want of a staid and equal[22] attention. It is a strange thing to see that the boldness of advocates should prevail with

13. Wringing the nose [blowing it violently] causes bleeding (Proverbs 30.33).
14. He shall rain snares upon them (see Psalms 11.6).
15. Unused for a long time.
16. It is a judge's duty to consider not only the circumstances, but also the time of an act (Ovid, *Tristia*, I.1.37).
17. Alluding to Psalms 150.5 (Praise him with sounding cymbals; praise him with loud clashing cymbals!).   18. Understanding.   19. Anticipate.
20. Irrelevancy.   21. Vainglory.   22. Equable.

judges, whereas they should imitate God, in whose seat they sit, who *represseth the presumptuous*, and *giveth grace to the modest*.[23] But it is more strange that judges should have noted favourites, which cannot but cause multiplication of fees, and suspicion of by-ways. There is due from the judge to the advocate some commendation and gracing,[24] where causes are well handled and fair pleaded, especially towards the side which obtaineth not;[25] for that upholds in the client the reputation of his counsel, and beats down in him the conceit[26] of his cause. There is likewise due to the public a civil reprehension of advocates, where there appeareth cunning counsel, gross neglect, slight information, indiscreet pressing, or an over-bold defence. And let not the counsel at the bar chop[27] with the judge, nor wind himself into the handling of the cause anew after the judge hath declared his sentence; but, on the other side, let not the judge meet the cause half-way, nor give occasion to the party to say his counsel or proofs were not heard.

Thirdly, for that that concerns clerks and ministers. The place of justice is an hallowed place, and therefore not only the bench, but the foot-pace[28] and precincts and purprise[29] thereof ought to be preserved without scandal and corruption. For certainly, *Grapes* (as the Scripture saith) *will not be gathered of thorns or thistles*;[30] neither can justice yield her fruit with sweetness amongst the briars and brambles of catching and polling[31] clerks and ministers. The attendance of courts is subject to four bad instruments. First, certain persons that are sowers of suits, which make the court swell, and the country pine. The second sort is of those that engage courts in quarrels of jurisdiction, and are not truly *amici curiae*, but *parasiti curiae*,[32] in puffing a court up beyond her bounds, for their own scraps and advantage. The third sort is of those that may be accounted the left hands of courts: persons that are full of nimble and sinister tricks and shifts, whereby they pervert the plain and direct courses of courts, and bring justice into oblique lines and labyrinths. And the fourth is the poller[33] and exacter of fees; which justifies the common resemblance of the courts of justice to the bush

23. James 4.6 and 1 Peter 5.5   24. Sign of approval.   25. Does not win.
26. High opinion.   27. Bandy words.
28. Dais (on which the judge's seat was set).   29. Area about the court.
30. Matthew 7.16.   31. Grasping and plundering.
32. Not truly friends, but parasites of the court.   33. Plunderer.

whereunto while the sheep flies for defence in weather,[34] he is sure to lose part of his fleece. On the other side, an ancient clerk, skilful in precedents, wary in proceeding, and understanding in the business of the court, is an excellent finger of a court, and doth many times point the way to the judge himself.

Fourthly, for that which may concern the sovereign and estate. Judges ought above all to remember the conclusion of the Roman Twelve Tables, *Salus populi suprema lex*,[35] and to know that laws, except they be in order to that end, are but things captious, and oracles not well inspired. Therefore it is an happy thing in a state when kings and states do often consult with judges, and again, when judges do often consult with the king and state: the one, when there is matter of law intervenient[36] in business of state, the other, when there is some consideration of state intervenient in matter of law. For many times the things deduced to judgement may be *meum* and *tuum*, when the reason and consequence thereof may trench to point of estate.[37] I call matter of estate, not only the parts of sovereignty, but whatsoever introduceth any great alteration or dangerous precedent, or concerneth manifestly any great portion of people. And let no man weakly conceive that just laws and true policy have any antipathy, for they are like the spirits and sinews, that one moves with the other. Let judges also remember that Solomon's throne was supported by lions on both sides:[38] let them be lions, but yet lions under the throne, being circumspect that they do not check or oppose any points of sovereignty. Let not judges also be so ignorant of their own right, as to think there is not left to them, as a principal part of their office, a wise use and application of laws. For they may remember what the Apostle[39] saith of a greater law than theirs: *Nos scimus quia lex bona est, modo quis ea utatur legitime.*[40]

34. Rough weather.
35. The welfare of the people is the supreme law (not from the Twelve Tables, laws formulated in Rome about 450 B.C., but from Cicero, *On Laws*, III.3).
36. Intervening.
37. The matters brought for judgement may be simply ones of property, but the principle and consequences involved may touch on something to do with the state.
38. Alluding to 1 Kings 10.19–20.   39. St Paul.
40. We know that the law is good, provided a man use it lawfully (1 Timothy 1.8).

57.
Of Anger

To seek to extinguish anger utterly is but a bravery[1] of the Stoics.[2] We have better oracles: *Be angry, but sin not. Let not the sun go down upon your anger*.[3] Anger must be limited and confined, both in race[4] and in time. We will first speak how the natural inclination and habit to be angry may be attempered and calmed. Secondly, how the particular motions of anger may be repressed, or at least refrained from doing mischief. Thirdly, how to raise anger or appease anger in another.

For the first: there is no other way but to meditate and ruminate well upon the effects of anger, how it troubles man's life. And the best time to do this is to look back upon anger when the fit is throughly[5] over. Seneca saith well that *anger is like ruin, which breaks itself upon that it falls*.[6] The Scripture exhorteth us *to possess our souls in patience*.[7] Whosoever is out of patience is out of possession of his soul. Men must not turn bees,

animasque in vulnere ponunt.[8]

Anger is certainly a kind of baseness; as it appears well in the weakness of those subjects in whom it reigns: children, women, old folks, sick folks. Only men must beware that they carry their anger rather with scorn than with fear, so that they may seem rather to be above the injury than below it: which is a thing easily done if a man will give law to himself in it.

For the second point: the causes and motives of anger are chiefly three. First, to be too sensible of hurt, for no man is angry that feels not himself hurt; and therefore tender and delicate persons must needs be oft angry, they have so many things to trouble them

Text: 1625

1. Showy attempt.   2. See Essay 2, note 18.   3. Ephesians 4.26.
4. Scope.   5. Thoroughly.   6. *On Anger*, I.1.2.
7. See Luke 21.19.   8. And lay down their lives in the wound (Virgil, *Georgics*, IV.238).

which more robust natures have little sense of. The next is the apprehension and construction[9] of the injury offered to be, in the circumstances thereof, full of contempt; for contempt is that which putteth an edge upon anger, as much or more than the hurt itself. And therefore, when men are ingenious in picking out circumstances of contempt, they do kindle their anger much. Lastly, opinion of the touch of a man's reputation[10] doth multiply and sharpen anger. Wherein the remedy is, that a man should have, as Consalvo[11] was wont to say, *telam honoris crassiorem.*[12] But in all refrainings of anger, it is the best remedy to win time, and to make a man's self believe that the opportunity of his revenge is not yet come, but that he foresees a time for it; and so to still himself in the meantime and reserve it.

To contain[13] anger from mischief, though it take hold of a man, there be two things whereof you must have special caution. The one, of extreme bitterness of words, especially if they be aculeate and proper;[14] for *communia maledicta*[15] are nothing so much; and again, that in anger a man reveal no secrets, for that makes him not fit for society. The other, that you do not peremptorily break off in any business in a fit of anger; but howsoever you show bitterness, do not act anything that is not revocable.

For raising and appeasing anger in another: it is done chiefly by choosing of times, when men are frowardest and worst disposed, to incense them. Again, by gathering (as was touched before) all that you can find out to aggravate the contempt. And the two remedies are by the contraries. The former, to take good times, when first to relate to a man an angry business, for the first impression is much. And the other is to sever, as much as may be, the construction of the injury from the point of contempt,[16] imputing it to misunderstanding, fear, passion, or what you will.

9. Interpretation.   10. The opinion that one's reputation has been impugned.
11. Gonzalo, Hernandez de Cordova, Spanish general, d. 1515.
12. A thicker web of honour (the saying is untraced, but Bacon quotes it elsewhere: see *Works*, VII.150).   13. Restrain.
14. Stinging and personal.   15. General revilings.
16. From any implication of contempt.

which more robust natures have little sense of. The next is the
apprehension and construction of the injury offered to be, in the
circumstance thereof, full of contempt: for contempt is that which
putteth an edge upon anger, as much or more than the hurt itself.
And therefore when men are ingenious in picking out circumstances of contempt, they do kindle their anger much. Lastly,
opinion of the touch of a man's reputation, doth multiply and

58.

Of Vicissitude of Things

Solomon saith, *There is no new thing upon the earth.*[1] So that
as Plato had an imagination, *that all knowledge was but
remembrance,*[2] so Solomon giveth his sentence,[3] *that all novelty is
but oblivion.*[4] Whereby you may see that the river of Lethe[5]
runneth as well above ground as below. There is an abstruse
astrologer that saith,[6] *If it were not for two things that are constant
(the one is, that the fixed stars ever stand at like distance one from
another, and never come nearer together nor go further asunder;
the other, that the diurnal motion perpetually keepeth time), no
individual would last one moment.* Certain it is, that the matter is in
a perpetual flux, and never at a stay. The great winding-sheets, that
bury all things in oblivion, are two: deluges and earthquakes. As for
conflagrations and great droughts, they do not merely[7] dispeople
and destroy. Phaethon's car went but a day.[8] And the three years'
drought in the time of Elias[9] was but particular,[10] and left people
alive. As for the great burnings by lightnings, which are often in the
West Indies,[11] they are but narrow.[12] But in the other two destruc-
tions, by deluge and earthquake, it is further to be noted, that the
remnant of people which hap[13] to be reserved are commonly
ignorant and mountainous people, that can give no account of the
time past, so that the oblivion is all one as if none had been left. If
you consider well of the people of the West Indies, it is very probable

Text: 1625

1. Ecclesiastes 1.9.   2. See *Phaedo*, 72E, and *Meno*, 81C–D.
3. Judgement.   4. Derived from Ecclesiastes 1.10–11.
5. River in Hades, the abode of the dead, whose waters, once drunk, caused
complete forgetfulness.
6. Perhaps the Italian philosopher Telesio (d. 1588) in his *On the Nature of
Things*.   7. Utterly.
8. Phaethon, the child of the sun, set heaven and earth on fire when he attempted
to drive his father's chariot.
9. Elijah the prophet: for the drought, see 1 Kings 17 and 18.
10. Partial (the meaning throughout the essay).
11. The entire American continent as well as the islands.
12. Limited.   13. Happen.

that they are a newer or a younger people than the people of the Old World. And it is much more likely that the destruction that hath heretofore been there was not by earthquakes (as the Egyptian priest told Solon concerning the island of Atlantis, *that it was swallowed by an earthquake*[14]), but rather that it was desolated by a particular deluge. For earthquakes are seldom in those parts. But on the other side, they have such pouring rivers as the rivers of Asia and Africa and Europe are but brooks to them. Their Andes likewise, or mountains, are far higher than those with us; whereby it seems that the remnants of generation of men were in such a particular deluge saved. As for the observation that Machiavel hath,[15] that the jealousy of sects doth much extinguish the memory of things, traducing Gregory the Great, that he did what in him lay to extinguish all heathen antiquities, I do not find that those zeals do any great effects, nor last long: as it appeared in the succession of Sabinian,[16] who did revive the former antiquities.

The vicissitude or mutations in the superior globe[17] are no fit matter for this present argument. It may be, Plato's *Great Year*,[18] if the world should last so long, would have some effect, not in renewing the state of like[19] individuals (for that is the fume[20] of those that conceive the celestial bodies have more accurate influences upon these things below than indeed they have), but in gross. Comets, out of question,[21] have likewise power and effect over the gross and mass of things, but they are rather gazed upon and waited upon in their journey than wisely observed in their effects, specially in their respective[22] effects; that is, what kind of comet, for magnitude, colour, version[23] of the beams, placing in the region of heaven, or lasting, produceth what kind of effects.

There is a toy[24] which I have heard, and I would not have it given over, but waited upon[25] a little. They say it is observed in the Low Countries (I know not in what part) that every five and thirty years the same kind and suit[26] of years and weathers comes about again, as

14. Plato, *Timaeus*, 25D. See also Essay 35, note 22.

15. Machiavelli, *Discourses*, II.5 (where Pope Gregory is said to have ordered the destruction of pagan poems, histories and idols).

16. Succeeded Gregory as Pope; he permitted some revival of paganism.

17. Upper sphere, the heavens. See Essay 15, note 12.

18. The space of time required for all heavenly bodies to revolve back to the places they had when the world began (see *Timaeus*, 39 C–E).   19. The same.

20. Vain notion.   21. Without doubt.   22. Different.

23. Turning about.   24. Trifle.   25. Considered.   26. Sequence.

great frosts, great wet, great droughts, warm winters, summers with little heat, and the like; and they call it the *Prime*. It is a thing I do the rather mention, because, computing backwards, I have found some concurrence.

But to leave these points of nature, and to come to men. The greatest vicissitude of things amongst men is the vicissitude of sects and religions. For those orbs[27] rule in men's minds most. The true religion is *built upon the rock*; the rest are tossed upon the waves of time. To speak[28] therefore of the causes of new sects, and to give some counsel concerning them, as far as the weakness of human judgement can give stay to so great revolutions.

When the religion formerly received is rent by discords, and when the holiness of the professors of religion is decayed and full of scandal, and withal the times be stupid, ignorant, and barbarous, you may doubt[29] the springing up of a new sect, if then also there should arise any extravagant and strange spirit to make himself author thereof. All which points held when Mahomet published his law. If a new sect have not two properties, fear it not, for it will not spread. The one is the supplanting or the opposing of authority established, for nothing is more popular than that. The other is the giving licence to pleasures and a voluptuous life. For as for speculative heresies (such as were in ancient times the Arians',[30] and now the Arminians'[31]), though they work mightily upon men's wits, yet they do not produce any great alterations in states, except it be by the help of civil[32] occasions. There be three manner of plantations of new sects: by the power of signs and miracles, by the eloquence and wisdom of speech and persuasion, and by the sword. For martyrdoms, I reckon them amongst miracles, because they seem to exceed the strength of human nature, and I may do the like of superlative and admirable holiness of life. Surely there is no better way to stop the rising of new sects and schisms than to reform abuses; to compound the smaller differences; to proceed mildly and not with sanguinary persecutions; and rather to take off the principal authors

---

27. Spheres of influence (astrological term).   28. It remains for me to speak.
29. Fear.
30. Fourth-century religious sect, founded by Arius of Alexandria, who denied the equality of the Father and the Son in the Christian Trinity.
31. Followers of Arminius (Jakob Harmensen, d. 1609), the Dutch Protestant theologian who opposed Calvin's view of predestination (that God had determined the salvation or damnation of individuals before their creation).   32. Political.

by winning and advancing them than to enrage them by violence and bitterness.

The changes and vicissitude in wars are many, but chiefly in three things: in the seats or stages of the war, in the weapons, and in the manner of the conduct. Wars in ancient time seemed more to move from east to west, for the Persians, Assyrians, Arabians, Tartars (which were the invaders) were all eastern people. It is true, the Gauls were western, but we read but of two incursions of theirs, the one to Gallo-Graecia,[33] the other to Rome. But east and west have no certain points of heaven,[34] and no more have the wars, either from the east or west, any certainty of observation. But north and south are fixed, and it hath seldom or never been seen that the far southern people have invaded the northern, but contrariwise. Whereby it is manifest that the northern tract of the world is in nature the more martial region, be it in respect of the stars of that hemisphere, or of the great continents that are upon the north; whereas the south part, for aught that is known, is almost all sea; or[35] (which is most apparent) of the cold of the northern parts, which is that which, without aid of discipline, doth make the bodies hardest and the courages warmest.

Upon the breaking and shivering of a great state and empire, you may be sure to have wars. For great empires, while they stand, do enervate and destroy the forces of the natives which they have subdued, resting upon their own protecting forces; and then when they fail also, all goes to ruin, and they become a prey. So was it in the decay of the Roman empire; and likewise in the empire of Almaigne,[36] after Charles the Great,[37] every bird taking a feather; and were not unlike to befall to Spain, if it should break. The great accessions and unions of kingdoms do likewise stir up wars. For when a state grows to an over-power, it is like a great flood that will be sure to overflow: as it hath been seen in the states of Rome, Turkey, Spain, and others. Look when the world hath fewest barbarous peoples, but such as commonly will not marry or generate, except they know means to live (as it is almost everywhere at this day, except Tartary), there is no danger of inundations of people. But when there be great shoals of people, which go on to

33. Galatia (in Asia Minor).

34. East and west are not marked in the heavens by a particular star (in the way that north is fixed by the polar star).   35. Or because.   36. Germany.

37. Charlemagne, d. 814, king of the Franks, and Roman emperor.

populate without foreseeing means of life and sustentation, it is of necessity that once in an age or two they discharge a portion of their people upon other nations; which the ancient northern people were wont to do by lot, casting lots what part should stay at home, and what should seek their fortunes. When a warlike state grows soft and effeminate, they may be sure of a war. For commonly such states are grown rich in the time of their degenerating, and so the prey inviteth, and their decay in valour encourageth a war.

As for the weapons, it hardly falleth under rule and observation; yet we see even they have returns and vicissitudes. For certain it is, that ordnance[38] was known in the city of the Oxidrakes in India,[39] and was that which the Macedonians called thunder and lightning, and magic. And it is well known that the use of ordnance hath been in China above 2,000 years. The conditions of weapons and their improvement are, first, the fetching afar off,[40] for that outruns the danger, as it is seen in ordnance and muskets. Secondly, the strength of the percussion, wherein likewise ordnance do exceed all arietations[41] and ancient inventions. The third is, the commodious use of them, as that they may serve in all weathers, that the carriage may be light and manageable, and the like.

For the conduct of the war: at the first, men rested[42] extremely upon number. They did put the wars likewise upon main force and valour, pointing days for pitched fields,[43] and so trying it out upon an even match; and they were more ignorant in ranging and arraying their battles.[44] After, they grew to rest upon number rather competent than vast; they grew to advantages of place, cunning diversions, and the like; and they grew more skilful in the ordering of their battles.

In the youth of a state, arms do flourish; in the middle age of a state, learning; and then both of them together for a time; in the declining age of a state, mechanical arts and merchandise. Learning hath his[45] infancy, when it is but beginning and almost childish; then his youth, when it is luxuriant and juvenile; then his strength of years when it is solid and reduced;[46] and lastly, his old age, when

38. Gunpowder and artillery.
39. The story of Oxidrakes was perhaps derived from Philostratus, *Life of Apollonius*, II.33.
40. Hitting the target from a good distance away.
41. Attacks with battering-rams.   42. Relied.
43. Appointing days for pitched battles.   44. Battalions, bodies of troops.
45. Its.   46. Disciplined.

it waxeth dry and exhaust.[47] But it is not good to look too long upon these turning wheels of vicissitude, lest we become giddy. As for the philology of them,[48] that is but a circle of tales, and therefore not fit for this writing.

47. Exhausted.
48. As for the stories (of how the wheels of vicissitude, or fortune, have turned).

APPENDICES:

The *Essays*:
Fragments, Versions and Parallels

Bacon was one of those thinkers who found what he wanted to say early on, and then said it a lot of times throughout his life. His thought doesn't really evolve, so much as fill out. The things he was convinced of in the early 1590s, he was equally sure of in his last years. On the occasions when he tried to change tack, as with his natural history experiments in the 1620s, he could be painfully limited. But when he stuck to his first principles – attack the Schoolmen, encourage the monarch to become a Solomon of science, break down the social and psychological obstructions to clear thought – he could be unbeatable. What did change about him was his writing: he got better and better at it, in part because he learnt how to hang on to things that were good. When he had written something well, or wittily, or quoted one of the ancients to good effect, he stored the words away and brought them back in another piece. Pluto's helmet of secrecy is in the 1625 essay *Of Delays*, but it had already appeared twice before, in 'Perseus' in *The Wisdom of the Ancients* (1609), and in the Latin version of *The Advancement of Learning* (1623). For sure, this is only a chip in the mosaic of his work, but what is true of the details (and many of them) is true of the design. To counsel a prince in a Christmas jamboree in 1594 was to use a deliberative or persuasive rhetoric: pay for a science centre, a Baconian counsellor tells a festive prince, and become a real god of learning, not one just for the poets. But the dimensions and intricacies of counsel, and how princes are to receive and use it, make up a companion piece to his own efforts of persuasion. The essay *Of Counsel* not only complements but completes the activity of the writer-statesman (we should not forget the 1625 subtitle for the *Essays*: 'Counsels, Civil and Moral'). So it is with the interpretations of classical myth in *The Wisdom of the Ancients*. In these Bacon fathoms the mysteries of the ancient fables, and their ways back into Greek knowledge before Plato; but the stories of heroes and gods, and those social deities, the Roman emperors, are no less explored in the *Essays*. Writing, rewriting, moving passages from one work to another, hoping that one day everything would come together – Bacon's work is of a piece, and in pieces. In these appendices there is a selection which should suggest what part the *Essays* have in Bacon's grand design, and in his writing.

Appendix 1:
Writing the *Essays*

The drafts and published pieces in this section show how Bacon developed and may have planned the *Essays*, and, in the dedications, what he thought of them himself. The original spellings and punctuation have been preserved here (except in A.2) to give some idea of what is lost, and gained, in modernizing Bacon's texts. Long *s* is replaced with square *s*, and *u*, *v*, *i* and *j* are normalized to current usage. Obvious mistakes have been corrected. R. S. Crane and Stanley Fish, in the studies listed on pp. 50–51, have useful things to say about the evolution of the *Essays* between 1597 and 1625.

A. Dedicating the *Essays*

Bacon dedicated the final edition of the *Essays* to George, Duke of Buckingham, in the 1620s the most powerful man in England after the King. In his earlier dedications, the rank of the recipients and their influence was much less considerable. The 1597 edition was addressed to his brother Anthony, and the 1612 edition to Sir John Constable, a close friend and the husband of Bacon's sister-in-law, Dorothy Barnham. Behind these fraternal dedications, however, were two other, major figures. Before 1612 Bacon had intended to address his revised *Essays* to Henry, Prince of Wales, but he was forced to drop this idea when the Prince died in November of that year. A draft of what would have been the printed dedication to Henry is preserved in a manuscript in the British Library (Sloane MS 4259, folio 155). It is printed below from Spedding, *Letters and Life*, IV.340–41. After Prince Henry's death, and at the last moment, the dedication of the 1612 *Essays* was transferred to Sir John Constable.

Fifteen years earlier, in 1597, there was a much odder transfer of interest in the *Essays*. On 30 January, in the printed dedication, Bacon addressed them to his brother, but only nine days later Anthony himself wrote a letter to Robert, Earl of Essex, in effect surrendering the dedication to him:

I am bold, and yet out of a most entire and dutiful love wherein my german brother [i.e. Francis] and myself stand infinitely bound unto your Lordship, to present unto you the first sight and taste of such fruit as my brother was constrained to gather, as he professeth himself, before they were ripe, to prevent stealing; and withal most humbly to beseech your Lordship, that as my brother in token of a mutual firm brotherly affection hath bestowed by dedication the property of them upon myself, so your Lordship, to whose disposition and commandment I have entirely and inviolably vowed my poor self, and whatever appertaineth unto me, either in possession or right, – that your Lordship, I say, in your noble and singular kindness towards us both, will vouchsafe first to give me leave to transfer my interest unto your Lordship, then humbly to crave your honourable acceptance and most worthy protection.

(*Works*, VI.521–2)

This letter must have accompanied a copy of the *Essays*. Evidently, in 1597, Bacon felt that he could not present them directly to Essex (as he should have done, in all loyalty), and so he used his brother as a screen for a surreptitious and roundabout dedication. Perhaps this behaviour kept Bacon safe from the Earl's enemies: even at this distance, though, it looks like (in Bacon's own words) 'the wisdom of rats, that will be sure to leave a house somewhat before it fall'.

1. Dedication to the 1597 *Essays*

To M. Anthony Bacon
his deare Brother.

Loving and beloved Brother, I doe nowe like some that have an Orcharde il neighbored, that gather their fruit before it is ripe, to prevent stealing. These fragments of my conceites were going to print; To labour the staie of them had bin troublesome, and subject to interpretation; to let them passe had beene to adventure the wrong they mought receive by untrue Coppies, or by some garnishment, which it mought please any that should set them forth to bestow upon them. Therefore I helde it best discreation to publish them my selfe as they passed long agoe from my pen, without any further disgrace, then the weaknesse of the Author. And as I did ever hold, there mought be as great a vanitie in retiring and withdrawing mens conceites (except they bee of some nature) from the world, as in obtruding them: So in these particulars I have played my selfe the Inquisitor, and find nothing to my understanding in them contrarie or infectious to the state of Religion, or manners, but rather (as I suppose) medicinable. Only I disliked now to put them out because they will bee like the late new halfe-pence, which though the Silver were good, yet the peeces were small. But since they would not stay with their Master, but would needes travaile abroade, I have preferred them to you that are next myself, Dedicating them, such as they are, to our love, in the depth whereof (I assure you) I sometimes wish your infirmities translated uppon my selfe, that her Majestie mought have the service of so active and able a mind, & I mought be with excuse confined to these contemplations & studies for which I am fittest, so commende I you to the preservation of the divine Majestie. From my Chamber at Graies Inne, this 30. of Januarie. 1597.

Your entire Loving brother.

2. Dedication intended for the 1612 *Essays*, but not published

TO THE MOST HIGH AND EXCELLENT PRINCE, HENRY, PRINCE OF WALES, DUKE OF CORNWALL, AND EARL OF CHESTER.

It may please your Highness,

Having divided my life into the contemplative and active part, I am desirous to give his Majesty and your Highness of the fruits of both, simple though they be.

To write just treatises requireth leisure in the writer, and leisure in the reader, and therefore are not so fit, neither in regard of your Highness' princely affairs, nor in regard of my continual services; which is the cause that hath made me choose to write certain brief notes, set down rather significantly than curiously, which I have called *Essays*. The word is late, but the thing is ancient. For Seneca's epistles to Lucilius, if one mark them well, are but *Essays*, that is, dispersed meditations, though conveyed in the form of epistles. These labours of mine I know cannot be worthy of your Highness, for what can be worthy of you? But my hope is, they may be as grains of salt, that will rather give you an appetite than offend you with satiety. And although they handle those things wherein both men's lives and their pens are most conversant, yet (what I have attained I know not) but I have endeavoured to make them not vulgar, but of a nature whereof a man shall find much in experience, and little in books; so as they are neither repetitions nor fancies. But howsoever, I shall most humbly desire your Highness to accept them in gracious part, and to conceive, that if I cannot rest, but must shew my dutiful and devoted affection to your Highness in these things which proceed from myself, I shall be much more ready to do it in performance of any your princely commandments. And so wishing your Highness all princely felicity I rest,

Your Highness's most humble servant.

3. Dedication to the 1612 *Essays*

To my loving brother, Sir John Constable Knight.

My last Essaies I dedicated to my deare brother Master Anthony
Bacon, *who is with God. Looking amongst my papers this vacation, I
found others of the same Nature: which if I my selfe shall not suffer to
be lost, it seemeth the World will not; by the often printing of the
former. Missing my Brother, I found you next; in respect of bond of
neare alliance, and of straight friendship and societie, and particularly
of communication in studies. Wherein I must acknowledge my selfe
beholding to you. For as my businesse found rest in my contemplations; so my contemplations ever found rest in your loving conference
and judgement. So wishing you all good, I remaine*

Your loving brother and friend.

B.   Versions of the *Essays*

Of Suitors appears in all four of the early versions, *1597, MS, 1612* and *1625* (editions described above, pp. 46–7). Since there are no significant variations between *MS* and *1612*, the manuscript version has been omitted. All three texts of the essay *Of Fortune* and the two of *Of Vainglory*, are printed here.

The texts begin overleaf, in parallel columns.

1597

Of Sutes.

Manie ill matters are undertaken, and many good matters with ill mindes.

Some embrace Sutes which never meane to deale effectually in them. But if they see there may be life in the matter by some other meane, they will be content to winne a thanke or take a second reward.

Some take holde of Sutes onely for an occasion to crosse some other, or to make an information wherof they could not otherwise have an apt precept, without care what become of the Sute, when that turne is served.

Nay some undertake Sutes with a full purpose to let them fall, to the ende to gratifie the adverse partie or competitor.

Of Suitors

1612	1625
Of Sutors.	Of Sutours.

Manie ill matters are undertaken, and many good matters with ill mindes.

Many ill Matters and Projects are undertaken; And Private *Sutes* doe Putrifie the Publique Good. Many Good Matters are undertaken with Bad Mindes; I meane not onely Corrupt Mindes; but Craftie Mindes, that intend not Performance.

Some embrace suits which never meane to deale effectually in them, but if they see there may be life in the matter by some other meane, they will be content to winne a thanke, or take a second reward, or at least to make use in the meane time of the Sutors hopes.

Some embrace *Sutes*, which never meane to deale effectually in them; But if they see, there may be life in the Matter, by some other meane, they will be content to winne a Thanke, or take a Second Reward, or at least to make Use, in the meane time, of the *Sutours* Hopes.

Some take hold of suits only for an occasion to crosse some other, or to make an Information whereof they could not otherwise have apt pretext, without care what become of the suite when that turne is served.

Some take hold of *Sutes*, onely for an Occasion, to Crosse some other; Or to make an Information, whereof they could not otherwise have apt Pretext; without Care what become of the *Sute*, when that Turne is served: Or generally, to make other Mens Businesse, a Kinde of Entertainment, to bring in their owne.

Nay, some undertake suits with a full purpose to let them fall, to the end to gratifie the adverse party or competitor.

Nay, some undertake *Sutes*, with a full Purpose, to let them fall; To the end, to gratifie the Adverse Partie, or Competitour.

1597

Surely there is in   sorte a right in everie Sute, either a right of equitie, if it be a Sute of controversie; or a right of desert, if it bee a Sute of petition. If affection leade a man to favor the wrong side in justice, let him rather use his countenance to compound the matter then to carrie it. If affection lead a man to favour the lesse worthy in desert, let him doe it, without depraving or disabling the better deserver.

In Sutes a man doth not well understand, it is good to referre them to some friend of trust and judgement, that may reporte whether he may deale in them with honor.

Suters are so distasted with delaies and abuses, that plaine dealing in denying to deale in Sutes at first, and reporting the successe barely, and in challendging no more thankes then one hath deserved, is growen not onely honourable but also gracious.

In Sutes of favour the first comming ought to take little place, so far forth consideration may bee had of his trust, that if intelligence of the matter coulde not otherwise have beene had but by him, advantage be not taken of the note.

1612

Surely there is in   sort a right in every suit; either a right of equity, if it be a suit of controversie or a right of desart, if it be a suit of petition. If affection leade a man to favour the wrong side in justice, let him rather use his countenance to compound the matter then to carry it. If affection leade a man to favor the lesse worthy in desart, let him doe it without depraving or disabling the better deserver.

In suits a man doth not well understand, it is good to referre them to some friend of trust and judgement, that may report whether hee may deale in them with honour.

Sutors are so distasted with delaies and abuses, that plaine dealing in denying to deale in suits at first, and reporting the successe barely, and in challenging no more thankes then one hath deserved, is growne not onlie honourable, but also gracious.

In suits of favour, the first comming ought to take little place: so farre forth consideration may be had of his trust, that if intelligence of the matter could not otherwise have been had, but by him, advantage be not taken of the note, but the party left to his other meanes.

1625

Surely, there is, in some sort, a Right in every *Sute*: Either a Right of Equity, if it be a *Sute* of Controversie; Or a Right of Desert, if it be a *Sute* of Petition. If Affection lead a Man, to favour the Wrong Side in Justice, let him rather use his Countenance, to Compound the Matter, then to Carry it. If Affection lead a Man, to favour the lesse Worthy in Desert, let him doe it without Depraving or Disabling the Better Deserver.

In *Sutes*, which a man doth not well understand, it is good to referre them, to some Frend of Trust and Judgement, that may report whether hee may deale in them with Honour: But let him chuse well his Referendaries, for else he may be led by the Nose.

Sutours are so distasted with Delayes, and Abuses, that Plaine Dealing, in denying to deale in *Sutes* at first, and Reporting the Successe barely, and in Challenging no more Thanks then one hath deserved, is grown not onely Honourable, but also Gracious.

In *Sutes* of Favour, the first Comming ought to take little Place: So farre forth Consideration may bee had of his Trust, that if Intelligence of the Matter, coulde not otherwise have beene had, but by him, Advantage bee not taken of the Note, but the Partie left to his other Meanes; and, in some sort, Recompenced for his Discoverie.

1597

To be ignorant of the value of a Sute is simplicitie, as well as to be ignorant of the right thereof is want of conscience.

Secrecie in Sutes is a great meane of obtaining, for voicing them to bee in forwardnes may discourage some kinde of suters, but doth quicken and awake others.

But tyming of the Sutes is the principall, tyming I saye not onely in respect of the person that shoulde graunt it, but in respect of those which are like to crosse it.

Nothing is thought so easie a request to a great person as his letter, and yet if it bee not in a good cause, it is so much out of his reputation.

1612

1625

To be ignorant of the value of a suit is simplicity, aswell as to bee ignorant of the right thereof, is want of conscience.

To be Ignorant of the value of a *Sute*, is Simplicitie; As well as to be Ignorant of the Right thereof, is Want of Conscience.

Secresie in suites is a great meane of obtaining; For voicing them to bee in forwardnesse, may discourage some kind of suitors, but doth quicken and awake others.

Secrecie in *Sutes*, is a great Meane of Obtaining; For voycing them, to bee in Forwardnesse, may discourage some Kinde of *Sutours*; But doth Quicken and Awake Others.

But timing of the suits is the principall. Timing I say not onely in respect of the person that should grant it, but in respect of those which are like to crosse it.

But Timing of the *Sute*, is the Principall. Timing, I say, not onely in respect of the Person, that should grant it, but in respect of those, which are like to Crosse it.

Let a man in the choise of his meane, rather chuse the fittest meane then the greatest meane, and rather them that deale in certaine things then those that are generall.

Let a Man, in the choice of his Meane, rather choose the Fittest Meane, then the Greatest Meane: And rather them, that deale in certaine Things, then those that are Generall.

The reparation of a deniall is sometimes equall to the first grant, if a man shew himselfe neither dejected, nor discontented *Iniquum petas vt æquum feras*, is a good rule where a man hath strength of favour; but otherwise a man were better rest in his suit; for hee that would have ventured at first to have lost the sutor, will not in the conclusion lose both the sutor and his owne former favor.

The Reparation of a Deniall, is somtimes Equall to the first Grant, If a Man shew himselfe, neither dejected, nor discontented. *Iniquum petas vt Æquum feras*; is a good Rule, where a Man hath Strength of Favour: But otherwise, a man were better rise in his *Sute*; For he that would have ventured at first to have lost the *Sutour*, will not in the Conclusion, lose both the *Sutour*, and his owne former Favour.

Nothing is thought so easie a request to a great person as his Letter; and yet if it be not in a good cause, it is so much out of his reputation.

Nothing is thought so Easie a Request, to a great Person, as his Letter; And yet, if it be not in a Good Cause, it is so much out of his Reputation.

There are no worse Instruments, then these Generall Contrivers of *Sutes*: For they are but a Kinde of Poyson and Infection to Publique Proceedings.

MANUSCRIPT

Of Fortune.

It cannott be denyed but outward
Accidentes conduce much to a Mans
fortune; favour; opportune death of
others; occasion fitting vertue. But
cheiflie the mould of a Mans fortune
is in himself.

And
the most frequent of external causes
is, That the folie of one Man, is the
fortune of another. Ffor noe Man
prospers so suddainly as by others
errours. *Serpens nisi Serpentem
comederit non fit Draco.* Overt and
apparent vertues bring fourth
praise, but there be hidden and sec-
rett vertues that bring forth *Fortune*; Certen deliveryes of a Mans
self, which have noe name; The
Spanish word *Desemboltura*
sheweth them best; when there be
noe stondes, nor restivenesse in a
Mans nature;

For so saieth *Livye* well after he had
described *Cato Major* in theis
wordes *In illo viro tantum robur
corporis, et animi fuit, ut quocunque loco natus esset fortunam
sibi facturus videretur,* he falleth
uponn that, that he had, *versatile
ingenium.* Certainly if a Man looke
sharply and accentively hee shall
see Fortune; for thoughe she be
blinde, yet she is not invisible. The
way of *Fortune* is like the Milken

Of Fortune

1612	1625

Of Fortune.

Of Fortune.

It cannot bee denied, but outward accidents conduce much to a Mans fortune. Favour, Oportune death of others; occasion fitting vertue. But chiefly the mould of a Mans fortune is in himselfe.

It cannot be denied, but Outward Accidents conduce much to *Fortune*: Favour, Opportunitie, Death of Others, Occasion fitting Vertue. But chiefly, the Mould of a Mans *Fortune*, is in his owne hands. *Faber quisque Fortunæ suæ*, saith the Poet.

And the most frequent of external causes is, that the folly of one man is the fortune of another. For no man prospers so sodenly, as by others errors. *Serpens nisi serpentem comederit non fit Draco*. Overt, and apparent vertues bring foorth praise, but there bee hidden and secret vertues that bring forth fortune. Certaine deliveries of a mans selfe which have no name. The Spanish word *Deremboltura* partlie expresseth them, when there be no stonds nor restivenesse in a mans nature.

And the most Frequent of Externall Causes is, that the Folly of one Man, is the *Fortune* of Another. For no Man prospers so suddenly, as by Others Errours. *Serpens nisi Serpentem comederit non fit Draco*. Overt, and Apparent vertues bring forth Praise; But there be Secret and Hidden Vertues, that bring Forth *Fortune*. Certaine Deliveries of a Mans Selfe, which have no Name. The Spanish Name, *Desemboltura*, partly expresseth them: When there be not Stonds, nor Restivenesse in a Mans Nature; But that the wheeles of his Minde keepe way, with the wheeles of his *Fortune*.

For so saith *Livie* well, after he had described *Cato Major* in these words. *In illo viro tantum robur corporis et animi fuit, ut quocunque; loco natus esset fortunam sibi facturus videretur*. He falleth upon that, that he had *Versatile ingenium*. Therefore if a man looke sharpely and accentively, hee shall see fortune; for though shee be blinde, yet shee is not invisible. The way of fortune is like the milken

For so *Livie* (after he had described *Cato Major*, in these words; *In illo viro, tantum Robur Corporis et Animi fuit, vt quocunque loco natus esset, Fortunam sibi facturus videretur;*) falleth upon that, that he had, *Versatile Ingenium*. Therefore, if a Man looke Sharply, and Attentively, he shall see *Fortune*: For though shee be Blinde, yet shee is not Invisible. The Way of *Fortune*, is like the *Milken*

MANUSCRIPT

way in the Sky, which is a meeting or knott of a number of smale Starres;

so are there a number of litle and scarce discerned vertues, or rather facultyes, and Customes, that make Men fortunate. The *Italians* have found out one of them; *Poco di Matto*; when they speake of one that cannott doe amisse.

And certainely there be not two more fortunate properties, then to have a litle of the foole, and not to much of the honest. Therefore extreame Lovers of theire Countrye, or Maisters, were never fortunate, neither can they be; For when a Man placeth his thoughtes without himself, he goeth not his owne way. An hastye *Fortune* maketh an Enterpriser, and Remover (the *French* hath it better *Entreprenant*, or *Remuant*,) but the exercised fortune maketh the Able man; Fortune is to be honoured and respected and it be but for her daughters, *Confidence* and *reputation*, for those two fœlicitye breedeth, the first in a Mans self, the later in others.

All wise Men to declyne the envy of theire owne vertues use to ascribe them to providence, and Fortune, for so they may the better assume them, and besides it is greatnes in a Man to be the Care of the higher powers.

1612

way in the skie, which is a meeting, or knot of a number of small starres; not seene asunder, but giving light together. So are there a number of little and scarse discerned vertues, or rather faculties and customes, that make men fortunate. The *Italians*   some of them, such as a man would little thinke, when they speake of one that cannot doe amisse, they will throw in into his other conditions, that he hath *Poco di matto.*

And certainly, there bee not two more fortunate properties, then to have a little of the foole, and not too much of the honest. Therefore extreme lovers of their Countrey, or Masters, were never fortunate, neither can they bee. For when a man placeth his thoughts without himselfe, hee goeth not his owne way. An hasty fortune maketh an enterpriser and remover; (the *French* hath it better *Enterprenant*, or *Remuant*) but the exercised fortune maketh the able man. Fortune is to bee honoured and respected, and it be but for her daughters, *Confidence* and *Reputation*; for those two felicity breedeth: the first, within a mans selfe; the later, in others towards him.

All wise men to decline the Envie of their owne vertues, use to ascribe them to providence, and fortune. For so they may the better assume them. And besides, it is greatnesse in a man to bee the care of the higher powers.

1625

Way in the Skie; Which is a Meeting or Knot, of a Number of Small Stars; Not Seene asunder, but Giving Light together. So are there, a Number of Little, and scarce discerned Vertues, or rather Faculties and Customes, that make Men *Fortunate*. The *Italians* note some of them, such as a Man would little thinke. When they speake of one, that cannot doe amisse, they will throw in, into his other Conditions, that he hath, *Poco di Matto.*

And certainly, there be not two more *Fortunate* Properties; Then to have a *Little* of the *Foole*; And not *Too Much* of the *Honest*. Therefore, Extreme Lovers of their Countrey, or Masters, were never *Fortunate*, neither can they be. For when a Man placeth his Thoughts without Himselfe, he goeth not his owne Way. An hastie *Fortune* maketh an Enterpriser, and Remover, (The *French* hath it better: *Entreprenant*, or *Remuant*) But the Exercised *Fortune* maketh the Able Man. *Fortune* is to be Honoured, and Respected, and it bee but for her Daughters, *Confidence*, and *Reputation*. For those two Felicitie breedeth: The first within a Mans Selfe; the Latter, in Others towards Him.

All Wise Men, to decline the Envy of their owne vertues, use to ascribe them to Providence and *Fortune*; For so they may the better assume them: And besides, it is Greatnesse in a Man, to be the Care, of the

1612

Of Vaine-glory.

It was pretily devised of *Æsop, The Flie sate upon the Axletree of the Chariot wheele, and said, What a dust doe I raise?* So are there some vaine persons, that whatsoever goeth alone, or moves upon greater meanes,   they thinke it is they that carry it. They that are glorious must needs be factious; for all bravery stands upon comparisons. They must needes be violent, to make good their owne vaunts. Neither can they bee secret, and therefore not effectuall; but according to the *French* proverb, *Beaucoup de bruit et peu de fruit,* Much bruit, little fruit. Yet certainly there is use of this quality in civill affaires. Where there is an opinion and fame to bee created, either of *Vertue* or *Greatnesse*: these men are good

1612 1625

Higher Powers. So *Caesar* said to
the Pilot in the Tempest, *Caesarem
portas, et Fortunam eius.* So *Sylla*
chose the Name of *Felix,* and not of
Magnus.

And it hath beene noted, that those
that ascribe openly to much to their
owne wisdome and policy, end
infortunate. It it written, that
Timotheus the *Athenian,* after hee
had in the account he gave to the
state of his government, often interlaced this speach. *And in this,
fortune had no part;* never prospered in any thing he undertooke
afterwards.

And it hath beene noted, that those,
that ascribe openly too much to
their owne Wisdome, and Policie,
end *Infortunate.* It is written, that
Timotheus the *Athenian,* after he
had, in the Account he gave to the
State, of his Government, often interlaced this Speech; *And in this
Fortune had no Part,* never prospered in any Thing he undertooke
afterwards. Certainly, there be,
whose *Fortunes* are like *Homers
Verses,* that have a Slide, and
Easinesse, more then the Verses of
other Poets: As *Plutarch* saith of
Timoleons Fortune, in respect of
that of *Agesilaus,* or *Epaminondas.*
And that this should be, no doubt it
is much, in a Mans Selfe.

Of Vainglory

1625

Of Vaine-Glory.

It was prettily Devised of *Æsope; The Fly sate upon the Axle-tree of the
Chariot wheele, and said, What a Dust doe I raise?* So are there some
Vaine Persons, that whatsoever goeth alone, or moveth upon greater
Means, if they have never so little Hand in it, they thinke it is they that
carry it. They that are *Glorious,* must needs be *Factious;* For all Bravery
stands upon Comparisons. They must needs be *Violent,* to make good
their owne Vaunts. Neither can they be *Secret,* and therefore not
Effectuall; but according to the *French* Proverb; *Beaucoup de Bruit, peu
de Fruit: Much Bruit, little Fruit.* Yet certainly there is Use of this Quali-
tie, in Civill Affaires. Where there is an Opinion, and Fame to be created
either of Vertue, or Greatnesse, these Men are good Trumpetters.

1612

Trumpeters. Again, as *Titus Livius* noteth in the case of *Antiochus* and the *Ætolians*, *There are sometimes greate effects of crosse lies*; as if a man that should interpose himselfe to negotiate between two.

should to either of them severally pretend, more interest then he hath in the other. And in this and the like kind, it often fals out, that somewhat is produced of nothing. For lies are sufficient to breed opinion, and opinion brings on substance.

But principally in cases of great enterprise, upon charge and adventure such composition of glorious natures doth put life into busines, and those that are of solid and sober natures have more of the ballast, then of the saile.

Certainely *Vaine-glory* helpeth to perpetuate a mans memory, and *Vertue* was never so beholding to humane nature, as it received his due at the second hand. Neither had the fame of *Cicero, Seneca, Plinius Secundus*, borne her age so well, if it had not beene joined with some vanity in themselves; like unto varnish, that makes seelings not onely shine, but last. But all this while, when I speake of *Vaine-glory*, I meane not of that property that *Tacitus* doth attribute to *Mucianus, Omnium quæ dixerat feceratque arte quadam ostentator*: For that proceedes not of vanity, but of a natural magnanimity and discretion; and in some persons is not onely comely, but gracious. For exusations, cessions, modesty it selfe well governed are but arts of ostentation: and amongst those Arts there is none better, then that which *Plinius Secundus* speaketh of, which is to be liberall of praise and commendation to others, in that wherein a mans selfe hath any perfection. For saith *Plinie* very wittily; *In commending another, you do your selfe right; for hee that you commend, is either superior to you in that you commend, or inferiour. If he be inferiour if he be to be commended; you much more: if he be superiour if hee be not to be commended; you much lesse.*

1625

Againe, as *Titus Livius* noteth, in the Case of *Antiochus*, and the *Ætolians; There are sometimes great Effects of Crosse Lies*: As if a Man, that   Negotiates between Two Princes, to draw them to joyne in a Warre against the Third, doth extoll the Forces of either of them, above Measure, the One to the Other: And sometimes, he that deales between Man and Man, raiseth his owne Credit, with Both, by pretending greater Interest, then he hath in Either. And in these, and the like Kindes, it often falls out, that *Somewhat* is produced of *Nothing*: For Lies are sufficient to breed Opinion, and Opinion brings on Substance. In Militar Commanders and Soldiers, *Vaine-Glory* is an Essentiall Point; For as Iron sharpens Iron, so by *Glory* one Courage sharpneth another. In Cases of great Enterprise, upon Charge and Adventure, a Composition of *Glorious* Natures, doth put life into Businesse; And those that are of Solide and Sober Natures, have more of the Ballast, then of the Saile. In Fame of Learning, the Flight will be slow, without some Feathers of *Ostentation. Qui de contemnendâ Gloriâ Libros scribunt, Nomen suum inscribunt. Socrates, Aristotle, Galen*, were Men full of *Ostentation*.

Certainly *Vaine-Glory* helpeth to Perpetuate a Mans Memory; And Vertue was never so Beholding to Humane Nature, as it received his due at the Second Hand. Neither had the Fame of *Cicero, Seneca, Plinius Secundus*, borne her Age so well, if it had not been joyned, with some *Vanity* in themselves: Like unto Varnish, that makes Seelings not onely Shine, but Last. But all this while, when I speake of *Vaine-Glory*, I meane not of that Property, that *Tacitus* doth attribute to *Mucianus; Omnium, quæ dixerat, feceratque, Arte quadam Ostentator*: For that proceeds not of *Vanity*, but of Naturall Magnanimity, and discretion: And in some Persons, is not onely Comely, but Gracious. For Excusations, Cessions, Modesty it selfe well Governed, are but Arts of *Ostentation*. And amongst those Arts, there is none better, then that which *Plinius Secundus* speaketh of; which is to be Liberall of Praise and Commendation to others, in that, wherein a Mans Selfe hath any Perfection. For saith *Pliny* very Wittily; *In commending Another, you doe your selfe right; For he that you Commend, is either Superiour to you, in that you Commend, or Inferiour. If he be Inferiour, if he be to be Commended, you much more: If he be Superiour, if he be not to be commended, you much lesse. Glorious* Men are the Scorne of Wise Men; the Admiration of Fooles; The Idols of Parasites; And the Slaves of their own Vaunts.

C. A fragment of an essay: *Of Fame*

The fragment *Of Fame* was first published by William Rawley, Bacon's chaplain, in his *Resuscitatio*, 1657, pp. 281–2 (from which the present text is taken, preserving the original spelling and punctuation). Rawley's book contains a life of Bacon, and certain writings which Bacon had not intended to publish but which he wanted preserved. Spedding, *Works*, VI. 519, describes *Of Fame* as a 'genuine and undoubted work of Bacon's, as far as it goes'.

The *Poets* make *Fame*[1] a *Monster*. They describe her, in Part, finely, and elegantly; and, in part, gravely, and sententiously.[2] They say, look how many *Feathers* she hath, so many *Eyes* she hath underneath: So many Tongues; So Many Voyces; She pricks up so many Ears.[3]

This is a *flourish*:[4] There follow excellent *Parables*;[5] As that, she gathereth strength in going; That she goeth upon the ground, and yet hideth her head in the Clouds. That, in the day time, she sitteth in a *Watch Tower*, and flyeth, most, by night: That she mingleth Things done, with things not done: And that she is a Terrour to great *Citties*: But that, which passeth all the rest, is: They do recount, that the *Earth*, *Mother* of the *Gyants*, that made War against *Jupiter*, and were by him destroyed, thereupon, in an anger, brought forth *Fame*: For certain it is, That *Rebels*, figured by the *Gyants*, and *Seditious Fames*, and *Libels*, are but *Brothers*, and *Sisters*; *Masculine*, and *Feminine*.[6] But now, if a Man can tame this *Monster*, and bring her to feed at the hand, and govern her, and with her fly[7] other ravening Fowle, and kill them, it is somewhat worth. But we are infected, with the stile of the *Poets*. To speak now, in a sad,[8] and serious manner: There is not, in all the Politiques,[9] a *Place*,[10] lesse handled, and more worthy to be handled, then this of *Fame*. We will, therefore, speak of these *points*. What are false *Fames*; And what are true *Fames*; And how they may be best discerned[11]; How *Fames*, may be sown, and raised; How they may be spread, and multiplyed; And how they may be checked, and layed dead. And other Things, concerning the *Nature* of *Fame*. *Fame*, is of that force, as there is, scarcely, any great Action wherein, it hath not, a great part; Especially, in the *War*. *Mucianus* undid *Vitellius* by a *Fame*, that he scattered; That *Vitellius* had in purpose, to remove the *Legions* of *Syria*, into *Germany*; And the Legions of *Germany*, into *Syria*:

---

1. Rumour.   2. Weightily and rich in meaning.
3. See Virgil, *Aeneid*, IV. 175–90.   4. An embellishment.
5. Comparisons.   6. See Essay 15, note 4.   7. Attack.   8. Grave.
9. Political writers.   10. Topic.   11. Distinguished.

whereupon the *Legions* of *Syria* were infinitely inflamed.[12] *Julius Cæsar*, took *Pompey* unprovided, and layed asleep his industry, and preparations, by a *Fame* that he cunningly gave out; How *Cæsars* own Souldiers loved him not; And being wearied with the Wars, and Laden with the spoyles of Gaul, would forsake him, as soon as he came into *Italy*.[13] *Livia*, setled all things, for the Succession, of her Son *Tiberius*, by continuall giving out, that her husband *Augustus*, was upon Recovery, and amendment.[14] And it is an usuall thing, with the *Basshawes*,[15] to conceale the Death of the Great *Turk* from the *Jannizaries*,[16] and men of War, to save the Sacking of *Constantinople*, and other *Towns*, as their Manner is. *Themistocles*, made *Zerxes*, King of *Persia* poast apace out of *Græcia*, by giving out, that the *Græcians*, had a purpose, to break his *Bridge*, of Ships, which he had made athwart *Hellespont*.[17] There be a thousand such like *Examples*; And the more they are, the lesse they need to be repeated; Because a Man, meeteth with them, every where: Therefore, let all Wise *Governors*, have as great a watch, and care, over *Fames*, as they have, of the *Actions*, and Designes themselves.

The rest was not Finished.

D.   A plan for an unwritten (or unpublished) essay

'Play' was first printed by Spedding, *Works*, VII.210–11, from a manuscript in Bacon's own hand (British Library MS, Harleian 7017, folio 110). Although Spedding concludes that this is a plan for an 'elaborate treatise' on the subject of play, it could just as well be the basis of an unwritten and much shorter essay, *Of Play*. The *sententiae* and proverbs are already written out, and in the right positions (there is a pointed opening and sharp conclusion), and the range of discussion is characteristic of the *Essays*. We cannot be sure, but this draft may well reveal how Bacon wrote up the *Essays* from the briefest of notes and quotations. Noticeably, the subject of play does not extend, in these jottings at least, to drama and the theatre. The text printed here is from Spedding, with Bacon's contractions expanded.

---

12. Tacitus, *Histories*, II.80.   13. *The Civil Wars*, I.6
14. Tacitus, *Annals*, I.5.   15. Turkish officials.
16. Bodyguard to the sultan.   17. Plutarch, *Themistocles*, XVI.4–5.

PLAY.

The syn against the holy ghost – termed in zeal by one of the fathers.

Cause of oths, quarrells, expence and unthriftines: ydlenes and indisposition of the mynd to labors.

Art of forgetting; cause of society, acquaintance, familiarity in frends; neere and ready attendance in servants; recreation and putting of melancholy.

Putting of malas curas et cupiditates.

Games of activity and passetyme; of act. of strength, quicknes; quick of ey, hand, legg, the whole mocon: strength of arme; legge; of activity, of sleight.

Of passetyme onely; of hazard; of play mixt.

Of hazard; meere hazard; cunnyng in making the game: Of playe; exercise of attention: of memory: of dissimulation: of discrecon.

Of many hands or of receyt: of few: of quick returne, tedious; of præsent judgment, of uncerten yssue.

Severall playes or ideas of play.

Frank play, wary play; venturous, not venturous; quick, slowe.

Oversight: Dotage: Betts: Lookers on: Judgment.

Groome porter: Christmas: Invention for hunger.

Oddes: stake: sett.

He that folowes his losses and giveth soone over at wynnings will never gayne by play.

Ludimus incauti studioque aperimur ab ipso.

He that playeth not the begynnyng of a game well at tick tack and the later end at yrish shall never wynne.

Frier Gilbert.

The lott; earnest in old tyme sport now, as musike out of Church to chamber.

Appendix 2:
Counsels for the Prince

In Praise of Knowledge

Source: On 17 November 1592 Robert, Earl of Essex, presented a 'device' (or courtly entertainment) to Queen Elizabeth to celebrate the anniversary of her accession. The device, entitled *A Conference of Pleasure*, consists of four speeches: the first praises the worthiest virtue (fortitude), the second the worthiest affection (love), the third the worthiest power (knowledge), and the fourth the worthiest person (Queen Elizabeth). The third speech is printed here from *Letters and Life*, I.123–6, with some small changes to the text.

In Praise of Knowledge

Silence were the best celebration of that which I mean to commend; for who would not use silence where silence is not made, and what crier can make silence in such a noise and tumult of vain and popular opinions?

My praise shall be dedicated to the mind itself. The mind is the man and the knowledge of the mind. A man is but what he knoweth. The mind itself is but an accident[1] to knowledge, for knowledge is a double of that which is; the truth of being and the truth of knowing is all one.

Are not the pleasures of the affections greater than the pleasures of the senses? And are not the pleasures of the intellect greater than the pleasures of the affections? Is not knowledge a true and only natural pleasure, whereof there is no satiety? Is it not knowledge that doth alone clear the mind of all perturbation? How many things are there which we imagine not? How many things do we esteem and value otherwise than they are! This ill-proportioned estimation, these vain imaginations, these be the clouds of error that turn into the storms of perturbation. Is there any such happiness as for a man's mind to be raised above the confusion of things, where he may have the prospect of the order of nature and the error of men?[2]

1. Is not essential.
2. Probably an allusion to Lucretius, *On the Nature of Things*, II.1–10, a passage which Bacon paraphrases in the essay *Of Truth*, p. 62 above.

But is this a vein only of delight and not of discovery? Of contentment and not of benefit? Shall he not as well discern the riches of nature's warehouses, as the benefit of her shop? Is truth ever barren? Shall he not be able thereby to produce worthy effects, and to endow the life of man with infinite commodities?

But shall I make this garland to be put upon a wrong head? Would anybody believe me, if I should verify this upon the knowledge that is now in use? Are we the richer by one poor invention, by reason of all the learning that hath been these many hundred years? The industry of artificers maketh some small improvements of things invented; and chance sometimes in experimenting maketh us to stumble upon somewhat which is new; but all the disputation of the learned never brought to light one effect of nature before unknown. When things are known and found out, then they can descant upon them, they can knit them into certain causes, they can reduce them to their principles. If any instance of experience stand against them, they can range it in order by some distinctions. But all this is but a web of the wit, it can work nothing. I do not doubt but that common notions, which we call reason, and the knitting of them together, which we call logic, are the art of reason and studies. But they rather cast obscurity than gain light to the contemplation of nature. All the philosophy of nature which is now received, is either the philosophy of the Grecians, or that other of the Alchemists. That of the Grecians had the foundation in words, in ostentation, in confutation, in sects, in schools, in disputations. The Grecians were (as one of themselves saith) *you Grecians, ever children*.[3] They knew little antiquity; they knew (except fables) not much above five hundred years before themselves; they knew but a small portion of the world. That of the alchemists hath the foundation in imposture, in auricular traditions and obscurity; it was catching hold of religion, but the principle of it is, *Populus vult decipi*.[4] So that I know no great difference between these great philosophies, but that the one is a loud crying folly, and the other a whispering folly. The one is gathered out of a few vulgar observations, and the other out of a few experiments of a furnace. The one never faileth to multiply words, and the other ever faileth to multiply gold.

Who would not smile at Aristotle, when he admireth the eternity and invariableness of the heavens, as there were not the like in the bowels of the earth? Those be the confines and borders of these two kingdoms, where the continual alteration and incursion are. The superficies and upper parts of the earth are full of varieties. The superficies and lower parts of the heavens (which we call the middle region of the air) is full of

3. The words addressed to Solon, the sixth-century Athenian statesman and poet, by an Egyptian priest. Plato, *Timaeus*, 22 BC.
4. The people want to be deceived.

variety. There is much spirit in the one part that cannot be brought into mass. There is much massy body in the other place that cannot be refined to spirit. The common air is as the waste ground between the borders.

Who would not smile at the astronomers, I mean not these new carmen which drive the earth about,[5] but the ancient astronomers, which feign the moon to be the swiftest of the planets in motion, and the rest in order, the higher the slower; and so are compelled to imagine a double motion; whereas how evident is it, that that which they call a contrary motion is but an abatement of motion. The fixed stars overgo Saturn, and so in them and the rest all is but one motion, and the nearer the earth the slower; a motion also whereof air and water do participate, though much interrupted.

But why do I in a conference of pleasure enter into these great matters, in sort that pretending to know much, I should forget what is seasonable? Pardon me, it was because all other things may be endowed and adorned with speeches, but knowledge itself is more beautiful than any apparel of words that can be put upon it.

And let me not seem arrogant, without respect to these great reputed authors. Let me so give every man his due, as I give Time his due, which is to discover truth. Many of these men had greater wits, far above my own, and so are many in the universities of Europe at this day. But alas, they learn nothing there but to believe: first to believe that others know that which they know not; and after that themselves know that which they know not. But indeed facility to believe, impatience to doubt, temerity to answer, glory to know, doubt to contradict, end to gain, sloth to search, seeking things in words, resting in part of nature; these, and the like, have been the things which have forbidden the happy match between the mind of man and the nature of things, and in place thereof have married it to vain notions and blind experiments. And what the posterity and issue of so honourable a match may be, it is not hard to consider. Printing, a gross invention; artillery, a thing that lay not far out of the way; the needle,[6] a thing partly known before; what a change have these three made in the world in these times; the one in state of learning, the other in state of the war, the third in the state of treasure, commodities and navigation. And those, I say, were but stumbled upon and lighted upon by chance.

Therefore, no doubt the sovereignty of man lieth hid in knowledge; wherein many things are reserved, which kings with their treasure

5. i.e. those astronomers who follow Copernicus and believe that the earth revolves round the sun. The *ancient astronomers* are those who accept the Ptolemaic theory of the universe (that the sun and planets rotate around the earth), and adjust their theory, where necessary, to explain irregularities in planetary movements. See Essay 15, note 12, and Essay 17, note 8.   6. The magnetic needle.

cannot buy, nor with their force command; their spials[7] and intelligencers can give no news of them, their seamen and discoverers cannot sail where they grow. Now we govern nature in opinions, but we are thrall unto her in necessity; but if we would be led by her in invention, we should command her in action.

Advising the Study of Philosophy

Source: The Christmas festivities for 1594 at Gray's Inn included six speeches addressed to a Prince of Purpoole, a mock prince elected by the students to hold court, receive ambassadors and be the object of advice and entertainment. The speeches were delivered by counsellors, who argued in turn for 'the Exercise of War', 'the Study of Philosophy', 'Eternizement and Fame by Buildings and Foundations', 'Absoluteness of State and Treasure', 'Virtue and a Gracious Government', and 'Pastimes and Sports'. The second speech is printed here from *Letters and Life*, I.334–5, again with some slight alterations to the text.

Advising the Study of Philosophy

It may seem, most excellent Prince, that my Lord which now hath spoken,[1] did never read the just censures of the wisest men, who compared great conquerors to great rovers[2] and witches, whose power is in destruction and not in preservation; else would he never have advised your Excellency to become as some comet or blazing star, which should threaten and portend nothing but death and dearth, combustions and troubles of the world. And whereas the governing faculties of men are two, force and reason, whereof the one is brute and the other divine, he wisheth you for your principal ornament and regality the talons of the eagle to catch the prey, and not the piercing sight which seeth into the bottom of the sea. But I contrariwise will wish unto your Highness the exercise of the best and purest part of the mind, and the most innocent and meriting conquest, being the conquest of the works of nature; making this proposition, that you bend the excellency of your spirits to the searching out, inventing, and discovering of all whatsoever is hid and secret in the world; that your Excellency be not as a lamp that shineth to others and yet seeth not itself, but as the Eye of the World, that both carrieth and useth light.

Antiquity, that presenteth unto us in dark visions the wisdom of

7. Spies.
1. i.e. the counsellor advising 'the Exercise of War' in the first speech.
2. Robbers.

former times, informeth us that the governments of kingdoms have always had an affinity with the secrets and mysteries of learning. Amongst the Persians, the kings were attended on by the Magi.[3] The Gymnosophists[4] had all the government under the princes of Asia; and generally those kingdoms were accounted most happy, that had rulers most addicted to philosophy. The Ptolemies in Egypt may be for instance; and Solomon was a man so seen in the universality of nature that he wrote an herbal of all that was green upon the earth. No conquest of Julius Caesar made him so remembered as the Calendar. Alexander the Great wrote to Aristotle upon the publishing of the *Physics*, that he esteemed more of excellent men in knowledge than in empire.

And to this purpose I will commend to your Highness four principal works and monuments of yourself. First, the collecting of a most perfect and general library, wherein whatsoever the wit of man hath heretofore committed to books of worth, be they ancient or modern, printed or manuscript, European or of other parts, of one or other language, may be made contributory to your wisdom. Next, a spacious, wonderful garden, wherein whatsoever plant the sun of divers climates, out of the earth of divers moulds, either wild or by the culture of man, brought forth, may be, with that care that appertaineth to the good prospering thereof, set and cherished: this garden to be built about with rooms to stable in all rare beasts and to cage in all rare birds; with two lakes adjoining, the one of fresh water, the other of salt, for like variety of fishes. And so you may have in small compass a model of universal nature made private. The third, a goodly huge cabinet, wherein whatsoever the hand of man by exquisite art or engine hath made rare in stuff, form, or motion; whatsoever singularity, chance, and the shuffle of things hath produced; whatsoever nature hath wrought in things that want life and may be kept; shall be sorted and included. The fourth such a still-house, so furnished with mills, instruments, furnaces, and vessels as may be a palace fit for a philosopher's stone.[5] Thus, when your Excellency shall have added depth of knowledge to the fineness of your spirits and greatness of your power, then indeed shall you be a Trismegistus;[6] and then when all other miracles and wonders shall cease by reason that you shall have discovered their natural causes, yourself shall be left the only miracle and wonder of the world.

3. Members of the priestly caste, renowned for their skill in magic and astrology.
4. Ancient Hindu religious sect. See Essay 39, note 12.
5. The substance sought by the alchemists. It was thought to be able to change base metals into gold, and to cure diseases.
6. Hermes Trismegistus was thought to be an ancient Egyptian priest, philosopher and king, who had written works of great wisdom and learning in the distant past (well before Plato and Aristotle). The writings were in fact of the second and third centuries A.D.

Appendix 3:

The Wisdom of the Ancients

Source: First published in 1609, *De Sapientia Veterum* (Of the Wisdom of the Ancients) is a collection of thirty-one explications of classical fable. The ones printed here are taken, with slight alterations, from the translation by Spedding in *Works*, VI.714–17, 720–22, and 745–53. The standard study of how Bacon put these interpretations together is by C. W. Lemmi, *The Classic Deities in Bacon*, Baltimore, 1933.

PERSEUS
or
WAR

Perseus was sent, it is said, by Pallas to cut off the head of Medusa, from whom many nations in the westernmost parts of Spain suffered grievous calamities – a monster so dreadful and horrible that the mere sight of her turned men into stone. She was one of the Gorgons; and the only one of them that was mortal, the others not being subject to change. By way of equipment for this so noble exploit, Perseus received arms and gifts from three several gods. Mercury gave him wings for his feet; Pluto gave him a helmet; Pallas a shield and a mirror: And yet though so well provided and equipped, he did not proceed against Medusa directly, but went out of his way to visit the Graeae. These were half-sisters to the Gorgons, and had been born old women with white hair. They had but one eye and one tooth among them, and these they used to wear by turns; each putting them on as she went abroad, and putting them off again when she came back. This eye and tooth they now lent to Perseus. Whereupon, judging himself sufficiently equipped for the performance of his undertaking, he went against Medusa with all haste, flying. He found her asleep, but not daring to face her (in case she should wake) he looked back into Pallas's mirror, and taking aim by the reflexion, cut off her head. From the blood which flowed out of the wound, there suddenly leaped forth a winged Pegasus. The severed head was fixed by Perseus in Pallas's shield, where it still retained its power of striking stiff, as if thunder or planet stricken, all who looked on it.

The fable seems to have been composed with reference to the art and judicious conduct of war. And first, for the kind of war to be chosen, it sets forth (as from the advice of Pallas) three sound and weighty precepts to guide the deliberation.

The first is, not to take any great trouble for the subjugation of the neighbouring nations. For the rule to be followed in the enlarging of a patrimony does not apply to the extension of an empire. In a private property, the vicinity of the estates to each other is of importance; but in extending an empire, occasion, and facility of carrying the war through, and value of conquest, should be regarded instead of vicinity. We see that the Romans, while they had hardly penetrated westward beyond Liguria,[1] had conquered and included in their empire eastern provinces as far off as Mount Taurus.[2] And therefore Perseus, though he belonged to the east, did not decline a distant expedition to the uttermost parts of the west.

The second is that there be a just and honourable cause of war: for this begets alacrity as well in the soldiers themselves, as in the people, from whom the supplies are to come: also it opens the way to alliances, and conciliates friends; and has a great many advantages. Now there is no cause of war more pious than the overthrow of a tyranny under which the people lies prostrate without spirit or vigour, as if turned to stone by the aspect of Medusa.

Thirdly, it is wisely added that whereas there are three Gorgons (by whom are represented wars), Perseus chose the one that was mortal, that is, he chose such a war as might be finished and carried through, and did not engage in the pursuit of vast or infinite projects.

The equipment of Perseus is of that kind which is everything in war, and almost ensures success; for he received swiftness from Mercury, secrecy of counsel from Pluto, and providence from Pallas. Nor is the circumstance that those wings of swiftness were for the heels and not for the shoulders without an allegorical meaning, and a very wise one. For it is not in the first attack, so much as in those that follow up and support the first, that swiftness is required; and there is no error more common in war than that of not pressing on the secondary and subsidiary actions with an activity answerable to the vigour of the beginnings. There is also an ingenious distinction implied in the images of the shield and the mirror (for the parable of Pluto's helmet which made men invisible needs no explanation) between the two kinds of foresight. For we must have not only that kind of foresight which acts as a shield, but that other kind likewise which enables us (like Pallas's mirror) to spy into the forces and movements and counsels of the enemy.

1. The area of Italy around Genoa and Leghorn.
2. The mountain ridge of Asia Minor.

But Perseus, however provided with forces and courage, stands yet in need of one thing more before the war be commenced, which is of the highest possible importance – he must go round to the Graeae. These Graeae are treasons; which are indeed war's sisters, yet not sisters german, but as it were of less noble birth. For wars are generous; treasons degenerate and base. They are prettily described, in allusion to the perpetual cares and trepidations of traitors, as old and white from their birth. Their power (before they break out into open revolt) lies either in the eye or the tooth; for all factions when alienated from the state, both play the spy and bite. And the eye and tooth are as it were common to them all: the eye because all their information is handed from one to another, and circulates through the whole party; the tooth, because they all bite with one mouth and all tell one tale – so that when you hear one you hear all. Therefore Perseus must make friends of those Graeae, that they may lend him their eye and tooth – the eye for discovery of information, the tooth to sow rumours, raise envy, and stir the minds of the people.

These matters being thus arranged and prepared, we come next to the carriage of the war itself. And here we see that Perseus finds Medusa asleep, for the undertaker of a war almost always, if he is wise, takes his enemy unprepared and in security. And now it is that Pallas's mirror is wanted. For there are many who before the hour of danger can look into the enemy's affairs sharply and attentively; but the chief use of the mirror is in the very instant of peril, that you may examine the manner of it without being confused by the fear of it; which is meant by the looking at it with eyes averted.

The conclusion of the war is followed by two effects: first the birth and springing up of Pegasus, which obviously enough denotes fame, flying abroad and celebrating the victory. Secondly the carrying of Medusa's head upon the shield, for this is incomparably the best kind of safeguard. A single brilliant and memorable exploit, happily conducted and accomplished, paralyses all the enemies' movements, and mates malevolence itself.

ORPHEUS
or
PHILOSOPHY

The story of Orpheus, which though so well known has not yet been in all points perfectly well interpreted, seems meant for a representation of universal Philosophy. For Orpheus himself – a man admirable and truly divine, who being master of all harmony subdued and drew all things after him by sweet and gentle measures – may pass by an easy metaphor for philosophy personified. For as the works of wisdom surpass in dignity and power the works of strength, so the labours of Orpheus surpass the labours of Hercules.

Orpheus, moved by affection for his wife who had been snatched from him by an untimely death, resolved to go down to Hell and beg her back again of the Infernal Powers; trusting to his lyre. Nor was he disappointed. For so soothed and charmed were the infernal powers by the sweetness of his singing and playing, that they gave him leave to take her away with him; but upon one condition – she was to follow behind him, and he was not to look back until they had reached the confines of light. From this however in the impatience of love and anxiety he could not refrain. Before he had quite reached the point of safety, he looked back, and so the covenant was broken, and she suddenly fell away from him and was hurried back into Hell. From that time Orpheus betook himself to solitary places, a melancholy man and averse from the sight of women; where by the same sweetness of his song and lyre he drew to him all kinds of wild beasts, in such manner that putting off their several natures, forgetting all their quarrels and ferocity, no longer driven by the stings and furies of lust, no longer caring to satisfy their hunger or to hunt their prey, they all stood about him gently and sociably, as in a theatre, listening only to the concords of his lyre. Nor was that all: for so great was the power of his music that it moved the woods and the very stones to shift themselves and take their stations decently and orderly about him. And all this went on for some time with happy success and great admiration, till at last certain Thracian women, under the stimulation and excitement of Bacchus, came where he was. And first they blew such a hoarse and hideous blast upon a horn that the sound of his music could no longer be heard for the din: whereupon, the charm being broken that had been the bond of that order and good fellowship, confusion began again; the beasts returned each to his several nature and preyed one upon the other as before; the stones and woods stayed no longer in their places: while Orpheus himself was torn to pieces by the women in their fury, and his limbs scattered about the fields. At whose death, Helicon (river sacred to the Muses) in grief and indignation buried his waters under the earth, to reappear elsewhere.

The meaning of the fable appears to be this. The singing of Orpheus is of two kinds; one to propitiate the infernal powers, the other to draw the wild beasts and the woods. The former may be best understood as referring to natural philosophy, the latter to philosophy moral and civil. For natural philosophy proposes to itself, as its noblest work of all, nothing less than the restitution and renovation of things corruptible, and (what is indeed the same thing in a lower degree) the conservation of bodies in the state in which they are, and the retardation of dissolution and putrefaction. Now certainly if this can be effected at all, it cannot be otherwise than by due and exquisite attempering and adjustment of parts in nature, as by the harmony and perfect modulation of a lyre. And yet being a thing of all others the most difficult, it commonly fails of effect; and fails (it may be) from no cause more than from curious and premature meddling and impatience. Then Philosophy finding that her great work is too much for her, in sorrowful mood, as well becomes her, turns to human affairs; and applying her powers of persuasion and eloquence to insinuate into men's minds the love of virtue and equity and peace, teaches the peoples to assemble and unite and take upon them the yoke of laws and submit to authority, and forget their ungoverned appetites, in listening and conforming to precepts and discipline. Whereupon soon follows the building of houses, the founding of cities, the planting of fields and gardens with trees; insomuch that the stones and the woods are not unfitly said to leave their places and come about her. And this application of Philosophy to civil affairs is properly represented, and according to the true order of things, as subsequent to the diligent trial and final frustration of the experiment of restoring the dead body to life. For true it is that the clearer recognition of the inevitable necessity of death sets men upon seeking immortality by merit and renown. Also it is wisely added in the story, that Orpheus was averse from women and from marriage; for the sweets of marriage and the dearness of children commonly draw men away from performing great and lofty services to the commonwealth, being content to be perpetuated in their race and stock, and not in their deeds.

But howsoever the works of wisdom are among human things the most excellent, yet they too have their periods and closes. For so it is that after kingdoms and commonwealths have flourished for a time, there arise perturbations and seditions and wars; amid the uproars of which, first the laws are put to silence, and then men return to the depraved conditions of their nature, and desolation is seen in the fields and cities. And if such troubles last, it is not long before letters also and philosophy are so torn in pieces that no traces of them can be found but a few fragments, scattered here and there like planks from a shipwreck; and then a season of barbarism sets in, the waters of Helicon being sunk under the ground, until, according to the appointed vicissitude of things, they break out and issue forth again, perhaps among other nations, and not in the places where they were before.

PROMETHEUS
or
THE STATE OF MAN

Tradition says that Man was made by Prometheus, and made of clay; only that Prometheus took particles from different animals and mixed them in. He, desiring to benefit and protect his own work, and to be regarded not as the founder only but also as the amplifier and enlarger of the human race, stole up to heaven with a bundle of fennel-stalks in his hand, kindled them at the chariot of the sun, and so brought fire to the earth and presented it to mankind. For this so great benefit received at his hands, men (it is said) were far from being grateful; so far indeed, that they conspired together and impeached him and his invention before Jupiter. This act of theirs was not so taken as justice may seem to have required. For the accusation proved very acceptable both to Jupiter and the rest of the gods; and so delighted were they, that they not only indulged mankind with the use of fire, but presented them likewise with a new gift, of all others most agreeable and desirable – perpetual youth. Overjoyed with this, the foolish people put the gift of the gods on the back of an ass. The ass on his way home, being troubled with extreme thirst, came to a fountain; but a serpent, that was set to guard it, would not let him drink unless he gave in payment whatever that was that he carried on his back. The poor ass accepted the condition, and so for a mouthful of water the power of renewing youth was transferred from men to serpents. After mankind had lost their prize, Prometheus made up his quarrel with them; but retaining his malice, and being bitterly incensed against Jupiter, he did not scruple to tempt him with deceit, even in the act of sacrifice. Having slain (it is said) two bulls, he stuffed the hide of one of them with the flesh and fat of both, and bringing them to the altar, with an air of devotion and benignity offered Jupiter his choice. Jupiter, detesting his craft and bad faith, but knowing how to requite it, chose the mock bull; then bethinking him of vengeance, and seeing that there was no way to take down the insolence of Prometheus except by chastising the human race (of which work he was extravagantly vain and proud), ordered Vulcan to make a fair and lovely woman. When she was made, each of the gods bestowed upon her his several gift, whence she was called Pandora. Then they placed in her hands an elegant vase, in which were enclosed all mischiefs and calamities; only at the bottom there remained Hope. With her vase in her hand she repaired first of all to Prometheus, to see if he would take and open it, which he, cautious and cunning, declined. Thus rejected she went away to Epimetheus, Prometheus's brother, but of a character entirely different, who opened it without hesitation. But as soon as he saw all the mischiefs rushing out, growing wise when it was too late, he struggled to get the lid on again as fast as possible; but it was all he could do to keep in the last of the party, which was Hope, that lay at the bottom. In the end Jupiter seized Prometheus, and upon many and grave charges – as that of old he had stolen fire, that he had made a mock of Jupiter's majesty in that deceitful sacrifice, that he had scorned and rejected his gift, together with another not mentioned before, that he had attempted to ravish Minerva – threw him into chains and condemned him to perpetual tortures. For by Jupiter's command he was dragged to Mount Caucasus, and there bound fast to a column so that he could not stir. And there was an eagle which gnawed and consumed his liver by day; but what was eaten in the day grew again in the night, so that matter was never wanting for the torture to work upon. Yet they say that this punishment had its end at last; for Hercules sailed across the ocean in a cup that was given to him by the Sun, came to Caucasus, shot the eagle with his arrows, and set Prometheus free. In honour of Prometheus there were instituted in some nations games called torch-races, in which the runners carried lighted torches in their hands; and if any went out the bearer stood aside, leaving the victory to those that followed; and the first who reached the goal with his torch still burning received the prize.

This fable carries in it many true and grave speculations both on the surface and underneath. For there are some things in it that have been long ago observed, others have never been touched at all.

Prometheus clearly and expressly signifies Providence: and the one thing singled out by the ancients as the special and peculiar work of Providence was the creation and constitution of Man. For this one reason no doubt was, that the nature of man includes mind and intellect, which is the seat of providence; and since to derive mind and reason from principles brutal and irrational would be harsh and incredible, it follows almost necessarily that the human spirit was endued with providence not without the precedent and intention and warrant of the greater providence. But this was not all. The chief aim of the parable appears to be, that Man, if we look to final causes, may be regarded as the centre of the world; insomuch that if man were taken away from the world, the rest would seem to be all astray, without aim or purpose, to be like a besom without a binding, as the saying is, and to be leading to nothing. For the whole world works together in the service of man, and there is nothing from which he does not derive use and fruit. The revolutions and courses of the stars serve him both for distinction of the seasons and distribution of the quarters of the world. The appearances of the middle sky afford him prognostications of weather. The winds sail his ships and work his mills and engines. Plants and animals of all kinds are made to furnish him either with dwelling and shelter or clothing or food or medicine, or to lighten his labour, or to give him pleasure and comfort; insomuch that all things seem to be going about man's business and not their own. Nor is it without meaning added that in the mass and composition of which man was made, particles taken from the different animals were infused and mixed up with the clay; for it is most true that of all things in the universe man is the most composite, so that he was not without reason called by the ancients the little world. For though the Alchemists, when they maintain that there is to be found in man every mineral, every vegetable, &c., or something corresponding to them, take the word *microcosm* in a sense too gross and literal, and have so spoiled the elegance and distorted the meaning of it, yet that the body of man is of all existing things both the most mixed and the most organic, remains not the less a sober and solid truth. And this is indeed the reason it is capable of such wonderful powers and faculties; for the powers of simple bodies, though they be certain and rapid, yet being less refracted, broken up, and counteracted by mixture, they are few; but abundance and excellence of power resides in mixture and composition. Nevertheless we see that man in the first stage of his existence is a naked and defenceless thing, slow to help himself, and full of wants. Therefore Prometheus applied himself with all haste to the invention of fire, which in all human necessities and business is the great minister of relief and help; insomuch that if the soul be the form of forms and the hand the instrument of instruments, fire may rightly be called the help of helps and the mean of means. For through it most operations are effected, through it the arts mechanical and the sciences themselves are furthered in an infinite variety of ways.

Now the description of the manner in which the theft of fire was accomplished is apt and according to the nature of the thing. It was by applying a stalk of fennel to the chariot of the Sun. For fennel is used as a rod to strike with. The meaning therefore clearly is that Fire is produced by violent percussions and collisions of one body with another; whereby the matter they are made of is attenuated and set in motion, and prepared to receive the heat of the celestial bodies, and so by clandestine processes, as by an act of theft, snatches fire as it were from the chariot of the Sun.

There follows a remarkable part of the parable. Men, we are told, instead of gratulation and thanksgiving fell to remonstrance and indignation, and brought an accusation before Jupiter both against Prometheus and against Fire; and this act was moreover by him so well liked, that in consideration of it he accumulated fresh benefits upon mankind. For how should the crime of ingratitude towards their maker, a vice which includes in itself almost all others, deserve approbation and reward? And what could be the drift of such a fiction? But this is not what is meant. The meaning of the allegory is, that the accusation and arraignment by men both of their own nature and of art, proceeds from an excellent condition of mind and issues in good, whereas the contrary is hated by the gods, and unlucky. For they who extravagantly extol human nature as it is and the arts as received, who spend themselves in admiration of what they already possess, and hold up as perfect the sciences which are professed and cultivated, are wanting, first, in reverence to the divine nature, with the perfection of which they almost presume to compare, and next in usefulness towards man; as thinking that they have already reached the summit of things and finished their work, and therefore need seek no further. They on the other hand who arraign and accuse nature and the arts, and abound with complainings, are not only more modest (if it be truly considered) in their sentiment, but are also stimulated perpetually to fresh industry and new discoveries. And this makes me marvel all the more at the ignorance and evil genius of mankind, who being over-crowed by the arrogance of a few persons, hold in such honour that philosophy of the Peripatetics,[1] which was but a portion, and no large portion either, of the Greek philosophy, that every attempt to find fault with it has come to be not only useless, but also suspected and almost dangerous. Whereas certainly in my opinion both Empedocles and Democritus,[2] who complain, the first madly enough, but the second very soberly, that all things are hidden away from us, that we know nothing, that we discern nothing, that truth is drowned in deep wells, that the true and the false are strangely joined and twisted together (for the New Academy[3] carried it a great deal too far) are more to be approved than the school of Aristotle so confident and dogmatical. Therefore let all men know that the preferring of complaints against nature and the arts is a thing well pleasing to the gods, and draws down new alms and bounties from the divine goodness; and that the accusation of Prometheus, our maker and master though he be, yea sharp and vehement accusation, is a thing more sober and profitable than this overflow of congratulation and thanksgiving: let them know that conceit of plenty is one of the principal causes of want.

Now for the gift which men are said to have received as the reward of their accusation, namely the unfading flower of youth. It seems to show that methods and medicines for the retardation of age and the prolongation of life were by the ancients not despaired of, but reckoned rather among those things which men once had and by sloth and negligence let slip, than among those which were wholly denied or never offered. For they seem to say that by the true use of fire, and by the just and vigorous accusation and conviction of the errors of art, such gifts might

1. i.e. Aristotelian philosophy.

2. Greek philosophers of the fifth and fourth centuries B.C. See Essay 16, note 7, and p. 281 below. 3. See Essay 1, note 4.

have been compassed; and that it was not the divine goodness that was wanting to them therein, but they that were wanting to themselves; in that having received this gift of the gods, they committed the carriage of it to a lazy and slow-paced ass. By this seems to be meant experience, a thing stupid and full of delay, whose slow and tortoise-like pace gave birth to that ancient complaint that *life is short and art is long*. And for my own part I certainly think that those two faculties – the Dogmatical and the Empirical – have not yet been well united and coupled, but that the bringing down of new gifts from the gods has ever been left either to the abstract philosophies, as to a light bird, or to sluggish and tardy experience, as to an ass. And yet it must be said in behalf of the ass, that he might perhaps do well enough, but for that accident of thirst by the way. For if a man would put himself fairly under the command of experience, and proceed steadily onward by a certain law and method, and not let any thirst for experiments either of profit or ostentation seize him by the way and make him lay down and unsettle his burthen in order that he may taste them – such a man I do think would prove a carrier to whom new and augmented measures of divine bounty might be well enough entrusted.

As for the transfer of the gift to serpents, it seems to be an addition merely for ornament; unless it were inserted in shame of mankind, who with that fire of theirs and with so many arts, cannot acquire for themselves things which nature has of herself bestowed on many other animals.

The sudden reconciliation of men with Prometheus after the frustration of their hope, contains likewise a wise and useful observation. It alludes to the levity and rashness of men in new experiments; who if an experiment does not at once succeed according to wish, are in far too great a hurry to give up the attempt as a failure, and so tumble back to where they were and take on with the old things again.

Having thus described the state of man in respect of arts and matters intellectual, the parable passes to Religion; for with the cultivation of the arts came likewise the worship of things divine, and this was immediately seized on and polluted by hypocrisy. Therefore under the figure of that double sacrifice is elegantly represented the person of the truly religious man and the hypocrite. For in the one there is the fat, which is God's portion, by reason of the flame and sweet savour, whereby is meant affection and zeal burning and rising upward for the glory of God. In him are the bowels of charity, in him wholesome and useful meat. In the other is found nothing but dry and bare bones, with which the skin is stuffed out till it looks like a fair and noble victim; whereby are signified those external and empty rites and ceremonies with which men overload and inflate the service of religion: things rather got up for ostentation than conducing to piety. Nor is it enough

for men to offer such mockeries to God, but they must also lay and
father them upon himself, as though he had himself chosen and
prescribed them. It is against such a kind of choice that the prophet in
God's person remonstrates, when he says, *Is this such a fast as I have
chosen, that man should afflict his soul for one day and bow his head
like a bulrush?*[4]

After touching the state of Religion, the parable turns to morals and
the conditions of human life. Pandora has been generally and rightly
understood to mean pleasure and sensual appetite, which, after the
introduction of civil arts and culture and luxury, is kindled up as it were
by the gift of fire. To Vulcan therefore, who in like manner represents
fire, the making of Pleasure is imputed. And from her have flowed forth
infinite mischief upon the minds, the bodies, and the fortunes of men,
together with repentance when too late; nor upon individuals only, but
upon kingdoms also and commonwealths. For from this same fountain
have sprung wars and civil disturbances and tyrannies. But it is worth
while to observe how prettily and elegantly the two conditions and as it
were pictures or models of human life are set forth in the story, under
the persons of Prometheus and Epimetheus. The followers of Epimetheus are the improvident, who take no care for the future but think
only of what is pleasant at the time; and on this account it is true that
they suffer many distresses, difficulties, and calamities, and are engaged in a perpetual struggle with them; and yet in the mean time they
indulge their genius, and amuse their minds moreover, as their ignorance allows them to do, with many empty hopes, in which they take
delight as in pleasant dreams, and so sweeten the miseries of life. The
school of Prometheus on the other hand, that is the wise and fore-
thoughtful class of men, do indeed by their caution decline and remove
out of their way many evils and misfortunes; but with that good there is
this evil joined, that they stint themselves of many pleasures and of the
various agreeableness of life, and cross their genius, and (what is far
worse) torment and wear themselves away with cares and solicitude and
inward fears. For being bound to the column of Necessity, they are
troubled with innumerable thoughts (which because of their flightiness
are represented by the eagle), thoughts which prick and gnaw and
corrode the liver: and if at intervals, as in the night, they obtain some
little relaxation and quiet of mind, yet new fears and anxieties return
presently with the morning. Very few therefore are they to whom the
benefit of both portions falls – to retain the advantages of providence
and yet free themselves from the evils of solicitude and perturbation.
Neither is it possible for anyone to attain this double blessing, except by
the help of Hercules; that is, fortitude and constancy of mind, which

4. From Isaiah 58.5.

being prepared for all events and equal to any fortune, foresees without fear, enjoys without fastidiousness, and bears without impatience. It is worth noting too that this virtue was not natural to Prometheus, but adventitious, and came by help from without. For it is not a thing which any inborn and natural fortitude can attain to; it comes from beyond the ocean, it is received and brought to us from the Sun; for it comes of Wisdom, which is as the Sun, and of meditation upon the inconstancy and fluctuations of human life, which is as the navigation of the ocean: two things which Virgil has well coupled together in those lines:

> Blessèd is he whose mind had power to probe
> The causes of things and trample underfoot
> All terrors and inexorable fate
> And the clamour of devouring Acheron.[5]

Most elegantly also is it added for the consolation and encouragement of men's minds, that that mighty hero sailed in a cup or pitcher; lest they should too much mistrust the narrowness and frailty of their own nature, or plead it in their own excuse, as though it were altogether incapable of this kind of fortitude and constancy: the true nature of which was well divined by Seneca, when he said, *It is true greatness to have in one the frailty of man and the security of God.*[6]

But I must now return to a part which, that I might not interrupt the connexion of what precedes, I have purposely passed by. I mean that last crime of Prometheus, the attempt upon the chastity of Minerva. For it was even for this offence – certainly a very great and grave one – that he underwent that punishment of the tearing of his entrails. The crime alluded to appears to be no other than that into which men not unfrequently fall when puffed up with arts and much knowledge – of trying to bring the divine wisdom itself under the dominion of sense and reason: from which attempt inevitably follows laceration of the mind and vexation without end or rest. And therefore men must soberly and modestly distinguish between things divine and human, between the oracles of sense and of faith; unless they mean to have at once a heretical religion and a fabulous philosophy.

The last point remains – namely the races with burning torches instituted in honour of Prometheus. This again, like that fire in memory and celebration of which these games were instituted, alludes to arts and sciences, and carries in it a very wise admonition, to this effect – that the perfection of the sciences is to be looked for not from the swiftness or ability of any one inquirer, but from a succession. For the strongest and swiftest runners are perhaps not the best fitted to keep

<hr>

5. Virgil, *Georgics*, II.490–93 (translation by L. P. Wilkinson, Penguin, 1982, p. 93).   6. *Epistles*, LIII.12; also quoted in *Of Adversity*, p. 74.

their torch alight; since it may be put out by going too fast as well as too slow. It seems however that these races and games of the torch have long been intermitted; since it is still in their first authors – Aristotle, Galen, Euclid, Ptolemy – that we find the several sciences in highest perfection, and no great matter has been done, nor hardly attempted, by their successors. And well were it to be wished that these games in honour of Prometheus, that is of Human Nature, were again revived; that the victory may no longer depend upon the unsteady and wavering torch of each single man, but competition, emulation, and good fortune be brought to aid. Therefore men should be advised to rouse themselves, and try each his own strength and the chance of his own turn, and not to stake the whole venture upon the spirits and brains of a few persons.

Such are the views which I conceive to be shadowed out in this so common and hackneyed fable. It is true that there are not a few things beneath which have a wonderful correspondency with the mysteries of the Christian faith. The voyage of Hercules especially, sailing in a pitcher to set Prometheus free, seems to present an image of God the Word[7] hastening in the frail vessel of the flesh to redeem the human race. But I purposely refrain myself from all licence of speculation in this kind, lest peradventure I bring strange fire to the altar of the Lord.

7. i.e. Christ. Bacon refers to the voyage of Hercules in *Of Adversity*, p. 74 (see note 7).

Appendix 4:
Idols of the Mind

Source: Book I of the *Novum Organum*, published in 1620, consists of one hundred and thirty 'Aphorisms concerning the Interpretation of Nature and the Kingdom of Man'. The ones printed here, as 1–23, are XXXIX–LXI in Spedding's translation, *Works*, IV.53–63.

1

There are four classes of Idols which beset men's minds. To these for distinction's sake I have assigned names – calling the first class *Idols of the Tribe*; the second, *Idols of the Cave*; the third, *Idols of the Market-place*; the fourth, *Idols of the Theatre*.

2

The formation of ideas and axioms by true induction is no doubt the proper remedy to be applied for the keeping off and clearing away of idols. To point them out, however, is of great use, for the doctrine of Idols is to the Interpretation of Nature what the doctrine of the refutation of Sophisms is to common Logic.

3

The Idols of the Tribe have their foundation in human nature itself, and in the tribe or race of men. For it is a false assertion that the sense of man is the measure of things. On the contrary, all perceptions as well of the sense as of the mind are according to the measure of the individual and not according to the measure of the universe. And the human understanding is like a false mirror, which, receiving rays irregularly, distorts and discolours the nature of things by mingling its own nature with it.

4

The Idols of the Cave are the idols of the individual man. For every one (besides the errors common to human nature in general) has a cave or den of his own, which refracts and discolours the light of nature; owing either to his own proper and peculiar nature; or to his education and conversation with others; or to the reading of books, and the authority of those whom he esteems and admires; or to the differences of impressions, accordingly as they take place in a mind preoccupied and predisposed or in a mind indifferent and settled; or the like. So that the spirit of man (according as it is meted out to different individuals) is in fact a thing variable and full of perturbation, and governed as it were by chance. Whence it was well observed by Heraclitus that men look for sciences in their own lesser worlds, and not in the greater or common world.[1]

5

There are also Idols formed by the intercourse and association of men with each other, which I call Idols of the Market-place, on account of the commerce and consort of men there. For it is by discourse that men associate, and words are imposed according to the apprehension of the vulgar. And therefore the ill and unfit choice of words wonderfully obstructs the understanding. Nor do the definitions or explanations wherewith in some things learned men are wont to guard and defend themselves, by any means set the matter right. But words plainly force and overrule the understanding, and throw all into confusion, and lead men away into numberless empty controversies and idle fancies.

6

Lastly, there are Idols which have immigrated into men's minds from the various dogmas of philosophies, and also from wrong laws of demonstration. These I call Idols of the Theatre, because in my judgement all the received systems are but so many stage-plays, representing worlds of their own creation after an unreal and scenic fashion. Nor is it only of the systems now in vogue, or only of the ancient sects and philosophies, that I speak; for many more plays of the same kind may yet be composed and in like artificial manner set forth, seeing that errors the most widely different have nevertheless causes for the most part alike. Neither again do I mean this only of entire systems, but also of many principles and axioms in science, which by tradition, credulity, and negligence have come to be received.

But of these several kinds of Idols I must speak more largely and exactly, that the understanding may be duly cautioned.

7

The human understanding is of its own nature prone to suppose the existence of more order and regularity in the world than it finds. And though there be many things in nature which are singular and un-matched, yet it devises for them parallels and conjugates and relatives

1. Heraclitus is reported to have said: 'Although the account is shared, most men live as though their thinking were a private possession' (in Sextus Empiricus, *Adversus Mathematicos*, VIII.133: see Charles H. Kahn, *The Art and Thought of Heraclitus*, Cambridge, 1979, p. 29).

which do not exist. Hence the fiction that all celestial bodies move in perfect circles; spirals and dragons being (except in name) utterly rejected. Hence too the element of Fire with its orb is brought in, to make up the square with the other three which the sense perceives. Hence also the ratio of density of the so-called elements is arbitrarily fixed at ten to one. And so on of other dreams. And these fancies affect not dogmas only, but simple notions also.

8

The human understanding when it has once adopted an opinion (either as being the received opinion or as being agreeable to itself) draws all things else to support and agree with it. And though there be a greater number and weight of instances to be found on the other side, yet these it either neglects and despises, or else by some distinction sets aside and rejects; in order that by this great and pernicious predetermination the authority of its former conclusions may remain inviolate. And therefore it was a good answer that was made by one who when they showed him hanging in a temple a picture of those who had paid their vows as having escaped shipwreck, and would have him say whether he did not now acknowledge the power of the gods – 'Aye,' asked he again, 'but where are they painted that were drowned after their vows?' And such is the way of all superstition, whether in astrology, dreams, omens, divine judgements, or the like; wherein men, having a delight in such vanities, mark the events where they are fulfilled, but where they fail, though this happen much oftener, neglect and pass them by. But with far more subtlety does this mischief insinuate itself into philosophy and the sciences, in which the first conclusion colours and brings into conformity with itself all that come after, though far sounder and better. Besides, independently of that delight and vanity which I have described, it is the peculiar and perpetual error of the human intellect to be more moved and excited by affirmatives than by negatives; whereas it ought properly to hold itself indifferently disposed towards both alike. Indeed in the establishment of any true axiom, the negative instance is the more forcible of the two.

9

The human understanding is moved by those things most which strike and enter the mind simultaneously and suddenly, and so fill the imagination; and then it feigns and supposes all other things to be somehow, though it cannot see how, similar to those few things by which it is surrounded. But for that going to and fro to remote and heterogeneous instances, by which axioms are tried as in the fire, the intellect is altogether slow and unfit, unless it be forced thereto by severe laws and overruling authority.

10

The human understanding is unquiet; it cannot stop or rest, and still presses onward, but in vain. Therefore it is that we cannot conceive of any end or limit to the world, but always as of necessity it occurs to us that there is something beyond. Neither again can it be conceived how eternity has flowed down to the present day, for that distinction which is commonly received of infinity in time past and in time to come can by no means hold; for it would thence follow that one infinity is greater than another, and that infinity is wasting away and tending to become finite. The like subtlety arises touching the infinite divisibility of lines, from the same inability of thought to stop. But this inability interferes more mischievously in the discovery of causes: for although the most general principles in nature ought to be held merely positive, as they are discovered, and cannot with truth be referred to a cause; nevertheless the human understanding being unable to rest still seeks something prior in the order of nature. And then it is that in struggling towards that which is further off it falls back upon that which is more nigh at hand, namely, on final causes: which have relation clearly to the nature of man rather than to the nature of the universe, and from this source have strangely defiled philosophy. But he is no less an unskilled and shallow philosopher who seeks causes of that which is most general, than he who in things subordinate and subaltern omits to do so.

11

The human understanding is no dry light,[2] but receives an infusion from the will and affections, whence proceed sciences which may be called 'sciences as one would.' For what a man had rather were true he more readily believes. Therefore he rejects difficult things from impatience of research; sober things, because they narrow hope; the deeper things of nature, from superstition; the light of experience, from arrogance and pride, lest his mind should seem to be occupied with things mean and transitory; things not commonly believed, out of deference to the opinion of the vulgar. Numberless in short are the ways, and sometimes imperceptible, in which the affections colour and infect the understanding.

12

But by far the greatest hindrance and aberration of the human understanding proceeds from the dullness, incompetency, and deceptions of the senses; in that things which strike the sense outweigh things which do not immediately strike it, though they be more important. Hence it is that speculation commonly ceases where sight

2. Derived from a saying by Heraclitus. See above, p. 31, and note 23.

ceases, insomuch that of things invisible there is little or no observation. Hence all the working of the spirits inclosed in tangible bodies lies
hid and unobserved of men. So also all the more subtle changes of form
in the parts of coarser substances (which they commonly call alteration,
though it is in truth local motion through exceedingly small spaces) is in
like manner unobserved. And yet unless these two things just mentioned be searched out and brought to light, nothing great can be
achieved in nature, as far as the production of works is concerned. So
again the essential nature of our common air, and of all bodies less dense
than air (which are very many), is almost unknown. For the sense by
itself is a thing infirm and erring; neither can instruments for enlarging
or sharpening the senses do much; but all the truer kind of interpretation of nature is effected by instances and experiments fit and apposite;
wherein the sense decides touching the experiment only, and the
experiment touching the point in nature and the thing itself.

13

The human understanding is of its own nature prone to abstractions
and gives a substance and reality to things which are fleeting. But to
resolve nature into abstractions is less to our purpose than to dissect her
into parts; as did the school of Democritus,[3] which went further into
nature than the rest. Matter rather than forms should be the object of
our attention, its configurations and changes of configuration, and
simple action, and law of action or motion; for forms are figments of the
human mind, unless you will call those laws of action forms.

14

Such then are the idols which I call *Idols of the Tribe*, and which take
their rise either from the homogeneity of the substance of the human
spirit, or from its preoccupation, or from its narrowness, or from its
restless motion, or from an infusion of the affections, or from the
incompetency of the senses, or from the mode of impression.

15

The *Idols of the Cave* take their rise in the peculiar constitution,
mental or bodily, of each individual, and also in education, habit, and
accident. Of this kind there is a great number and variety, but I will
instance those the pointing out of which contains the most important
caution, and which have most effect in disturbing the clearness of the
understanding.

3. Pre-Socratic philosopher, the pupil of Leucippus (see aphorism 19). He
believed that the universe was made up of atoms brought together by chance rather
than the will of a creator. For Bacon's views on the pre-Socratics, see *Thoughts and
Conclusions*, p. 84 (Farrington translation; full reference, p. 49 above).

16

Men become attached to certain particular sciences and speculations, either because they fancy themselves the authors and inventors thereof, or because they have bestowed the greatest pains upon them and become most habituated to them. But men of this kind, if they betake themselves to philosophy and contemplations of a general character, distort and colour them in obedience to their former fancies: a thing especially to be noticed in Aristotle, who made his natural philosophy a mere bond-servant to his logic, thereby rendering it contentious and well nigh useless. The race of chemists[4] again out of a few experiments of the furnace have built up a fantastic philosophy, framed with reference to a few things; and Gilbert[5] also, after he had employed himself most laboriously in the study and observation of the loadstone, proceeded at once to construct an entire system in accordance with his favourite subject.

17

There is one principal and as it were radical distinction between different minds, in respect of philosophy and the sciences, which is this: that some minds are stronger and apter to mark the differences of things, others to mark their resemblances. The steady and acute mind can fix its contemplations and dwell and fasten on the subtlest distinctions: the lofty and discursive mind recognizes and puts together the finest and most general resemblances. Both kinds however easily err in excess, by catching the one at gradations, the other at shadows.

18

There are found some minds given to an extreme admiration of antiquity, others to an extreme love and appetite for novelty; but few so duly tempered that they can hold the mean, neither carping at what has been well laid down by the ancients, nor despising what is well introduced by the moderns. This however turns to the great injury of the sciences and philosophy, since these affectations of antiquity and novelty are the humours of partisans rather than judgements; and truth is to be sought for not in the felicity of any age, which is an unstable thing, but in the light of nature and experience, which is eternal. These factions therefore must be abjured, and care must be taken that the intellect be not hurried by them into assent.

4. i.e. the alchemists, whose search for the philosopher's stone and the elixir of life combined pseudo-chemical theories with religious mysteries and language (satirized most notably in Ben Jonson's play *The Alchemist*).

5. William Gilbert, d. 1603, wrote the first scientific account of the magnet. He went on later to suggest that virtually everything could be explained in terms of the magnet and magnetic fields.

19

Contemplations of nature and of bodies in their simple form break up and distract the understanding, while contemplations of nature and bodies in their composition and configuration overpower and dissolve the understanding: a distinction well seen in the school of Leucippus and Democritus as compared with the other philosophies. For that school is so busied with the particles that it hardly attends to the structure, while the others are so lost in admiration of the structure that they do not penetrate to the simplicity of nature. These kinds of contemplation should therefore be alternated and taken by turns; that so the understanding may be rendered at once penetrating and comprehensive, and the inconveniences above mentioned, with the idols which proceed from them, may be avoided.

20

Let such then be our provision and contemplative prudence for keeping off and dislodging the *Idols of the Cave*, which grow for the most part either out of the predominance of a favourite subject, or out of an excessive tendency to compare or to distinguish, or out of partiality for particular ages, or out of the largeness or minuteness of the objects contemplated. And generally let every student of nature take this as a rule – that whatever his mind seizes and dwells upon with peculiar satisfaction is to be held in suspicion, and that so much the more care is to be taken in dealing with such questions to keep the understanding even and clear.

21

But the *Idols of the Market-place* are the most troublesome of all: idols which have crept into the understanding through the alliances of words and names. For men believe that their reason governs words, but it is also true that words react on the understanding; and this it is that has rendered philosophy and the sciences sophistical and inactive. Now words, being commonly framed and applied according to the capacity of the vulgar, follow those lines of division which are most obvious to the vulgar understanding. And whenever an understanding of greater acuteness or a more diligent observation would alter those lines to suit the true divisions of nature, words stand in the way and resist the change. Whence it comes to pass that the high and formal discussions of learned men end oftentimes in disputes about words and names; with which (according to the use and wisdom of the mathematicians) it would be more prudent to begin, and so by means of definitions reduce them to order. Yet even definitions cannot cure this evil in dealing with natural and material things, since the definitions themselves consist of words, and those words beget others: so that it is necessary to recur to individual instances, and those in due series and order; as I shall say presently when I come to the method and scheme for the formation of notions and axioms.

22

The idols imposed by words on the understanding are of two kinds. They are either names of things which do not exist (for as there are things left unnamed through lack of observation, so likewise are there names which result from fantastic suppositions and to which nothing in reality corresponds), or they are names of things which exist, but yet confused and ill-defined, and hastily and irregularly derived from realities. Of the former kind are Fortune, the Prime Mover, Planetary Orbits, Element of Fire, and like fictions which owe their origin to false and idle theories. And this class of idols is more easily expelled, because to get rid of them it is only necessary that all theories should be steadily rejected and dismissed as obsolete.

But the other class, which springs out of a faulty and unskilful abstraction, is intricate and deeply rooted. Let us take for example such a word as *humid*, and see how far the several things which the word is used to signify agree with each other; and we shall find the word *humid* to be nothing else than a mark loosely and confusedly applied to denote a variety of actions which will not bear to be reduced to any constant meaning. For it both signifies that which easily spreads itself round any other body; and that which in itself is indeterminate and cannot solidize; and that which readily yields in every direction; and that which easily divides and scatters itself; and that which easily unites and collects itself; and that which readily flows and is put in motion; and that which readily clings to another body and wets it; and that which is easily reduced to a liquid, or being solid easily melts. Accordingly when you come to apply the word, if you take it in one sense, flame is humid; if in another, air is not humid; if in another, fine dust is humid; if in another, glass is humid. So that it is easy to see that the notion is taken by abstraction only from water and common and ordinary liquids, without any due verification.

There are however in words certain degrees of distortion and error. One of the least faulty kinds is that of names of substances, especially of lowest species and well-deduced (for the notion of *chalk* and of *mud* is good, of *earth* bad); a more faulty kind is that of actions, as to *generate*, *to corrupt*, *to alter*; the most faulty is of qualities (except such as are the immediate objects of the sense) as *heavy*, *light*, *rare*, *dense*, and the like. Yet in all these cases some notions are of necessity a little better than others, in proportion to the greater variety of subjects that fall within the range of the human sense.

23

But the *Idols of the Theatre* are not innate, nor do they steal into the understanding secretly, but are plainly impressed and received into the mind from the play-books of philosophical systems and the perverted rules of demonstration. To attempt refutations in this case would be merely inconsistent with what I have already said: for since we agree neither upon principles nor upon demonstrations there is no place for argument. And this is so far well, inasmuch as it leaves the honour of the ancients untouched. For they are no wise disparaged – the question between them and me being only as to the way. For as the saying is, the lame man who keeps the right road outstrips the runner who takes a wrong one. Nay it is obvious that when a man runs the wrong way, the more active and swift he is the further he will go astray.

But the course I propose for the discovery of sciences is such as leaves but little to the acuteness and strength of wits, but places all wits and understandings nearly on a level. For as in the drawing of a straight line or a perfect circle, much depends on the steadiness and practice of the hand, if it be done by aim of hand only, but if with the aid of rule or compass, little or nothing; so is it exactly with my plan. But though particular confutations would be of no avail, yet touching the sects and general divisions of such systems I must say something; something also touching the external signs which show that they are unsound; and finally something touching the causes of such great infelicity and of such lasting and general agreement in error; that so the access to truth may be made less difficult, and the human understanding may the more willingly submit to its purgation and dismiss its idols.

Appendix 5:
A Poetical Essay

Source: The poem is transcribed in a good many seventeenth-century manuscripts. Thomas Farnaby printed a version of it in 1629, and ascribed it to Bacon. It is printed here from *Works*, VII.271–2. The poem, based on a Greek epigram, is Bacon's most notable piece of verse: an essay in strange metres and rhythms on the frustrations and inanity of life.

The world's a bubble, and the life of man
        less than a span;
In his conception wretched, from the womb
        so to the tomb:
Curst from the cradle, and brought up to years
        with cares and fears.
Who then to frail mortality shall trust,
But limns the water, or but writes in dust.

Domestic cares afflict the husband's bed,
        or pains his head.
Those that live single take it for a curse,
        or do things worse.
Some would have children; those that have them moan,
        or wish them gone.
What is it then to have or have no wife,
But single thraldom, or a double strife?

Yet since with sorrow here we live opprest,
        what life is best?
Courts are but only superficial schools
        to dandle fools.
The rural parts are turned into a den
        of savage men.
And where's the city from all vice so free,
But may be term'd the worst of all the three?

Our own affections still at home to please
        is a disease:

To cross the seas to any foreign soil
              perils and toil.
Wars with their noise affright us: when they cease,
              we are worse in peace.
What then remains, but that we still should cry
Not to be born, or being born to die.